D1447637

THE SEVENTH MEMBER STATE

THE
SEVENTH
MEMBER
STATE

Algeria, France, and the
European Community

MEGAN BROWN

HARVARD UNIVERSITY PRESS

Cambridge, Massachusetts
London, England
2022

FIRST PRINTING

Library of Congress Cataloging-in-Publication Data
Names: Brown, Megan, 1985– author.
Title: The seventh member state : Algeria, France, and the European
community / Megan Brown.
Description: Cambridge, Massachusetts : Harvard University Press, 2022. |
Includes bibliographical references and index.
Identifiers: LCCN 2021036183 | ISBN 9780674251144 (cloth)
Subjects: LCSH: European Economic Community. | Treaty Establishing the
European Economic Community (1957 March 25) | Postcolonialism—
Algeria—History. | Algeria—History—1830–1962. | Algeria—
History—1962–1990. | France—Foreign relations—Algeria. | Algeria—
Foreign relations—France. | Europe—Foreign Relations—Algeria. |
Algeria—Foreign relations—Europe.
Classification: LCC HC241.25.A4 B76 2022 | DDC 337.44065—dc23
LC record available at https://lccn.loc.gov/2021036183

To my parents, who made me sign up for
French class in the seventh grade

Contents

Abbreviations

AASM	Associated African States and Madagascar
CELPUF	Comité d'études et de liaison du patronat de l'Union française / Study and Liaison Committee of the Employers of the French Union
DAEF	Direction des affaires économiques et financières du Ministère des affaires étrangères / Ministry of Foreign Affairs, Economic and Financial Division
DE-CE	Ministry of Foreign Affairs, Economic and Financial Division (DAEF), Service of Economic Cooperation / DAEF, Service de coopération économique
DELFRA	French embassy or consulate in a given capital or city
DG VIII	Directorate General VIII, overseeing the European Overseas Development Fund
Diplomatie	Ministry of Foreign Affairs
DOM	Départements d'outre-mer / French Overseas Departments (French Guiana, Guadeloupe, Martinique, Réunion; status obtained March 19, 1946)
DREE	DAEF, Direction des relations économiques extérieures / Ministry of Foreign Affairs, Economic and Financial Division (DAEF), Direction of External Economic Relations
EC	European Communities (ECSC, EEC, and Euratom, merged 1967)
ECJ	European Court of Justice
ECSC	European Coal and Steel Community (Treaty of Paris, 1951)
EDC	European Defense Community
EEC	European Economic Community (Treaty of Rome, 1957)

EPC	European Political Community
ERP	European Recovery Program
EU	European Union (Treaty of Maastricht, 1992)
Euratom	European Atomic Energy Community (Treaty of Rome, 1957)
FED	Fonds européen de développement / European Development Fund
FEDOM	Fonds européen de développement pour les pays et territoires d'outre-mer / European Overseas Development Fund
FIDES	Fonds d'investissement pour le développement économique et social / Investment Fund for Economic and Social Development
FLN	Front de libération nationale / National Liberation Front
GATT	General Agreement on Tariffs and Trade
GPRA	Gouvernement provisoire de la République algérienne / Provisional Government of the Algerian Republic
MFE	Mouvement fédéraliste européen / European Federalist Movement
MIDFA	Musulman indépendant pour la défense du fédéralisme algérien / Independent Muslim for the Defense of Algerian Federalism
MRP	Mouvement républicain populaire/Popular Republican Movement
MTLD	Mouvement pour le triomphe des libertés démocratiques / Movement for the Triumph of Democratic Liberties
NATO	North Atlantic Treaty Organization
OEEC	Organisation for European Economic Co-operation
PCF	Parti communiste français / French Communist Party
PRL	Parti républicain de la liberté / Republican Party of Liberty
RPF	Rassemblement du peuple français / Rally of the French People
SFIO	Section française de l'Internationale ouvrière / French Section of the Workers' International
SGCI	Secrétariat général du comité interministériel pour les questions de coopération économique européenne / General Secretary of the Interministerial Committee Responsible for Questions of European Economic Cooperation
The Six	Belgium, France, Italy, Luxembourg, the Netherlands, West Germany
TOM	Territoires d'outre-mer / French Overseas Territories
UDMA	Union démocratique du manifeste algérien / Democratic Union of the Algerian Manifesto

Timeline

1944, January– February	Brazzaville Conference
1945, May 8	Victory in Europe Day; demonstrations in Sétif and Guelma lead to weeks of violence and repression
1946, October	Constitution approved; foundation of the French Fourth Republic and the French Union
1946, December	War in Indochina begins
1947, September 20	French National Assembly approves *statut organique de l'Algérie*
1951, April 18	The Six sign the Treaty of Paris, establishing the ECSC
1954, March–May	Battle of Dien Bien Phu, ultimately leading to French departure from the region
1954, August	French National Assembly rejects the EDC
1954, November 1	Coordinated FLN attacks launch the Algerian War
1955, April	Asian-African Conference held in Bandung, Indonesia
1956, March	Moroccan and Tunisian independence
1956, June	French National Assembly passes the *loi-cadre Defferre*
1957, February	UN General Assembly holds its first debate on the Algerian War
1957, March 25	The Six sign the Treaties of Rome, establishing the EEC and Euratom
1958	Foundation of the French Fifth Republic and the French Community; independence of Guinea following rejection by popular referendum of French Community membership
1960	Independence of most French Community states and Belgian Congo

1962, March 18	France and GPRA sign the Evian Accords
1962, July 5	Algerian independence day
1963, January	First French veto of British EEC membership
1963, July	EEC and AASM sign first Yaoundé Convention
1967, July	1965 Merger Treaty goes into effect, unifying ECSC, EEC, and Euratom under EC
1967, September	Second French veto of British membership
1973, January	Denmark, Ireland, and the United Kingdom accede to the EC in first enlargement
1973, October	Start of oil crisis
1975, February	EEC and seventy-one African, Caribbean, and Pacific states sign first Lomé Convention
1976, April 26	EEC and Algeria sign Co-operation Agreement

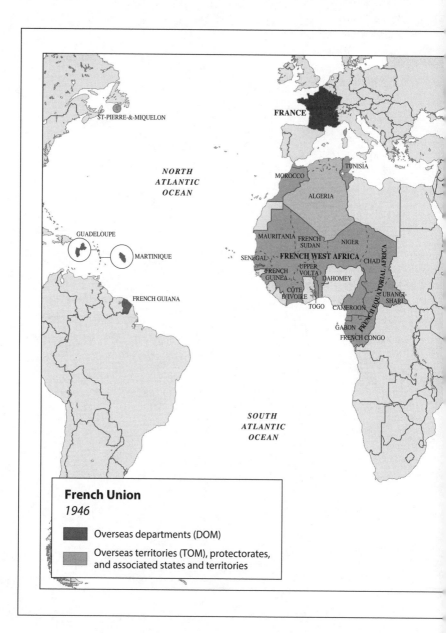

ST-PIERRE-&-MIQUELON

FRANCE

NORTH
ATLANTIC
OCEAN

TUNISIA

MOROCCO

ALGERIA

GUADELOUPE

MARTINIQUE

MAURITANIA   FRENCH
                SUDAN   NIGER

SENEGAL   FRENCH WEST AFRICA   CHAD

FRENCH   UPPER
GUINEA   VOLTA   DAHOMEY

CÔTE
D'IVOIRE

FRENCH GUIANA

TOGO   CAMEROON

UBANGI-
SHARI

GABON

FRENCH CONGO

SOUTH
ATLANTIC
OCEAN

French Union
1946

Overseas departments (DOM)

Overseas territories (TOM), protectorates,
and associated states and territories

Map 1   Global reach of the French Union after World War II

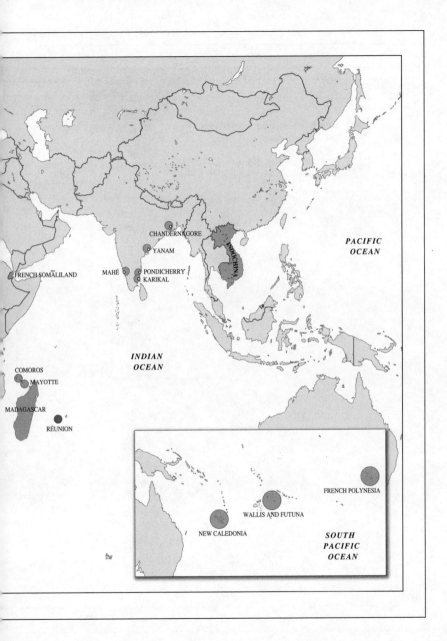

PACIFIC
OCEAN

CHANDERNAGORE

YANAM

INDOCHINA

FRENCH SOMALILAND

MAHÉ

PONDICHERRY
KARIKAL

INDIAN
OCEAN

COMOROS

MAYOTTE

MADAGASCAR

RÉUNION

FRENCH POLYNESIA

WALLIS AND FUTUNA

NEW CALEDONIA

SOUTH
PACIFIC
OCEAN

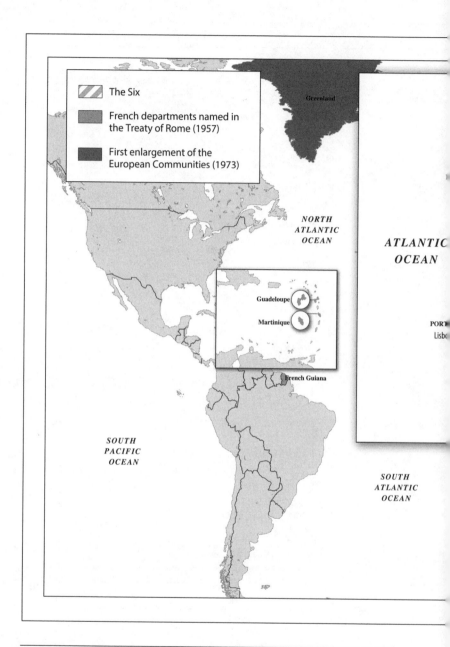

Map 2   Integrated Europe, with France's overseas departments, plus 1973 enlargement

In the very beginning lies chaos, but a chaos rich in life. It is the fertile primeval slime, where a being is coming into existence, still monstrous, but endowed with a principle of unity, and strong enough to dispel impossibilities, to acquire the essential organs. What are the efforts of the awakened centuries if we compare them to the spontaneous tendencies of the embryonic age, mysterious age when a being in the process of making itself cuts off a useless appendage, creates a nervous system, grows a limb?

—Ernest Renan, *Histoire des origines du christianisme*

Introduction

A Kaleidoscopic Approach
to European Integration

"We always talk about French Algeria," Mohamed Bentaïeb, a representative of the department of Algiers declared at the National Assembly in Paris in August 1947. "Yes, of course, but one thing strikes me: I have never heard talk of French Paris or French Toulouse. Algeria is French and Muslim. When you speak of French Algeria, you offend both [populations], creating divisions when you cry: '*vive l'Algérie française!*'" With this bold remark during a debate about a proposed law that would relegate Muslim Algerians to a separate electoral college, Bentaïeb, a member of the centrist Mouvement républicain populaire (MRP) party who hailed from a wealthy Orléansville (Chlef) family, dared his fellow deputies to assert that Algerians warranted different treatment than their fellow French citizens. He punctuated his remarks with a question that now appears prophetic: "Is it necessary to cry so loudly that Algeria is French? No one has said the contrary."[1] The law soon passed, codifying unequal representation.

Bentaïeb undoubtedly knew that the answer to his provocative question was not so cut and dry. From the first attacks on

Algerian soil in 1830 and for decades to follow, French forces engaged in "pacification" campaigns in Algeria, with the period of violent conquest coming to a close in parts of the Sahara only at the turn of the twentieth century. Two years prior to Bentaïeb's speech, on May 8, 1945, violence erupted in the Algerian cities of Sétif and Guelma during celebrations marking Germany's surrender and the end of World War II in Europe. When demonstrators unfurled banners and started chanting for the release of the exiled Algerian nationalist leader Messali Hadj, police attacked the crowds. By the end of the month, French military and civilian forces killed an estimated 2,000 Algerians in the region of Guelma alone, or many more, depending on whose tally one follows. Algerians themselves killed 102 European settlers, mainly in and around Sétif.[2] Although in these events' aftermath some observers noted that Algerian nationalism posed a major threat to the French presence there, on the international stage the French experienced little pressure to relinquish their southern Mediterranean departments in the years immediately following the war.[3] Within less than a decade, however, the cries about Algeria's Frenchness that Bentaïeb called extraneous became a desperate necessity for French officials, as anti-imperial nationalists ramped up both armed resistance and diplomatic challenges to over a century of French imperial rule.

As these voices grew louder, French officials sought audiences that would be obligated to heed their claims. Nascent unified European institutions provided just such a venue to remind the world that Algeria was French. In the process, these officials wrote Algeria into the fabric of integrated Europe itself. The postwar years represented a high period of European integration, during which time the governments of mainly western European states entered into agreements that eased customs rates and opened the door to merge some sectors of their economies. These treaties, which together laid the foundation of today's European Union (EU), first intertwined the affairs of Belgium, France, Italy, Luxembourg, the Netherlands, and West Germany, known collectively as the Six. When French officials picked up their pens to sign these accords, the France they represented was not a nation-state but an empire. Most consequential of all, along with its colonial territories, France maintained a firm grip on the departments of Algeria, organized since the mid-nineteenth century as legal, administrative equivalents to continental departments like the Dordogne or Vosges. Beyond France, Belgium, Italy, and the Netherlands also still possessed colonies or administered United Nations (UN) trust territories for over a decade after World War II's end. When they signed the texts establishing the institutions in question—the European Coal and Steel Community (ECSC) in 1951 and then the European Economic Community (EEC) in 1957—four of the Six maintained imperial interests. Rather than viewing European integration as the rescue of the nation-state, in the famed formulation of historian Alan S. Milward, the majority of the Six's extracontinental interests must lead us to consider instead how European integration could serve for its founders—and chiefly for France— as the rescue of the imperial nation-state.[4]

European Integration as an Imperial Project

The title of this book starts from a seemingly ahistorical point, identifying Algeria as the seventh member state of the nascent institutions of integrated Europe, although the Six are typically credited as its founders. As I demonstrate, Algeria was very much

a part of the European project and remained so well after its independence from France in 1962. How could a majority Muslim
state on the southern shores of the Mediterranean become a
member state of an emergent unified Europe? Because for nearly
a century, it had already been an integral part of France itself. Since
1848, French law treated the northern regions of Algeria as departments, meaning they were administered like the French metropole, or continental European French territory. By the turn of
the twentieth century, all European settlers born in Algeria, regardless of whether they traced their lineage to Nantes or Naples,
counted as French citizens.[5] Using a logic based on racialized arguments about Islam, the citizenship regime excluded nearly all
of Algeria's Indigenous population with the exception of a minus-
cule handful of Muslims with outstanding military records or degrees from French universities and the majority of its Jews, who
gained French citizenship in 1870 through a legislative decision
in Paris.[6] Algerian territory, not peoples, was undeniably French
in this view. Gradually, French officials looked to extend more
rights to those noncitizen populations, although never without
great pushback from the European settlers, who comprised roughly
10 percent of Algeria's population. French officials in Paris perceived the settlers as a formidable and reactionary voting bloc, particularly after a surge of anti-Republican action in Algeria in the
1930s and under the Vichy regime.[7] The French debt to its colonies during the war and the discrediting, with Nazi Germany's defeat, of overt racism and civilizational claims led officials to revisit
the meaning of French citizenship following the end of hostilities
in Europe.[8] They pursued reforms to the empire, reformulated as
the French Union under the new constitutional regime of the
Fourth Republic (1946–1958). Despite this commitment to reform,

French authorities were slow to jettison their long-held beliefs about what populations were capable or deserving of full citizenship, beliefs predicated on racist ideologies now recast in developmentalist terms. After the war, French officials preferred even German prisoners of war to North African laborers, whom a high-ranking civil servant called "undesirable." The head of a government committee on population and family questions argued that the new legal reforms did not grant Algerians citizenship and demanded a numerical quota on their migration to the metropole.[9]

The imperial reforms of the French Fourth Republic introduced ambiguity into the relationship between Algeria's departments and continental France. Together with the overseas departments of French Guiana, Guadeloupe, Martinique, and Réunion (DOM), Algeria's departmental status distinguished it from the rest of the French Union—places like Indochina and French West Africa. Ambiguity emerged because officials in Paris wavered on whether Algerian Muslims actually could enjoy the full rights of French metropolitan citizens, as Bentaïeb's critique of the second college made clear, while contemporaneous debates about citizenship across the French Union wrought further consternation among continental French politicians wary of introducing a form of republican citizenship that might be truly universal.[10] The constitution's wording lacked clarity about Algeria's exact administrative status, which allowed French officials to level a range of claims about its juridical regime depending on what best served their administrations' domestic and foreign policy needs. This became particularly useful when the National Liberation Front (FLN) launched the first attacks in the Algerian War of Independence (1954–1962), a war whose battles were fought both in the streets and in the highest international institutions, such as the UN.

French officials' uneven attempts to expand citizenship rights to people across the French Union coincided with the golden age of postwar European integration. Officials, notably from the Ministry of Foreign Affairs but also from the Ministry of Overseas France and an interministerial committee responsible for European affairs, came to view European integration negotiations as a venue for asserting the legitimacy of Algérie française. By insisting that a supranational treaty name Algeria as a constitutive part of France, they effectively weaponized the treaty, making the geographic reach of the EEC a rejoinder to Algerian demands for independence.

This book calls for a new reading of the spatial boundaries of integrated Europe and a new periodization of decolonization itself. I assert an alternative administrative geography for the EEC, one that comprises the southern shores of the Mediterranean.[11] When it served their interests, French officials insisted that Algeria's status made it inextricable from continental France: a singular French Republic. This departmental status facilitated Algeria's integration with the EEC. The ambiguity of Algeria's position within the Republic, however, allowed these same officials to withhold Algerian territory and goods from integrated Europe when they saw fit. It also enabled the exclusion of Muslim Algerian people from the benefits of EEC membership. Representatives of the Six, including, for the most part, French officials, viewed Algerians' ability to count as European as suspect and undesirable, given their racial and religious identities. The French policy of including or excluding Algeria from integrated European institutions thus changed over time and was greatly impacted by the state of anti-imperial nationalism across the French Union and particularly in Algeria itself.

Algeria's European integration is a history of multiscalar sovereignty. French authorities remained deeply committed to maintaining their rule over Algeria, whose departments, they claimed, were equivalent to those of continental France. They also weighed the degree to which they would need to cede their own sovereignty to integrated Europe, both to remain relevant globally and to maintain a measure of sovereignty in their colonies. By internationalizing the cause of French Algeria through European institutions, they believed they could hold on to the region, although such a tactic could both help and hinder their aims.[12] Algerian nationalists, meanwhile, made demands for sovereignty that increasingly fell on sympathetic ears, particularly at the UN.[13]

In the early years of European integration, such as the founding of the ECSC, French officials actively argued against including Algeria, despite its departmental status, because they feared doing so would threaten French sovereignty there. As the Algerian War intensified in the late 1950s, they changed course and insisted Algeria be named in the Treaty of Rome, the foundational text of the EEC signed in 1957. This meant that for five years, until Algerian independence in July 1962, the EEC's regulations for trade and social security extended to Algeria and—possibly—Algerians. Because the treaty named Algeria, European officials were at a loss as to how to extricate the country from the EEC after its independence. Not until 1976, when the EEC and Algeria signed an accord outlining a new, pared-down relationship, did the Mediterranean serve as the border of Europe. The process of decolonization, this demonstrates, was slow. Just as critically, Algerians themselves could maneuver this process in their own favor.

To fully appreciate the impact of French Algeria's domestic legal status on an international scale—and the consequences of French officials' insistence that this status be recognized by the Six—it is imperative to look beyond 1962 as the singular year of Algeria's exit from France.[14] A close examination of French diplomatic endeavors both to stave off Algerian anti-imperial nationalism and to dominate European affairs reveals decisions impacted by war, international pressure, economic imperatives, and existential beliefs about the nature of French sovereignty. Understanding French officials' kaleidoscopic approach to European integration, by which I mean the frequently shifting ways that they represented Algeria's relationship to France and Europe, is critical to interpreting Europe's postwar years. By tracing these shifts over a thirty-year period, I underscore the *longue durée* nature of decolonization in which the end of imperial relations cannot be reduced to a celebratory independence day.

In the 1950s, 1960s, and possibly even 1970s, European citizenship appeared accessible to Algerians because they, like Savoyards and Alsatians, had lived in departments of the French Republic. That potentially all Algerians, regardless of their race or religion, could hold those rights underlines the significance of the French decision to include Algeria in its plan for European integration.[15] This is a messier history than is often told. Historian Yves Montarsolo concluded that "decolonization was foreshadowed insofar as long before independence, the line which today still separates the countries of the 'North' from those of the 'South' had been de facto drawn. The birth of the Common Market shattered the concept of the French Union . . . and the 'internal border' separating the metropole from the overseas territories had been even more clearly brought to light."[16] In fact, the case of Algeria shows

that such lines were drawn much later—years after formal decolonization—and remained hazy at best. The afterlives of France's
fateful decision to insist on Algeria's inclusion in the EEC invited
and continues to invite a barrage of questions about the limits of
Europe and who holds the right to claim European citizenship
status or identity.

Diplomacy in Grand Halls and Brief Telegrams

At its heart, this study is about diplomatic tactics and bureaucratic
decision making. It is populated by influential French officials like
Christian Pineau of the Ministry of Foreign Affairs (February
1956–May 1958), nicknamed the Quai d'Orsay because of its Parisian headquarters, and Gaston Defferre, the colorful minister of
overseas France (February 1956–May 1957), better known for his
decades as mayor of Marseille (1953–1986). Much of the decision
making, and the memoranda that influenced decisions by Pineau,
Defferre, and others, derived from mid-level bureaucrats who go
unnamed in the archives they helped create.[17] Diplomats, like
Georges Gorse, France's representative before the EEC (November
1959–June 1961), and civil servants, like the Corsican development
official Jacques Ferrandi, shared an institutional culture with these
anonymous officials. Like most postwar French authorities, they
had come of age during the Third Republic (1870–1940) and were
educated to embrace a commonsense belief in France's imperial
mission and global might.[18] This esprit de corps can be traced in
the movement of officials from posts in Africa to posts in Brussels
during and after formal decolonization.[19]

Joining these French figures are members of the European diplomatic corps, in particular the Six's ministers of foreign affairs,

their diplomatic representatives in Paris and Brussels, and—after July 1962—Algeria's foreign office as well. Brussels, although not the only seat of the integrated institutions, operated as the de facto capital of Europe. Analyzing sometimes combustive encounters, I trace the events and beliefs that undergirded French foreign policies impacting integrated Europe and Algeria. The general public enters little into this telling both because I emphasize the significance of the diplomatic stage and because of the relative indifference of the French population regarding European integration. In the mid-1950s, for example, less than 1 percent of respondents in a French survey ranked European questions as being of the utmost importance, as opposed to 67 percent for the unfolding crisis in North Africa.[20] This was a long-standing lack of interest. As one French official said in 1967, "European public opinion . . . ignores almost completely that, since its birth, Europe has kept specific relationships with more than 30 developing countries, among which 18 independent states."[21]

At the same time, the diplomatic wrangling at the center of this story did have human consequences. Algerian independence seemingly introduced a binary division of citizenship (Algerian versus French) that would create a sharp delineation of which state owed rights to which population. Yet for French and other European officials, that divide proved undesirable or challenging to enforce in some instances. Settlers who moved to the metropole, for example, would receive their full pension, although the place where they worked prior to July 1962 was no longer a part of France. The addition of European-wide labor and social security rights only further confused the situation. The rights the Treaty of Rome granted to citizens of the Six inserted a legal category of migrant that pushed beyond the binary of state citizenship. Only after Algeria's independence was the human impact of France's policy demands made known, as West German and Belgian nationals sought recognition for the years they labored in the now-nonexistent Algérie française. Their demands drew attention not only to the rupture of Algeria's formal independence but also to the slow and halting end of a European rights regime that in a limited capacity had extended there since 1957.

Such ramifications were far from the minds of the French administrators who crafted these policies in the mid-1950s. Despite a deafening silence about the Algerian War in the archival record related to European integration, civil servants in Paris, Brussels, and elsewhere exchanged a tremendous amount of correspondence about proposed European regulations for the movement of Algerian goods and, to a lesser degree, people, as well as proposed schemes for distributing European development funding to Algerian projects. Given the centrality of the Quai d'Orsay's role in the construction of integrated Europe, it comes as no surprise that bureaucrats there produced countless memoranda and correspondence on the thorniest questions of Algeria's relationship to the EEC. Quai d'Orsay officials depended on consular administrators across Europe, and particularly in Brussels, to relay information about the Six's reactions and to surveil local news as a gauge of how those populations perceived French policy. They also liaised with their counterparts in the Ministry of Overseas France and, at the Ministry of the Interior, officials responsible for Algerian affairs.

From memos so thick they require specialty staples, to lists of recipients that extend for multiple pages, to brief telegrams in all capital letters, the archival record can be rich and detailed even as it leaves much unsaid. As the sometimes meticulous accounts of correspondence will make clear, I have chosen to linger on what might appear to be the minutiae of negotiations. By analyzing the run-up to signing ceremonies, we can locate policy shifts and meditate on their significance. One example of this is the 1976 EEC-Algeria treaty, whose status as a key, and potentially era-ending, document only becomes clear if we trace just how circuitous the road to that accord actually was. Another example occurred in early 1957, just weeks ahead of the Treaty of Rome's signing, when French officials switched from a constitutionally dubious but conveniently occluding practice of tacitly including Algeria within regulations meant for the whole of the French Union, to a policy of explicitly demanding the integration of Algeria in the EEC. This about-face—highly consequential to the EEC's future relations with Algeria and the trajectory of France's imperial policies within integrated Europe—only reveals itself when we slow down and consider the seemingly mundane exchanges between often middling bureaucrats populating France's embassies and ministries.

The Eurafrican Economic Community

Like the UN, integrated Europe's institutions can trace their roots to pre–World War II ideologies focused on the maintenance of empire.[22] The French pursuit of linking Algeria to integrated Europe, although a postwar diplomatic endeavor, drew on an interwar ideology that appealed to statesmen and political thinkers alike. That ideology, known as Eurafrica, emphasized the geopolitical, or even geographical, union between Europe and Africa, largely to the former's benefit. While Eurafrica's overt paternalism fell out of fashion after World War II, the ideology lent itself to adaptation in the postwar era, now couched in a language of brotherhood. This recast Africans as (typically unequal) partners in Europe's renewal. Simultaneously, the expansion of rights and political representation to the French Union also invited some individuals from Africa to the debates about the proper relationship between the two continents.

In this postwar guise, Eurafrican ideology continued to emphasize the unbreakable bonds between the continents. French officials, including many of the African deputies who spoke about a Eurafrica of equals, did not approach European negotiations with decolonization on their minds. Rather, they sought to square French moves toward federation—the French Union, for example—with the drive to federate Europe and secure peace between France and West Germany. The late 1940s and early 1950s promised the rebirth of a type of French grandeur, now even more reliant on the empire, despite major challenges like Sétif and Guelma in 1945, as well as years-long conflicts in Madagascar (1947–1949) and Indochina (1946–1954). Securing the French Union alongside integrated Europe allowed French officials to cement their sovereignty in both.

Already in the interwar period, proponents of Eurafrica touted it as a third force between an ascendant United States and a menacing, young Soviet Union. Then, such a vision appealed to European states that lacked access to colonial resources and who feared being subsumed by their powerful neighbors. After World War II, Eurafrican fervor became a largely French preoccupation—a "primordial concern," in historian René Girault's words.[23] Integrated Europe would allow the Six to carve a path for a third way in an otherwise bipolar world. Contemporary observers viewed unified Europe as essential to maintaining Cold

War equilibrium.[24] France, French officials believed, must be at its helm. Integrating Europe and the Six's colonies in that endeavor would create a French-led bulwark between the two rival superpowers, complete with a large economy and access to the wealth of African resources, securing European relevance on the global stage. The other members of the Six bowed to French maneuvers to associate the French Union in the late 1950s because they understood the necessity of a French signature on any treaty forming an integrated European institution. They had already seen the collapse of other integration schemes, such as the European Defense Community (1954), when French officials refused to back the project.

I focus on the ECSC and the EEC because I am most interested in the lineage of what has become the best-known, and perhaps most controversial, European body: today's European Union. The postwar period witnessed a proliferation of integration schemes, beyond these organizations.[25] A range of European states united under the aegis of institutions like the Organisation for European Economic Co-operation (OEEC, 1948) and the Council of Europe (1949), the latter of which some pro-Europeanists came to despair would never be effectual, requiring the further steps of the ECSC and beyond. The successful institutions of the postwar, meaning those that actually emerged, tended to focus on economic regulation. For example, the OEEC formed to administer the European Recovery Program, known as the Marshall Plan. The ECSC, as we will see, focused on cementing favorable tariffs and managing resource access across the Six's (continental) borders. Although all dubbed "European" institutions, their membership varied. The Council of Europe included Turkey, a founding member of the OEEC, by 1950. The reality that Turkey's membership would be critical in major postwar institutions like the North Atlantic Treaty Organization (NATO, 1949), which it joined in 1952, highlights how geographies of "Europe" or the "West" could be constructed through diplomatic exchange. Indeed, the Six anticipated that when the EEC would enlarge to encompass more states, the first two would be Greece and Turkey.[26] West Germany's Federal Statistics Office listed Turkish people as Europeans in their migration statistics reports through 1973.[27] Yet Greece only acceded to the European Union in 1981, eight years after the first enlargement of the European Communities (EC), as the ECSC, EEC, and the European Atomic Energy Community (Euratom) were known after their 1967 merger. The question of Turkey's membership remains unresolved to this day.

As this book makes clear, even Algeria's independence from France did not spell the end of its imbrication with integrated Europe. Algeria's leaders quickly lobbied EEC officials, hoping to obtain assurances of the continuation of favorable trade and aid regulations. In so doing, they joined other African leaders, such as Togolese president Sylvanus Olympio, who saw new political institutions as venues for asserting independence while securing aid.[28] Algeria's particular status prior to 1962 armed its leaders with unique arguments for making such demands. Europe, however, represented one of many diplomatic configurations for these leaders. Officials in independent Algeria pursued a range of integration possibilities, including not just their ties with the EEC but also a type of Maghreb Union and an active participation in the Non-Aligned Movement.[29] This speaks to postwar internationalism and the array of possibilities for how geopolitics could be configured beyond the Cold War divide in the 1960s and 1970s.[30] Algeria's hard-won independence did not preclude Algerians from potentially benefiting from EEC membership, either through development aid or even the free movement of labor and its attendant social security regime. Such rights and benefits remained largely in the realm of the theoretical, but they indicate the surprising openings made by the French decision to push for Algeria's integration in the EEC years prior. Algerian diplomats approached Brussels bureaucrats with confidence, certain that the EEC owed their citizenry some of the benefits of European membership. It would take a new diplomatic accord, in 1976, to pry those rights away from them.

European Integration and Histories of Empire

When the reality that Algeria was named in the Treaty of Rome no longer served French or European interests, European officials not only wrote Algeria out of the EEC; its history as a part of its foundational territory was erased from memory.[31] European historian Kiran Klaus Patel suggests that the contemporary European Union's "exaggerated self-image exacerbates" how crises like 2016's Brexit vote are understood, treated by politicians and journalists as new phenomena rather than registering historical precedent like Algeria's exit. I suggest that the belief in Brexit's anomalous nature, which caused such consternation, was fairly genuine, given the remarkably thorough erasure of Algeria's EEC history from both European lore and scholarship until now. Even Patel, whose work has touched on Algeria's and Greenland's departures from the EEC, does not address the twisting path toward Algeria's inclusion in the EEC or its slow exit.[32] More generally, until recent years integrated Europe garnered little popular attention, allowing hagiographical celebrations of its founding fathers to pass as the metanarrative for what in actuality was a complex and contested history.[33] Although a flurry of scholarship in the past two decades has given sustained attention to empire and European integration, Algeria's European integration history has yet to be told, earning only scant mention in even the most detailed treatments of Eurafrica.[34] Despite this, some scholars have already asked if we must look "beyond Eurafrica."[35] This work demonstrates that there is still much more to explore about the relationship between empire and the European project. Far from a strange and brief blip in a grand history of European integration, the period in which Algeria was poised to be Europe's seventh member state was highly consequential and points to other futures that might have been— and why they were never realized. It is a history that, in Todd Shepard's words, has largely "remained in the shadows."[36] I aim to shed some light.

Building on our understanding of Africa's relationship to integrated Europe, this book challenges the perniciously persistent tendency in scholarship to divorce Algeria from histories of Africa's relationship to integrated Europe or only to highlight how regions of Africa beyond the Maghreb experienced European integration. This mirrors official discourse but not the realities of the integration process. Unlike later agreements between independent African states and the EEC, notably the subsequent Yaoundé (1963, 1969) and Lomé (first signed 1975) Conventions, until early 1957 French officials implicitly included Algeria in negotiations when they discussed future relations between Europe and what they labeled Black Africa. This only changed as the Algerian War dragged on and officials hatched their plan to instrumentalize the EEC treaty in their fight to maintain sovereignty and legitimacy in those departments. Grouping Algeria with French West and

Equatorial Africa and the rest of the French Union was juridically inaccurate, given its departmental status.

Fourth Republic law drew an awkward line between types of citizenship, declaring that citizens of the French Republic were citizens of the French Union but not vice versa. Ambiguous imperial legal definitions allowed French officials to operate with a degree of flexibility when they sought the most favorable accords possible between themselves and the other members of the Six. They did so while attempting to maintain an imperial order that, regardless of recent reforms, still privileged a tacitly racial hierarchy with white metropolitan France on top. With some important recent exceptions that attend to Algeria's relationship to European integration, the most influential works on empire and European institutions treat as a given the tidy divide between regions labeled North and sub-Saharan Africa, despite ample scholarship on the Sahara as a site of connectivity.[37]

To the extent that territory outside of the European continent arises in mainstream recollections of European integration, decolonization serves as a clean break, with a colonial before and a European after. Hence West German chancellor Konrad Adenauer's apocryphal declaration to French prime minister Guy Mollet after the embarrassment of the Suez Crisis in 1956: "Europe shall be your revenge."[38] An overemphasis of French pragmatism also helps to feed the argument that draws a line between France's imperial past and its European present. To cite an example of this type of contention, one historian described French business leaders during the war in Indochina as "forced to make a choice between Indochina and NATO—meaning, between empire and Europe. . . . The European spirit superseded the colonial spirit as a new vector for building the future."[39] In reality, such a stark choice did not exist. Events like Suez did not turn French authorities away from their tempestuous colonies and into Europe's warm embrace. Rather, in the years following the Suez Crisis, the French attempted to leverage their new membership in integrated Europe to rein in the insurgency in Algeria and elsewhere. In order to do so, French officials insisted that the Six accept naming Algeria as within the territorial reach of the EEC. I build on scholarship that emphasizes the durability and prehistories of European-African relations by demonstrating that the Treaty of Rome itself would become a means through which French officials could pursue surprising connections even after the formal independence of most of their empire, including Algeria.[40]

Frederick Cooper's work on the French Union demonstrates the opening and possibility of expanded rights and egalitarian citizenship from the end of World War II until the independence of much of France's empire in 1960.[41] Gary Wilder's account of urgent utopian futures lived and planned by the Martinican poet and politician Aimé Césaire and the Senegalese author and politician Léopold Sédar Senghor points to emancipatory visions that rejected the nation-state as the end point of self-determination.[42] In different ways, these historians and their actors invite us to linger on the possibility that postwar imperial reforms could have led to a fundamentally different way of organizing the world. I take inspiration from their accounts of opening and possibility, considering the ways that Algeria's inclusion within the EEC suggests an alternative geography to Europe and challenges the delineation of 1962 as a singular break between Algeria and France or Algeria and Europe.

This is a history of the foreclosure of utopian futures. It reveals the gradual limitation of possibilities for rights and autonomy in Algeria and beyond, despite legal realities dating to 1957 and earlier that appeared to open new pathways for inclusion in French and European affairs. At first glance, this appears to be an account of the creative potential of an expansive Europe, inclusive of empire, that officials were both capable of imagining and desirous of carrying out. When we dig deeper, it is also a reckoning of a European inability or unwillingness to think and act creatively when officials found their sovereignty threatened by their fellow Europeans and, worse still, by former colonial subjects. This is a story of futures that were not realized and possibilities that were abandoned. The study of unrealized plans and nonevents deepens our understanding of the past by revealing what historical actors anticipated for the future. Just as we can learn from Césaire's and Senghor's visions for futures beyond the nation-state, we can learn from what did not happen in Algeria's EEC history.[43] I point to moments when European officials struggled to justify denying rights to Algerians, but ultimately I track the gradual excision of Algeria from a European rights regime. This excision began even before Algeria's independence and allows us to trace the hardening of borders and the construction—from its inception—of an exclusionary Europe.

The EEC negotiation was France's counterstrike against Algerian nationalists' diplomatic revolution in which French officials wielded the Treaty of Rome as a weapon of their own. Unlike Algerian tactics, which focused on rousing international opinion and relied on coverage in major newspapers, the French tactic homed in on the assent of their near neighbors in hopes of safeguarding the empire through a new institutional framework.[44] This aligns with other studies of how French officials attempted to use international institutions, such as the World Health Organization, to reify the empire's borders.[45] It also supports the notion that France had "a more nuanced arsenal" than just military force to draw on during the Algerian War.[46] The French weaponization of the Treaty of Rome to bolster their claims to Algeria can be read as a pragmatic choice made by French authorities at a decisive moment. Beyond securing the apparent agreement of the Six that Algeria was France, French officials harnessed additional development funds that would, they believed, calm the crisis in Algeria. Without denying the calculated nature of their decision, I show that French officials were also responding in real time to challenges from their European partners and from Algerians, both of whom threatened French officials' sovereignty and forced them constantly to revisit and move their line in the sand.

Assumptions about French level-headedness and pragmatism at times dominate interpretations of this period, particularly through the repetition of claims by the economic historians Jacques Marseille and Daniel Lefeuvre.[47] Ever since Raymond Cartier's influential 1956 contention in *Paris-Match* that France's colonies cost more to maintain than they were worth, received wisdom has held that decolonization was a logical and financially discerning choice made by colonial administrations. Such a view negates anti-imperial activists' agency and pays undue homage to capitalism's inherent rationality.[48] It rewrites decolonization as a rear-guard rejection of empire by Europeans, not an active and generative achievement by the people who overthrew colonial rule. Recent work has persuasively undercut the claim that the empire was a costly endeavor for the French and that economic sense can explain a French-led decolonization.[49] I build on this revision by examining the political—including diplomatic—machinations meant to maintain the empire.

This book emphasizes Algeria's place at the core of French diplomatic efforts with the Six, spurred by the war but facilitated by decades-old assumptions and laws dictating Algeria's Frenchness. Irwin Wall's contention that "Algeria was at every step of the way from 1954 to 1962 central to French diplomacy" rings true in an examination of France's strategies in EEC negotiations, although it became more central as the war intensified and remained so for over a decade after Algerian independence.[50] Critical work has demonstrated that the history of postwar Europe must be decentered from the continent or look beyond Europe's geographic borders. Doing so opens new understandings of the economic interactions between integrated European institutions and Global South states acting in concert or alone.[51] I suggest that the history of European integration is inseparable from the history of French empire and, more specifically, that the story of Algeria's independence is bound up with the EU's institutional predecessors despite and sometimes because of efforts by Algerian nationalists themselves. With this lens, the origins of European policy vis-à-vis Algeria can be traced to the fight for French Algeria, revealing the power of diplomacy to shape long-term economic and political ties where we least expect them to be.

Thirty Years of Europe and Algeria?

This book is structured to demonstrate the overlapping timelines of European integration and Algerian decolonization, emphasizing their mutual impact.[52] After briefly discussing the origins of European unity ideology and its connection with imperialism from the mid-nineteenth century until the start of World War II, including through Eurafrican advocacy, Chapters 1 and 2 chart the roughly ten years following the 1944 liberation of France, which witnessed the first iterations of European integration. This period saw not only the successful establishment of the ECSC but also the major failures of the EDC and the European Political Community (EPC). These institutions, the Six understood, lived or died at the hands of the French, and the EDC's rejection in 1954 made clear that French officials were willing to withhold their favor. Lingering on these early years of European integration, I demonstrate that French officials wavered on whether associating Africa writ large or integrating Algeria specifically would assist or frustrate their imperial ambitions. This remained the case even with the administrative changes brought about by the fall of the Fourth Republic and the emergence of the Fifth Republic (1958–present). I also emphasize the ambiguity of French law vis-à-vis Algeria's juridical status, which could be as useful as it was confusing when administrators came to the European negotiating table.

Simultaneous to European integration, the postwar period witnessed French attempts to reform colonial administration, as the Fourth Republic reconfigured the empire as the French Union and people living there gained more rights in theory and, sometimes, in practice. The era also featured the expansion of anti-imperial activism across the French Union, such as, among other key events, Indochina's independence in 1954 after close to a decade of war and, on its heels, the start of the Algerian War of Independence. Chapters 3 and 4 turn to the foundation and implementation of the EEC in 1957. Unlike the first ten years of integration, when protectionist French officials insisted that the empire remained outside of Europe's scope, now Europe would be integral to the French plan to rescue its empire by providing diplomatic legitimacy and an influx of monetary aid. This was a direct response to the intensification of violence in Algeria and the FLN's successful harnessing of international opinion. I locate a pivot during the final weeks of EEC negotiations, in February 1957, only days after the UN General Assembly held its first open discussion about the Algerian War.

This served as a turning point and French officials changed their demands. Previously, they asked for the EEC to "associate" with the French Union, and they refrained from naming Algeria at all. Now they declared that they would not sign a treaty if it failed to integrate Algeria, meaning that EEC regulations would be guaranteed to reach these French departments. The French sine qua non—that Algeria be named in the Treaty of Rome as part of its territorial range—disconcerted and in some cases angered their European partners, but the Six viewed France's signature as more critical than any possible repercussions resulting from Algeria's inclusion in integrated Europe. It resulted in Article 227, a section of the treaty that explicitly encompassed Algerian territory within the confines of the EEC. By writing Algeria into the Treaty of Rome, French officials now had an international treaty affirming their right to maintain the warring territory.

This tactic did not stave off Algerian nationalists, however, and in 1962, the newly independent state emerged victorious from nearly eight years of war. Chapters 5 and 6 focus on independent Algeria's relationship to integrated Europe. Thanks to the French advocacy of the late 1950s, Algerians found themselves, or at least their territory, literally inscribed into the Treaty of Rome, a reality that their new leaders viewed as an opportunity. Neither French nor Algerian leaders envisioned a full break in diplomatic and economic relations, despite the nearly wholesale departure of European settlers and the Algerian decision to nationalize foreign holdings, but the nascent state's precise status under EEC law remained undefined. Algeria's position within Europe became of paramount concern. In Brussels, the Six worried about the possibility that Algeria could be a seventh member state of the EEC, even as they insisted that French officials shoulder the burden of clarifying what future relations between Algeria and the EEC should look like. In practice, the Six operated in piecemeal fashion, with some states maintaining the favorable tariffs promised by the Treaty of Rome when they traded with Algeria and others opting to treat it as a third-party state. Nevertheless, Algerian development projects continued to receive EEC funding, and the Six struggled to explain how its status should change. It took a full fourteen years after Algeria's independence for its leaders and EEC officials to cement a new treaty that definitively excised Algeria from the EEC. It did so with generic wording that failed to mention Algeria ever having been named in the Treaty of Rome. Even this treaty could not expunge from the record the reality that there was a human impact to Algeria's years in the EEC. European workers who had spent their careers in Algeria now fought to receive their pensions, earned in a part of the world that was no longer France. By then, the 1973 oil crisis had fundamentally shifted European relations with Arab states and the *trente glorieuses,* or thirty prosperous postwar years, had come to a close.[53] With the 1976 treaty, Algeria's status within the EEC was erased, and with it, integrated Europe recast itself as a wholly continental endeavor. As the conclusion suggests, the legacies of Algeria's European years lived on in later European border flashpoints, notably Brexit and the so-called migrant crisis, as well as in French attempts to exclude and otherize people of North African origin living in France.

In short, deciding whether or how independent Algeria would relate to a Europe to which it already in theory belonged would prove a thorny issue whose resolution dragged on for over a decade. In that time, it was not evident to the leaders of the EEC where the borders of Europe might be drawn and whose citizenry might be owed rights as Europeans. How did this impact the lives of Algerians themselves? In the French logic of colonial administration, when a worker traversed the Mediterranean from Marseille to Algiers, he had not "left France." Once France's European partners agreed that Algeria would be a part of the EEC, we might then wonder, what if the worker departing Algiers had made his way to Amsterdam?[54] Had he entered into Europe, or had he never left? And what would that mean for him and his family in Algeria? Such questions had the potential to subvert the very nature of a "European" institution. Indeed, for a time, it appeared that Algeria just might be the seventh member state of the European Economic Community.

1

Eurafrican Dreams, Imperial Realities

In August 1947, the Council of the Republic in Paris had before it a prospective law that would create an Algerian assembly with an equal number of seats for settler and Muslim representatives, pleasing neither would-be constituency. Despite their agreement on the loathsomeness of the proposed *statut organique de l'Algérie,* there was no love lost between representatives of each population. When Constantine-born Marcelle Devaud, a councillor for the Seine department, rhapsodized about Algeria's "centuries of history and past grandeur" inherited by the Fourth Republic, Chérif Saadane quickly interrupted to declare, "You speak of France's history, which is not our history. We are at the French parliament. We demand a parliament for ourselves and we will gladly leave these seats that we occupy here." Saadane represented the department of Algiers in the council, as Mohamed Bentaïeb, who opened this book criticizing the same law, did in the National Assembly. Devaud, a member of the conservative Parti ré-publicain de la liberté (PRL), retorted, "Monsieur Saadane, we do not find it inappropriate that you are with us [but] if you do not want to be our brothers, you are our guests and we ask you to respect this tribune just as we do." Devaud's remarks drew immediate outcry from the benches of the far left and would be referenced by outraged speakers for the remainder of the day. The recording secretary, a Socialist who represented French citizens in Morocco, reminded her that the Algerians present held "exactly the same rights as the other councillors of the Republic."[1] Devaud's dismissive and racist assertion—she defended herself against accusations of the latter—of Algerian "guests" in the Council of the Republic speaks to more than just prevailing settler colonial beliefs of the day. It also signals the complexity and ambiguity of the status of Algerians both within the French government and within France itself.

In the late 1940s, regardless of their disdain for Devaud, most deputies were unwilling to extend to Algerians the right of representation that was a given for French citizens in the metropole. If the French Republic was expansive enough to include Algeria, it could be reduced to a narrower version of France that forestalled full equality across the Mediterranean as well. The tribulations of World War II also created openings for people from France's empire to redefine their relationship to the metropole. With the administrative reorganization of the empire into the French Union in 1946, local authority grew and the possibility of suffrage and citizenship, albeit with limitations, drew more African peoples into France's political life. Demands for further local autonomy fit within emergent calls for federalism. Federalism, meaning the limited intertwining of the political and economic functions of states beholden to a degree to one centralized power, was one of the most salient ideas of the postwar period. Leaders in the French Union, from Ferhat Abbas of Algeria to Léopold Senghor of Senegal, advocated federalism for the French Union. Indeed, Saadane belonged to the reformist Union démocratique du manifeste algérien (UDMA) party, founded by Abbas and dedicated to pushing for a federalist relationship between Algeria and metropolitan France. In their embrace of the concept, advocates envisioned a future predicated not on metropolitan dominance but on egalitarian and autonomous futures within the French Union's framework.

In this same era, advocates of European integration dubbed themselves federalists. No discussion of European federalism is complete without an account of the place of empire in that history.[2] From its inception, modern dreams of joining the continent for peace included Africa and, in particular, a shared exercise in its domination. From Victor Hugo's exhorting of a United States of Europe in 1849 to the prolific interwar and postwar publications casting Africa as Europe's "last chance," the connections between European planning and empire proved durable. European federalists eventually found a name for the link between unified Europe and colonized Africa: Eurafrica. The coiner of the term, like Hugo and the others who preceded him, saw a collective European subjugation of Africa, through the shared exploitation of its resources and the opening of its territory to European migration, as central to the project of binding Europe. The dream of a federative Europe traced deep roots into the nineteenth century, but the horrific nature of World War II pushed authorities to make it a reality. Federalism here meant European powers binding themselves via trade agreements—and symbolically, in the case of the European Coal and Steel Community (ECSC), coupling their war industries—to eradicate competition and render future conflict impossible. By then, the advocates of federalism in the French

Union, like Senghor, insisted that European federalism must support a Eurafrica in which Africans were equal partners in the integration process.

After surveying the long life of Eurafrican ideology, this chapter turns to changes in French overseas administration and citizenship after World War II. As Devaud's incendiary remarks indicate, not all French officials believed that people in the French Union were ready or deserving of the rights of French citizenship. This reticence to accept French Union nationals as French citizens was compounded by the opaque nature of the legal language surrounding their rights under the Fourth Republic's constitution. Algeria, for example, although considered a part of the French Republic and organized into administrative departments like the metropole, appeared to some jurists to have been demarcated as overseas departments or territories, which would imply different forms of representation and rights. Indeed, while it was legally inaccurate to group Algeria with the rest of the French Union, officials did so when they discussed the empire on the international stage. Neglecting Algeria's peculiar status as a part of the French Republic allowed these officials to maintain an exclusively French grip over the region as they negotiated the boundaries of a European federation.

The ambiguity that arose in this period puzzled some legal scholars and caused concern among representatives of overseas populations. Whereas the unknowns drew alarm in some circles, for French officials in Paris the uncertainty also proved useful. It provided greater flexibility in how rights would extend to Overseas France and, at the negotiating table for European integration, facilitated their ability to draw a line between the France that would be included in Europe and the France that would be kept out. In the early steps of European institution building, French officials unevenly applied the principle that Algeria was a constitutive part of the Republic. This wavering allowed them to maintain exclusive access to Algerian resources and markets while also drawing on international funds to feed development projects in Algeria. The same went for the rest of the French Union. However, that very useful state of ambiguity made it increasingly difficult for French officials to deny rights to people in the French Union, including rights under European institutions.

Eurafrican ideology shifted from being a pan-European pursuit to tool for French mastery over its own colonial holdings. That change occurred at the end of World War II and amplified as French officials grew to fear challenges from anti-imperial nationalists. In tracking the shift to a French-focused Eurafrica, the international consequences, intended and otherwise, of reforms to the French Union come into focus. The domestic conditions of imperial reform, and specifically the turn toward federalism, opened particular pathways for French officials to demand Eurafrican policy when it suited their economic and political needs. The surprising elision of the supposedly firm legal distinctions between Algeria and the remainder of the French Union served that purpose well. French domestic debates about the meaning of the French Union and the best ways to represent its residents—regulations like the *statut organique de l'Algérie* and others—showcase the range of ways that representatives from Paris to Algiers to Dakar could harness the gray areas of imperial law to insist on concrete policies that would place France at the center of integrated Europe.

"Delightful Peace At Last"

France's beloved author Victor Hugo is often celebrated for his prophetic call for a United States of Europe, which he trumpeted during the 1849 Peace Conference held in Paris. By joining together, European states could stem future war and allocate resources to education and technology, rather than costly armies. Like statesmen a century later, Hugo saw his motherland as the center of that union, writing, "France is already Europe." Further, in its colonial enterprise, he declared, "We have not come to Africa to bring back Africa, but to bring Europe there." His rationale presaged later Eurafrican ideology, encouraging European states to "pour your overflowing population into Africa, and thereby solve your social issues: turn your proletarians into owners."[3] That Hugo tied "Europe" to a celebration of the French conquest of Algeria—he referred to the army in "Roman land"—is telling. European unity, even in the eyes of its earliest proponents, would be constructed in Africa as well as in the metropole.[4]

Efforts to strengthen European grandeur and find solutions to continental poverty and overpopulation through colonization went hand in hand with attempts to secure peace through treaties and to alleviate competition between Berlin, Paris, and beyond. In vision if not in name, Hugo had identified Eurafrica as a pivotal part of the unification of Europe. Although he centered Paris at Eurafrica's heart, the nascent ideology first encompassed the imperial aspirations of many European statesmen and thinkers, rendering it a truly pan-European concept. The offer of sharing access to Africa appealed to Europeans whose states lacked colonies or whose colonies were wrested from it, as in the case of Germany after World War I. A European pact to share Africa would decrease competition and labor issues across Europe by putting continentally bound states onto an even playing field with major empires and by opening supposedly empty African space to excess and underemployed European populations.[5]

As even the most cursory glance at the history of the nineteenth and twentieth centuries demonstrates, Hugo's dreams were far from realized. To name only the major conflagrations, the Crimean War, Franco-Prussian War, World War I, and World War II all embroiled European powers in the years and decades after his peace conference proclamation. Beyond the battlefield, politicians and industrialists alike looked warily at the rising economic and political might across the Atlantic: the United States.[6] These subsequent conflicts and anxieties convinced more elite Europeans that some form of unity could secure perpetual peace, particularly after the Great War.[7] Questions of self-determination, sovereignty, and empire were closely bound up in the pursuit of securing and maintaining world peace. Although this offered venues, particularly through the League of Nation's Permanent Mandates Commission, for minority populations and people from colonized places to make claims and decry mistreatment, the league ultimately reinforced the right of domination, shying away from declarations of racial equality and reticent to condemn imperial powers.[8]

The nightmarish casualties of World War I rendered campaigns for European unification all the more urgent. France had suffered over 1.6 million metropolitan and colonial military and civilian deaths, or 4.29 percent of its population. Germany lost 2.4 million people, or 3.82 percent of its population.[9] Those losses are roughly equivalent to the 2021 populations of Philadelphia and Houston, respectively, or of Vienna and Rome.[10] The blame placed on the German Empire is remembered as having the most influence on the aftermath of war, namely in the form of the so-called war guilt clause of the Treaty of Versailles. But the interwar period was also marked by the popularity of internationalism and, in particular, cooperation among Europeans. The respected French minister of foreign affairs Aristide Briand declared during a September 1929 meeting of the League of Nations Assembly, "I think that among peoples constituting geographical groups like the peoples of Europe, there should be some kind of federal bond. . . . This is a link I want to forge."[11] Such an idea was not Briand's innovation; he and his compatriots, including French prime minister Édouard Herriot, had been influenced by their relationship with Count Richard von Coudenhove-Kalergi, founder of the Pan-European Union.

Coudenhove-Kalergi cuts a fascinating historical figure. Perhaps best known today for his successful advocacy of "Ode to Joy" as the Council of Europe's anthem, he was born in Tokyo in 1894 to an Austro-Hungarian father and a Japanese mother.[12] He published the "Pan-Europa Manifesto" in 1923 and established the Pan-European Union the following year. He quickly became an influential thinker and lobbyist for the cause of Eurafrica, a turn of phrase he is credited with coining. In his view, the federation of Europe was both in need of and akin to empire. As he wrote in *Paneuropa*, the movement's publication, "Africa could provide Europe with raw materials for its industry, nutrition for its population, land for its overpopulation, labor for its unemployed, and markets for its products."[13] The emphasis on Africa's utility to the whole of Europe would be a common trope for the next half century. Coudenhove-Kalergi forwarded a plan at once idealistic and pragmatic. Comparing the pan-European movement to the

British Empire in a 1931 speech at Chatham House in London, home to the Royal Institute of International Affairs, he declared that both were "strong because [they were] based not only on ideals but also on interests."[14] Coudenhove-Kalergi's ideas inspired politicians and fellow political thinkers across Europe, like the German architect Herman Sörgel, who hatched a plan to dam the Strait of Gibraltar to create a literal supercontinent by shrinking the Mediterranean Sea, and the Italian author Paolo d'Agostino Orsini di Camerota.[15]

Meanwhile, people outside of Europe—and migrants to Europe from African and Asian colonies—theorized their own versions of solidarity and internationalism. These were based around regions or "civilizations" and were meant to counter Western-focused assertions of supremacy and global leadership. Speaking once again in Chatham House, now in June 1939, Coudenhove-Kalergi predicted that Asian peoples would form a union and declared that it was "possible the second World War will end with the union of the European race."[16] Given the influence of Japanese pan-Asianism at this time, such an assertion is unsurprising. Indeed, Europeanists could look beyond their borders to see other important models for forging transnational solidarity, notably the pan-Africanist movement, which was both transimperial and transatlantic. The interwar period also saw pan-Arabist pressure via journals such as *La Nation arabe* and North African student associations, as well as the emergence of pan-Islamist movements such as the Muslim Brotherhood, founded in 1928.[17] These forms of solidarity offered visions of what scholar Manu Goswami calls "a concrete and geopolitical futurity" that would be "non-imperial," with "equality as a point of departure rather than an abstract normative ideal or juridical status."[18] Such ideas inspired fear in European officials, for whom colonies provided economic and political power, military advantage, and international prestige. Even more menacingly, pan-Africanists and others were in dialogue with one another.[19] To combat this, advocates of European federalism envisioned Eurocentric cooperation that could answer dangerous anti-imperial nationalism *and* internationalism, keeping Europeans powerful and relevant in this deeply uncertain era.

The concept of Eurafrica proved remarkably malleable in the 1930s and 1940s, furnishing fascist thinkers with a vocabulary about European supremacy and partnership in a subjugated Africa. Coudenhove-Kalergi was himself a Freemason, and Nazi students burned his books in 1933. As the situation in Europe grew more dire, he railed against Europe falling "under the sway of a Bolshevist or nationalist dictatorship" and exhorted an embrace of "the great motherland of united nations and of free men."[20] Yet Europeanist and Eurafrican ideology meshed well with fascist geopolitical pretensions such as Mitteleuropa, Mittelafrika, and *lebensraum*. Nazi Germany even had its own precursor to the Schuman Plan, the foundational outline of European integration, in the Funk Plan, a 1940 proposal for the economic unification of Western Europe under the Reichsmark, only abandoned after Operation Barbarossa.[21] The celebration of the Mediterranean as a Eurafrican lake complemented fascist Italy's formulation of *mare nostrum,* or "our sea," meant, in the words of geographer Marco Antonsich, "to legitimize Italy's right to rule over the Mediterranean."[22] After visiting a colonial exhibition in Naples in 1940, Jesuit priest Vittorio Genovesi penned a poem in Latin titled "Mare Nostrum" that read in part, "soon, cultivated by our colonists, the earth of Ambracia flourishes / everywhere work proceeds busily so that the land, which had up to this point been afflicted by the terrible darkness of barbarity, finally begins to shine with civil custom." It concluded, "may Rome, as a guide, again lead the way and take up the reins again, so that the African people will shake off its awful darkness . . . and so Europe will be able to enjoy delightful peace at last."[23] Europe's mission, Genovesi argued, was to forge peace by "civilizing" and controlling Africans. Meanwhile in France, some Vichy collaborators, and at least one Algerian Muslim collaborator, saw Eurafrica as part of a new world order.[24] Not limited to republican and liberal thinkers, versions of European integration and Eurafrica appealed across political divides.

When the guns of World War II cooled, Eurafrica did not share the same fate as many of the ideologies that came to prominence in the interwar. This can be explained in part because its best-known proponents, like Coudenhove-Kalergi and the French economics professor and author Eugène Guernier, were not fascist sympathizers and survived the war with their ideological reputations intact. Perhaps due to its relatively unknown quality beyond the halls of power or because Adolf Hitler did not have time to act in Africa, celebrations of the concept continued at a fast clip, although now with a greater emphasis on brotherhood than domination. There was some pushback; one French politician complained that the term was "above all polluted by its usage by the German occupant. . . . We at least could make an effort of imagination and avoid using this word when we speak of any form of close association between Europe and Africa."[25] But Eurafrica only gained in popularity. Senegalese deputy Senghor dismissed criticism of its fascist links, writing in *Le Monde,* "What does it matter, if it is correct!" Echoing *mare nostrum* language, he declared it to be "one of those classic ideas that have always animated the vision of great men and great people. For the ancients, the Mediterranean was nothing other than an interior sea, a lake."[26] Senghor's advocacy of a confederal Eurafrica that could place African men on equal footing with their European counterparts was a far cry from Genovesi's rhapsodizing and harkened back to the interwar anti-imperial internationalisms that centered concrete demands for equality. Yet the repetition of language evinces the endurance of a belief in the unshakable and natural bond between the African and European continents.

French Eurafrica

The broad concept of Eurafrica may have survived World War II unscathed. The French relationship to its empire was another matter. The war and the Vichy regime's undermining of republican institutions rendered metropolitan French claims of civilizational superiority indefensible. Added to this was the acknowledgment that the metropole would not have been liberated from Nazi occupation without the military might of colonial troops who rallied behind Charles de Gaulle, thanks in part to French Guiana-born colonial administrator Félix Éboué's support for the general. This translated into two key shifts. First, Eurafrican advocacy saw a distinct change, as it now appeared to French officials to be a way of normalizing the empire and giving it a sheen of progress. From the mid-1940s onward, Eurafrica turned from being a pan-European program to one led by the French for French interests. Second, French officials recognized that the empire would need to reform. They enacted legislative changes, such as establishment of the French Union and new citizenship laws, to meet that need.

In 1944, de Gaulle convened the Brazzaville Conference (in present-day Republic of the Congo), hosted by Éboué, during which colonial administrators planned for reforms and some assimilatory practices, notably related to extending more rights to a select group of Africans educated in the French system and legally demarcated as *évolués,* literally "evolved" men. This signaled a new era in French imperialism, now focused on collaboration with—not domination over—African peoples. Rather than moving toward decolonization, early postwar France was on track to reframe the empire into a federative body that would maintain French sovereignty. Clotaire Bée, a jurist who in the 1950s would serve as an administrator in Madagascar, wrote in 1947 that "France does not have an empire, it is an empire . . . a Global France."[27] This Global France would lead in Africa and in Europe; Eurafrican ideology offered a route to master both.

With this new focus on a federative French Union, celebrations of Eurafrica had to shed their earlier language of African subservience to a pan-European power. To escape its tinge of fascism and adapt to postwar distaste for overt expressions of racial superiority, white thinkers now joined advocates like Senghor to cast Eurafrica as a guarantee of equality between Europe and Africa.[28] In July 1945, Robert Delavignette, director of the École nationale de la France d'outre-mer, formerly known as the École coloniale, rhapsodized that "such a union is the opposite of domination. . . . *Tomorrow, we all will be the natives of the same French Union.*"[29] Guernier, best known for his 1933 *L'Afrique: Champ d'expansion de l'Europe,* which detailed economic spheres of influence, turned in the postwar to a call for the creation of a "Eurafrican community." He wrote in 1953, "If we want to construct Europe like our ancestors constructed France, we must economically fuse Europe and Africa, which will lead one day to the search for a political framework built from justice, liberty, and progress, contenting both."[30] The rhetoric had shifted, from claiming Africa as the means of European expansion to casting Africa as the partner in a unification of Europe in which all parties must be appeased. That Africans would, in either scenario, be obligated to assist Europeans went unremarked on; to Guernier and others, it was a logical demand to make.

Given the association of both European federalism and Eurafrica with earlier plans for peace making, Eurafrica after the war appeared as a humanistic mode of defending France's imperial status while nodding to changing political tides. For metropolitan officials faced with challenges from the newly formed United Nations (UN), Eurafrican language became a useful vocabulary for defending what one statesman would later call France's African vocation. In 1950, an administrator in French West Africa wrote that the French were "simultaneously in a position of judge and defendant before the tribunal that is the United Nations, defending a project of which those participating know very little concerning the conditions and merits." By asserting that UN officials did not understand the situation in Africa, he portrayed French authorities as uniquely suited to addressing questions of empire. As Jessica Pearson has shown, French officials went to great lengths to argue that the UN did not have the authority to oversee the internal affairs of the empire, a claim similarly forwarded by British and Belgian UN delegates.[31] Casting Africans as equal participants in the pursuit of Eurafrica stood to minimize UN scrutiny of French imperial practice. For officials outside of continental France, Eurafrican advocacy opened conversations about rights across the French Union and beyond, allowing them to remind other French and European administrators that equal treatment and rights would be a precondition to African involvement in any future national or international institutions. For ideologues and political thinkers, this new version of Eurafrica returned France to its rightful place as the leader of Africa while shielding France from accusations of racism. Celebrations of France's unique capacity to straddle Europe and Africa—a Eurafricanist ideal—would allow it to do so.

Articles by the Prix Goncourt winner and staunch Europeanist Gaston Riou are a good example of the French reaction to UN scrutiny and the halting attempt to recast France's civilizing mission as a partnership of equals. In 1950, Riou wrote in *Hommes et mondes,* a literary and political journal, "Slavers, racists, that isn't us! France followed Grégoire in 1789, Schoelcher in 1848, Brazza and Éboué under the Third Republic. We have a lot of '*indigènes*' in our assembles, and we love them. At the helm of our Senate, we have elected a son of Guiana [Gaston Monnerville], and we love him." He quoted Guernier, who at the Cercle métropolitain de l'Empire française had recently declared, using a French term for diversity that denoted the offspring of interracial unions, "I believe in the excellence of *métissages*. In all domains, I believe in the virtue of mixes and fusions!" These ecstatic expressions allowed Riou to conclude, "Such is French colonialism, gentlemen of Lake Success [then home of the UN]. Such is French racism."[32] Riou appeared fixated on certain accusations in the UN, writing in a later issue of the same journal, "We challenge them to dare to say we are racists and slavers ever again."[33] His flattening of history—naming Éboué and the colonizer Pierre Savorgnan de Brazza in the same breath—and his patronizing declarations of love exemplify French tropes about humanism and universalism. Indeed, that Riou needed to name abolitionists of 1789 and 1848 inadvertently drew attention to France's shameful reenslavement of peoples in 1802, to say nothing of practices like the *corvée,* a forced labor system operative in parts of French West and Equatorial Africa until after World War II. It also accentuated the complete erasure of the history of Saint-Domingue (present-day Haiti) from accounts of the French Revolution.[34] This type of unswerving confidence in France's universalism made its leaders strong contenders to advocate for a version of Eurafrica whose egalitarian mask obscured self-serving interests, even as they also pursued genuine imperial reform.[35]

Interwar iterations of Eurafrica projected a supercontinent, a citadel for European power in response to both the United States and the ascendant Soviet Union. The Eurafrica-as-bulwark argument became more relevant as the Cold War intensified after World War II. For French thinkers, Eurafrica kept Europe at the center of global affairs, and France—with its expansive empire—at the center of Europe. Author Pierre Fistié warned in *Le Monde* that "if our countries do not want to be the Athens or Thebes of an Asian or Atlantic Macedonia, there is but one solution: attack the issue no longer in European terms, but in Eurafrican terms." He called North Africa the "cornerstone" of Eurafrica, a label vigorously rejected by *L'Algérie libre,* mouthpiece of Messali Hadj's Movement for the Triumph of Democratic Liberties (MTLD), which published a scathing response to Fistié's column.[36] Despite opposition, the concept of Eurafrica gained momentum as an answer to European woes. In the tellingly titled 1955 *L'Eurafrique: Notre dernière chance (Eurafrica: Our Last Chance),* Pierre Nord—better known for his spy novels—emphasized Eurafrica as the third force in the Cold War, as opposed to a lonely, small Western Europe, "crushed between the USSR and the USA." Only with Africa and with "the consent of Africans" could Europe emerge as an equal power, thanks in part to African mineral deposits necessary for the building of an atomic bomb.[37] Nord was right, although the outcome looked different than he had perhaps imagined. Overseas France proved integral to French nuclear ambitions when, in 1960, France exploded its first atomic bomb— Gerboise Bleue—near Reganne in the Algerian Sahara.[38] Calling for Eurafrica, thinkers like Nord offered administrators a pathway toward the renewal of French authority on the international stage.

In contrast to support from Senghor and other elected officials from the French Union, the notion of a Eurafrica also drew the ire of groups and politicians who questioned what it would mean for people in the French Union itself. In its rejection of Fistié's argument, *L'Algérie libre* called Eurafrica "a desperate attempt to resuscitate a corpse with a transfusion of young blood" and "a manifestation of an incorrigible passion for domination." Dismissing the very premise of Eurafrica, or the French Union itself, the author argued that North Africa "is linked to France only through the coercion of arms."[39] In 1957, the Guinean politician Diawadou Barry called Africa "the cake of European reconciliation," suggesting that the European project marked a new era of European neocolonialism.[40] These complaints were easily ignored. The drive to solve the issues of European harmony on the one hand and colonial unrest on the other hand led French officials to pursue Eurafricanist policy, in both name and deed, as a means of securing France's place internationally. In Fistié's effusive words: "There are not two problems, that of North Africa and that of the future of Europe. . . . They depend so closely on one another that they form a single issue: the creation of a political entity that will reap the heritage of our civilization."[41]

Imperial Reforms for a Eurafrican Future

Whether in Fistié's dire civilizational terms or in Nord's reference to African mineral deposits, these authors inadvertently highlighted the anxious current that ran under Eurafrican ideology: European states had long relied on their empires for prestige, yes, but now Europe's very survival depended on its access to Africa. Just as Victor Hugo predicted for his United States of Europe, Nord and others envisioned a Eurafrica led by the French. Fistié, in the article reviled by the MTLD, declared that French and North African people would carry the weight of Eurafrica, "the tremendous [terrible] but magnificent responsibility."[42] Such assertions arose in part because of a common French conviction that they ran their empire better than other European powers. Recent administrative reforms to the empire, notably stemming from the Brazzaville Conference and the foundation of the French Union, fit within a French tradition of celebrating assimilation.[43] Assimilationist ideology held that by imposing French cultural practice on overseas populations, these people would come to feel French, as seen in Riou's rhapsodic praise of "mixing."

For French thinkers, assimilation rendered French colonialism a singularly just project that radiated universalist light across the globe. It also helped to legitimize the French Union and Eurafrica. At times, assimilation was rewarded with political rights, as in the case of évolués. Nord, for one, used assimilation to explain the superiority of France's African presence. "Whereas no Congolese told me 'I am Belgian,'" he wrote, across the French Union, Africans insisted "with nearly the ease and directness of a Picard or Breton, without my pushing them, by chance during a conversation, 'I am French.'" To Nord, this was "proof of France's exceptional accomplishment in its colonizing work."[44] This trope proved popular among European federalists. Albert Gordiani, a prominent member of Lyon's federalist circles, told a group of young visitors from Bougie (Béjaïa), Algeria, that "the citizen of Dakar, whether Black or white, feels equally at ease in Paris, Lille, or Bordeaux as in his native Senegal because everywhere in the metropole, as overseas, reigns the same spirit of liberty and respect." Likewise, once these young people returned to "that French province which is Algeria, you will see that France remains worthy of our love, regardless of our race or our religion."[45] Nord and Gordiani's belief that Africans, in this moment of imperial restructuring, felt French and identified with the metropole fit well with overarching Eurafricanist claims about the blossoming partnership between the two continents. It ignored the unequal extension of rights, implicitly based on race, and the racial prejudice in the form of housing discrimination and more experienced by French Africans who traveled to the metropole for their studies or work.[46]

From the Brazzaville Conference and on, French officials in Paris and the empire wrestled with the thorny question of who could be considered "French." Historians have demonstrated that the upheaval of war leads to changes in citizenship regimes.[47] The wartime patriotism evinced by leaders like Éboué, coupled with the great sacrifice of colonial troops, many of whom languished in prisoner of war camps for much longer than their white counterparts, led to the further shakeup of French rights regimes in the second half of the 1940s.[48] With the concept of "empire" outmoded, the newly established Fourth Republic reconfigured its holdings into the more federated French Union, an administrative body comprising continental France, the Algerian departments, the overseas departments (DOM, the "old colonies"), the overseas territories (TOM), and associated states and territories, namely the protectorates of Morocco and Tunisia, Indochina, and the UN trusteeships of Togo and Cameroon. These different demarcations fell under the mandates of distinct ministries, although as we will see, there was more overlap than the *organigrammes,* or complex administrative hierarchy charts favored by the French, suggested. The demarcations also dictated different types of laws, including about how, if at all, French citizenship applied to a given locale's population.

Legal promises did not always actualize. Within months of decreeing that all metropolitan law would extend to the DOM (French Guiana, Guadeloupe, Martinique, and Réunion) by the following year, the National Assembly balked and instead declared in December 1946 that any law would need to be passed for its application there. The social security regime would not come to Martinique until 1949 and family allowances were only extended there in the early 1970s.[49] Yet in the eyes of its proponents, the French Union's federative promise and its invitation to a more egalitarian form of citizenship signaled an evolution in French imperial administration and suggested that France was edging closer to the realization of actual republican universalism. Leaders from the DOM and TOM saw this as an opportunity to assert their claims for autonomy and inclusion not just in French affairs but in the emergent realm of integrated European institutions as well. At the same time, the Fourth Republic's constitution and other legislation raised questions because of the vagaries of its wording.

On May 7, 1946, the National Constituent Assembly approved the *loi Lamine Guèye,* named for the Senegalese deputy who introduced it and declaring that "all residents [*ressortissants*] of the overseas territories (including Algeria) have the quality of citizen, just like the French nationals [*nationaux*] of the metropole and the overseas territories." In James E. Genova's assessment, the passage of the law created "potentially the most revolutionary and fluid context for the (re)definition of French citizenship and nationality since the Revolution of 1789."[50] The language of the *loi Guèye,* however, left room for interpretation. Was "quality of citizenship" equal to citizenship itself? Was Algeria, a grouping of departments, somehow also a TOM, as the parenthetical implied? The "quality of citizenship" offered promise and confusion. Analyzing this phrase's use in the interwar, Gary Wilder points out that "these obtuse formulations derived from the fact that colonial subjects were not foreign nationals who could be naturalized; they could not solicit a French nationality that they already legally possessed."[51] In other words, although holding a "quality of citizenship" sounded like an extension of rights, it also opened the door to the denial of rights. Further still, the *loi Guèye* inscribed these rights several months before the adoption and implementation of the new constitution founding the Fourth Republic and with it the French Union. As such, subsequent debates about the nature of the French Union called into question whether the law should apply to the trusteeships at all.

Before the *loi Guèye,* a right-wing member of the National Constituent Assembly's Committee on Overseas France suggested that Africans were not yet prepared for suffrage. Representatives from overseas holdings quickly refuted this argument, including

Senghor, who reminded the committee that the expansion of universal male suffrage in the metropole in 1848—the same year that the Second Republic extended French citizenship to men in the Quatre Communes of Senegal—largely concerned illiterate men. As debates about how to engage subjects in the emerging French Union continued, the "quality of citizenship" struck some lawmakers as the key to forming a multinational union, while others, notably Paul-Émile Viard, a jurist representing Algiers, advocated for more concrete wording. Senghor himself argued that French subjects should be understood as "simply citizens without specifying whether they are 'French citizens' or 'citizens of the French Union.' Usage will decide the label." Open-endedness would keep feasible and attainable a range of political futures, among them association and federation. Independence was not among the possibilities that Senghor listed. Despite tense debates, the *loi Guèye* came to form the basis of the constitution's citizenship law. It held for its proponents the possibility of inviting further rights, including universal suffrage and more local autonomy down the road. Yet the reluctance on the part of European French legislators to go further and guarantee equal rights underlined the deeply ingrained, racialized beliefs about who truly merited full rights as a part of a French polity.[52]

After decades in which, in Tyler Stovall's formulation, "imperial liberal democracy had a paradoxical cast—citizenship in the metropole, subjecthood in the colonies—and the difference was racial," these debates invited new assertions of who merited the rights of French citizenship, but the racialized distinctions that characterized the earlier era remained.[53] In October 1946, the constitution of the Fourth Republic enshrined the unclear wording of the "quality of citizen." On the domestic stage, the Fourth Republic introduced an ambiguity into the status of its citizenry and muddled Algeria's precise relationship to the republic. This caused consternation in some circles, particularly among jurists interpreting the constitution's language. Yet the vagaries proved useful. For French officials, the parenthetical inclusion of Algeria invited a wider range of options when they negotiated with their European partners. They could decide, as it suited their purpose, whether to assert Algeria's uniqueness or to pass it off as akin to other parts of the French Union.

Undefined Algeria

On an international level, adhering to the legal norm that Algeria comprised departments served French interests well, in part by allowing officials to draw on funds and safeguards aimed at the metropole. In the late 1940s, assertions of Algeria's Frenchness facilitated the funneling of Marshall Plan aid to Algeria and guaranteed it protections under the terms of the North Atlantic Treaty Organization (NATO). Similar claims would later allow the French to tap funds from European institutions to support development projects in Algeria. Embracing the vagaries of the Fourth Republic's constitution also allowed officials to elide Algeria's distinct status. In particular, by selectively omitting Algeria's departmental status when forging early European treaties, French officials hoped to stave off demands that they share access to Algerian goods and markets.

This useful state of ambiguity served the French well during international discussions, even as it made some jurists nervous about the lack of clarity. Algeria's mutable relationship to the metropole on the global stage—part of the metropole; tangential to it—relied on the complexity of domestic citizenship and administrative regimes in the Fourth Republic. We will now turn to Algeria and Algerians' legal position in France, looking at citizenship rights, the debates about the *statut organique,* during which Councillor Devaud uttered her notorious remarks, and then conversations by jurists and politicians teasing out exactly what Algeria's status might be. The domestic arena is critical for understanding why the French would in later years insist that Algeria, as an integral part of the Republic, must be included in integrated European institutions. It is also necessary to parse this domestic legal landscape to explain how the French could level that claim and to consider what types of ramifications might come from making such demands on their European partners.

The 1946 constitution appeared to extend major voting rights to considerably larger numbers of people overseas, a prospect that did not sit well with all metropolitan officials. In practice, newly enfranchised people were prevented from casting ballots in the first election in which they were technically allowed to vote, and as the example of the Algerian *statut organique* makes clear, the legislature quickly erected barriers to equal representation. As for the "quality of citizen," socialist minister of Overseas France Marius Moutet argued that holding the *rights* of a citizen did not render a person a citizen.[54] Citizens of the French Republic were also citizens of the French Union. French Union citizens were not citizens of the French Republic and thus would not have a voice in metropolitan elections. The political assimilation of individuals across the French Union had its limits: limits delineated by metropolitan officials and, unspoken, based on perceptions of racial difference.

The citizenship question proved particularly consequential and complex for the departments of Algeria. Since 1848, successive French regimes had administered the north of Algeria as departments integrated to the metropole; most of its residents, in contrast, were not integrated as French citizens. Algeria's Muslim and until 1870, except in the Sahara, Jewish residents were denied full citizenship rights and instead held rights under what the French labeled personal status. Under French law, personal status denoted one's right to be subject to the laws and courts of their religious community, meaning Muslim, Jewish, or in the case of the French Establishments in India, Hindu customary law. Often presented by French authorities as a choice that could be opted out of at any time by a person who wished to enjoy full French citizenship under civil status, in reality it was neither desirable nor possible for most Algerians to shed their personal status.[55] Religious persuasion alone did not determine one's status, as white European converts to Islam maintained their French civil status. Nor was personal status wholly incompatible with full citizenship, as the Senegalese Frenchmen of the Quatre Communes could attest. The numbers of Algerians who successfully renounced their personal status are staggeringly low. From 1865 to 1915, only 2,396 Algerian Muslims became French through naturalization.[56] Attempts at making French citizenship more attainable in Algeria, most famously the 1936 Blum-Viollette proposal, which would have granted roughly 24,000 Muslims the right to French citizenship with personal status, were met with outrage from Algeria's settler population and did not come to be.

Beyond their lack of rights, Algerian Muslims had much to protest in the interwar period. As Algeria's population grew precipitously, from 4.5 million in 1926 to 5.5 million in 1936, urban shantytowns drew families subsisting on paltry wages and people in rural areas struggled with hunger. Meanwhile, anti-imperial or reformist movements arose in different colonies and among émigré populations in imperial metropoles. One key movement of the interwar was the Étoile nord-africaine, founded by Messali Hadj in 1926. North African laborers in Paris marched with communist and socialist trade unions in February 1934 to protest the right-wing riots and again on Bastille Day 1936, now to support the Popular Front. It was under this political climate that the Blum-Viollette bill failed. When the French government banned the Étoile nord-africaine in 1937, it was quickly replaced by the Algerian People's Party (PPA), a radical, populist nationalist group.[57] In Algiers and other cities, Muslim Algerian veterans of World War I used reminders of their sacrifice to demand political reform or outright independence; European settler veterans mobilized their own service to uphold existing hierarchies.[58]

World War II stood to change the relative intransigence of French citizenship law in Algeria and the rest of the empire. The North African theater of war proved critical to France's liberation and the defeat of both Vichy and Nazi forces.[59] The cost of the war was high in Algeria and served as a turning point for Algerian nationalism and the discrediting of French claims of universalism past and future. Allied troops invaded Morocco and Algeria in November 1942, and by May 1943, they had captured Tunis. Resistance work in Algiers and elsewhere helped to secure the victory, but in reality, much of the burden of the war fell on civilians whose own access to food and other supplies was severely curtailed as infrastructure was redirected to the war effort. When

136,000 demobilized Algerians returned home, they found, in the words of historian Martin Evans, that the "disjunction between the ideal of anti-Nazi liberation and the reality of French Algeria could not have been more startling."[60]

It was in this period that the events of May 8, 1945 in Sétif and Guelma occurred. During demonstrations celebrating Germany's capitulation on VE Day, marchers unfurled banners and shouted slogans in support of Messali Hadj, who had been deported to Brazzaville two weeks prior. The peaceful demonstration in Sétif devolved as scuffles and then shots broke out. As panic spread, Algerians killed forty-eight Europeans and the police shot into the Algerian crowds. On May 8 and the days that followed, Algerians killed 102 Europeans in the Sétif region. In the coming weeks, settlers, then the French military, killed 6,000 to 8,000 Muslim Algerians.[61] The vicious quelling of Algerian nationalist protests, whose own violence French authorities characterized as nothing but fanatical, apolitical barbarity, added to Muslims' feelings of alienation and distrust of the French state and the settler population.[62] In Guelma, the European population set up an extrajudicial tribunal to try suspect Muslim Algerians, not unlike the illegal court martials of the early days of the liberation. Until the end of June, settlers—with police, gendarmes, and militia members working together—carried out what one commissioner called "a revolt." From May 13 to 16, settler forces with the complicity of the local police and gendarmes killed over eighty Muslims per day. The French state would soon extend amnesty to the Europeans involved in the massacres. Historian Jean-Pierre Peyroulou concluded his detailed study of Guelma and its aftermath by arguing that the French state "contributed to making the colonial state irreformable" when it acquiesced to the settler population.[63]

At the time, however, officials in Paris and Algeria did not realize the missteps they were making, guided by their continued conviction that colonial authority and settler rule was just, even as they touted reform. As such, French counterinsurgent brute force accompanied promises of legal reform meant to favor Algeria's majority Muslim population.

These reforms began even before the end of the war in Europe. On March 7, 1944, the provisional government abolished the *indigénat,* the punitive regime of legalized repression and racial-religious discrimination that existed in a variety of forms across the empire. De Gaulle assured Algerians that they would enjoy equal rights to settlers. In theory, they could engage in free circulation to the metropole, although in practice, securing employment remained difficult.[64] The 1944 ordinance extended franchise in the second college to Algerian men over age twenty-one, while an additional 60,000—mainly decorated veterans or those who held civil service posts—received French citizenship while retaining their personal status. Thanks to the Fourth Republic's constitution, those 60,000 French citizens "in the status" were soon joined by the rest of Algeria's Muslim population as citizens of the French Union.[65]

The expansion of citizenship rights to Algerians raised uncomfortable questions for French authorities about representation and equality in these French departments. In an attempt to clarify Algerian rights given the ambiguity of the constitution, on September 20, 1947, the French National Assembly adopted the *statut organique de l'Algérie,* which created an Algerian Assembly with an equal number of representatives from the first college, comprising mainly Europeans and elected by roughly 532,000 people, and the second college, elected by 1.3 million Muslim Algerian electors.[66]

As the debates before the law's adoption demonstrate, this outcome satisfied very few people in Algeria. Under French jurisprudence, organic laws are meant to clarify constitutional directives about the organization of public powers—in this case, the makeup of the assembly. To the European population, the new law allowed too many Algerian representatives for comfort. To the Algerians, sending only sixty representatives for their vastly larger constituency was still too few, an insultingly low number that maintained their underrepresentation in government.[67]

Debates about the statute in the National Assembly and the Council of the Republic merit a close examination because of the range of important questions they provoked. Represented in the debates were virulent settler ideologies, calls for Algerian autonomy, confusion over Algeria's legal status, and fears of a future in which France no longer presided over Algerian affairs. Most germane to this book, the debates about the statute showcase how the ambiguity of Algeria's status could be mobilized to make opposing claims, in this case, for or against numerically representative government. The debates also emphasize limitations among French officials who celebrated assimilation but proved unable to picture Muslim Algerians as truly deserving of the full rights of French citizenship. In Brussels, Algeria's unclear status would soon be exploited as a means of securing European material, political, and even psychological support to counter anti-imperial nationalists.

Discussions about the *statut organique* began in the National Assembly, then moved to the Council of the Republic, then returned to the National Assembly for a final vote.[68] Typical of the Algerian officials insulted by the lack of equal representation, deputy of Constantine Abdelkader Cadi of the Musulman indépendant pour la défense du fédéralisme algérien (MIDFA) group invoked anti-colonial uprisings in Indochina and Madagascar and implied that the statute would provoke similar events in Algeria because it was nothing but "the current status quo, barely disguised."[69] On the opposite side were politicians like Algiers deputy General Adolphe Aumeran (Républicains indépendants), a Philippeville (Skikda)-born settler who called Cadi's patriotism into question. Constantine deputy Hachemi Benchennouf (MIDFA) came to Cadi's defense, declaring, "The truth is that you are not used to having before you second college representatives who have the right to express their ideas. This appears unbelievable to you. Here, we are in France and not in Algeria."[70] This was an interesting subversion—deliberate or not—of the wartime pronouncement by former Constantine deputy and alleged collaborationist Joseph Serda, "Alger n'est pas Paris," blistered in the communist press as indicative of the "overt assertion of separation from France" that originated not from Muslim nationalists, but from "the French (!)"[71] Serda's utterance, in turn, echoed a 1925 warning by communist representative Paul Henriet that "we are no longer in France," emphasizing the particularly repressive conditions of Algeria that made its political situation vastly different than the metropole's.[72] Benchennouf came closer to Henriet's claim, using the distinction to imply that the metropole was republican and imbued with the equality stymied by settlers in Algeria.

The notion of being "in France" rather than Algeria was legally complex, thanks in no small part to the lack of clarity in the constitution of the Fourth Republic. When the Council of the Republic debated the statute, Constantine councillor El-Hadi Mostefaï (UDMA) leveled a similar accusation, declaring that

Algerians were waiting for "a night of August 4," a reference to the nascent National Assembly voting to abolish the feudal order in 1789. He challenged those who claimed that "Algeria is nothing but the prolongation of France. Really? But it would be the opposite of this beautiful and sweet France, because everything that constitutes French grandeur in the eyes of the world is banished or unknown there."[73] Grandeur, here, meant republicanism and equality. Algerian representatives harnessed celebrations of French universalism to undercut claims that Algeria was unequivocally French soil.

As it stood under French law, Algeria was caught between being considered metropolitan or DOM. Mostefaï contended that the proposed statute would do little to clear up confusion, instead "giving ambiguity official recognition. . . . Lacking in this French Union a place of its own, it is condemned to sit at the end of the table, a poor relation, as a subject lacking the right to one day climb the steps that lead to freedom."[74] Like Benchennouf, Mostefaï painted a picture of a just France from which Algeria was excluded. He introduced into the conversation a fear about the confusion engendered by Algeria's ambiguous juridical status within the French Union. Given that the legislature was unable to delineate clearly under what legal regime Algerians were protected or even granted rights, the very core of the French Union, and its federative promise to its citizens, was compromised. Deputy Cadi and his colleagues countered the proposed statute with a federalist alternative that would guarantee representative rights and authority for the majority Muslim population, here meaning a federation between Muslim and settler populations that would require the buy-in from both as a means of securing the equal treatment of the former. Cadi was one of eight members of MIDFA, which espoused a nationalist—if moderate—set of goals meant to usher in equality between all populations in Algeria.

After its discussion of and votes to amend the statute, the Council of the Republic sent the law back to the National Assembly for a final discussion of their recommendations and the vote. Speaking on behalf of Algerian communists, Constantine deputy Abderrahmane (Chérif) Djemad declared that the group would vote against the statute because "the project leaves Algeria under the regime from which it has suffered too much." The Ivorian deputy Félix Houphouët-Boigny announced that African communists would also vote against it, arguing that initiatives such as Algerian women's suffrage and Arabic language instruction would require a two-thirds majority in the Algerian Assembly—meaning the support of a sizable number of settler representatives—which would doom such reforms to be "once again, postponed indefinitely." Houphouët-Boigny asked, "Do you believe that it is with divided peoples that you will form a true French union?" and decried the statute, "which does not satisfy in the slightest the legitimate aspirations of the vast majority of Algerian people."[75] This criticism did not sway the majority of National Assembly, which adopted the statute by a vote of 325 to 86. President Vincent Auriol proclaimed it law on September 20, 1947.[76] Houphouët-Boigny was right; the promised reforms were never realized.

The *statut organique* pleased few of the concerned parties. Despite their heated debates and the justified accusations of racism leveled against Devaud and some settler deputies, Algerian and settler alike united to cast their vote against the statute, rendering them strange bedfellows. Even after the purported reforms of the *statut organique,* which included a clause on free circulation of labor, Algerian laborers received French social security protections only if they worked in the metropole. They could not count on those same benefits or expect protection for their families if they returned to Algerian soil. The ineffectiveness of the statute and the Algerian Assembly it created did little to clarify Algeria's role within the French Republic or the French Union writ large. Indeed, Algeria's juridical status remained confused, as did the rights of Algerians, whose legal standing could shift if they moved to the metropole, for example. The ambiguity surrounding Algeria's status during the Fourth Republic puzzled jurists but would ultimately be a useful tool for French officials who believed the shifting ground could be leveraged when trying both to quell the nascent anti-imperial war and to negotiate European integration. But we are getting ahead of ourselves. For now, it is instructive to look at the jurists and officials who fretted over how to define Algeria in a legal sense, because their fears underlined the juridical confusion over Algeria's relationship to Paris.

Legal scholars, particularly in Algeria, took great interest in the postwar juridical status of Algeria and the rest of France's empire. Viard, dean of the law school of Algiers and a future National Assembly deputy (MRP), wrote in 1943 that France must be understood as a large, single body, "and when we say *France* here, we are no longer thinking of the Metropole." He went on to declare that the issue now was "to know in what manner the people of Greater France will participate in sovereignty."[77] Once the Fourth Republic's constitution was ratified, notions of sovereignty were compounded by attempts to parse out French Union citizenship, given the ambiguity of "the quality of French citizenship" held by overseas populations.

Jurist Jacques Lambert of the Algiers law faculty laid out the complicated, even convoluted, ways that Algeria could be understood under French law. Citing a variety of legal decisions from 1908 to 1935, Lambert demonstrated that "Algeria was not a colony." Instead, he argued, it was a *"sui generis* creation. One said, 'Algeria and the colonies.'" With the advent of the French Union, the question was, "What place in the French Republic does Algeria hold? Is it metropolitan France itself? That, we could say, is a physical absurdity. Algeria is therefore overseas. But is it 'overseas departments' or 'overseas territory?'" He cited scholars who had deemed it to be a DOM or TOM, or in the case of Viard, a composition of metropolitan departments. Although Moutet himself—the minister of Overseas France whose tenure oversaw the passage of the Fourth Republic's constitution and the *statut organique*— declared Algeria to be comprised of DOM, a legal reality upheld by the Conseil d'État in March 1947, Lambert argued that "doubt remains."[78] Jurists themselves, particularly those based in the metropole, added to this ambiguity by publishing law manuals about Overseas France, inclusive of Algeria.[79] While the Fourth Republic's constitution declared that the legal regimes of the DOM and metropole were the same, "save for exceptions determined by the law," Lambert argued that with the constitution's ratification, Algeria was not a DOM at all.[80]

Lambert's inconclusive attempt to parse Algeria's status is demonstrative of both the possibility of the postwar era, in which borders might be expansive, and also the challenges to such claims. The ambiguity of Algeria's status afforded French officials the space to deny Algerians rights and to exclude Algeria from European institutions when favorable for the metropole. That same ambiguity allowed French officials to push for protections for Algeria under the auspices of European frameworks, such as aid from the European Recovery Program (ERP), or Marshall Plan. Of the over $2.2 billion of the ERP that went to France between 1948 and 1951, the French government funneled $140 million, or more than 6 percent of the funds, to North Africa.[81] In the years to come, the mutability of Algeria's status—and the rights of Algerians themselves—caused friction with France's would-be European allies and sparked situations in which the French government appeared inadvertently poised to extend major labor or social rights to vast swaths of the Algerian populace. The ambiguity in the constitution's wording had its uses, but it also carried with it a risk. Then again, as Algerian disdain for the *statut organique* suggests, by this point anything offered by the French may have been too little, too late.

Beyond the *statut organique*, other debates about Algeria's and Algerians' status vis-à-vis the metropole played out in the legislature. In March 1948, a National Assembly session devolved during discussions of foreign relations, and specifically the "Muslim question," because representatives were able to harness the ambiguity of Algeria's status in order to direct the debate toward subjects they wished to pursue. Although ostensibly a debate slated to focus on the issue of Palestine on the eve of the foundation of the State of Israel, Algerian deputies swung the conversation to focus on Algeria's status in global politics and more.

In a foreshadowing of future issues with European integration, Alice Sportisse (Parti communiste français, PCF), who had represented Oran since the convening of the provisional government's First National Constituent Assembly in October 1945, warned that Franco-Italian accords now under negotiation would negatively impact Algerian workers, Muslim and otherwise. "It is not by chance," she argued, that the Algerian press, including the "Vichyist newspaper *L'Écho d'Alger*," celebrated the negotiations and tied them to talks between French and English representatives "in preparation for establishing the famous Eurafrica, an idea which is not new"—that is, a fascist idea. In spite of the beliefs of those who thought such a configuration would be the "third global force [*troisième force mondiale*]," Eurafrica had "only one meaning: to facilitate economic control at the same time as the installation of strategic bases of American imperialism in preparation for their anti-Soviet war."[82] Sportisse's ability to tie collaborationist ideology to American imperialism via Eurafrica was more than a semantic coup; it signaled that for some representatives, European cooperation in the colonies was insidious. So too was the pursuit of an internationalism that would summon global capitalism rather than worldwide communism. To Sportisse, this latest iteration of antiworker politics played out through the exploitation of empire. On a broader scale, it signaled the encroachment of a powerful and dangerous outside force looking to build its domination by grabbing at Algeria. The mobilization of the term *Eurafrica,* so popular with fascists, was a poor attempt to mask larger imperialist intentions.

Discussions linking Algeria to international questions inspired consternation among some representatives. When another PCF representative from Algeria, who spoke about trade unions rather than foreign affairs, caused Minister of Foreign Affairs Georges Bidault (MRP) to storm out of the chambers, Roland de Moustier of the right-wing PRL cried, "To the subject! This is a debate about foreign policy and not Algeria, which, until further notice, is French." Another PRL deputy soon exclaimed, "What is serious is wanting to treat Algeria as something other than French soil."[83] To the likes of de Moustier, who represented the metropolitan department of Doubs, even the insinuation that Algeria could be discussed when international issues were at hand represented a dangerous division of the French Republic.

Although PCF comments caused the ruckus, there was a potentially more dangerous idea floated that day. Earlier, Comoros deputy Saïd Mohamed Cheikh (Union démocratique et socialiste de la Résistance) declared, "According to us, France's Muslim policy cannot be discussed without including all of the countries of the French community permeated by Islam." The population of the Comoros, an Indian Ocean archipelago, was nearly 100 percent Muslim, and Cheikh did not shy away from tying it to a global Islamic community.[84] In his eyes, there existed a "Muslim world, which forms an indivisible whole." Later, he elaborated, "The Muslim question, whether asked about the interior of or outside of the French community, is indivisible."[85] The assertion that a supranational or transnational Islam existed within and beyond the borders of a federated French Union might have given Fourth Republic representatives pause. But unlike Sportisse, who could not speak without constant interruption, Cheikh's speech passed by relatively unremarked on. Did Cheikh's status as a deputy of the tiny Comoros make his contention appear less threatening? Did the other deputies chalk it up as religious sentiment that had little geopolitical meaning?

Had the deputies stopped to consider Cheikh's argument, they may have seen a more consequential implication in his "indivisible" claim. If the postwar period is hailed as the epoch of European unity, it is just as critically a high period of solidarity between non-European peoples. Cheikh was alluding to one in a range of possible transnational formulations that decentered Europe, here pan-Islam. Other attempts at *grands ensembles,* such as pan-Africanism and pan-Arabism, also extended their arms to Algeria. In the late

1940s, French officials recognized the menace of such thinking but failed to compute the broadness of its appeal. After all, they blamed the political violence of May 1945 on fanaticism and, as is clear from the PRL deputies' interjections, balked at even the suggestion that Algerian questions related to foreign affairs. Instead, most officials mentally separated French international interests from the governance of Algeria and the French Union. This would prove highly consequential as they pursued the first major stage of European integration, during which time they chose to exclude Algeria from their map of France and, by extension, Europe.

Constructing an Integrated Postwar Era

Shortly after World War II's end, French officials debated the meaning of the French Union and attempted to parse out how this new administrative body fit into both metropolitan and international affairs. At the same time, European administrators began gathering to plan for new stages of European integration. They would not follow Coudenhove-Kalergi's ambitious blueprint. The earliest stages were deeply focused on trade policy and tariff rates. Nevertheless, a semblance of Pan-Europa emerged. The first major step was the ECSC, which symbolically and practically tied together France and West Germany's war industries. Further plans for integration followed swiftly on the ECSC's heels. The ECSC covered only metropolitan French territory, a decision that led to consternation in some overseas circles. It was also a decision that may have contradicted the *statut organique,* whose Article 11 declared, "Treaties made with foreign powers rightfully apply in Algeria, as do the laws or decrees that are established."[86] Algeria's exclusion from the ECSC demonstrates that this precept was not followed.

The attempted federalism of the French Union was but one version of integration emerging after World War II, an era in which supranational cooperation was de rigueur. Belgium, the Netherlands, and Luxembourg formed the Benelux customs union while their respective governments were in exile in 1944. Across Europe, federalists regrouped and opened new lines of collaboration in hopes of seeing a unified Western European body come into being.[87] In order to manage the ERP's allocation, eighteen European states joined together from 1948 to 1949 to form the Organisation for European Economic Co-operation (OEEC), superseded by the Organisation for Economic Co-operation and Development (OECD) in the early 1960s.[88] The OEEC member states created the European Payments Union, which would facilitate European currency conversion through the setting of exchange rates. The postwar push for supranational organizing had begun. Critically, these examples of postwar European institutions have their own imperial histories, such as the Marshall Plan's financing of African projects.[89]

The Council of Europe also pursued Eurafrican policy, which would have shared African resources between the member states, culminating in the September 1952 Strasbourg Plan. Britain's representative said at the time, "It is clear that we have to think of these overseas territories not as the possessions of any one country; they have to be integrated with all the countries of Europe and all the overseas territories."[90] French representative of Guinea Raphaël Saller summed up the plan's inception as an attempt to address the reality that "Europe was not self-sufficient," based on the belief that "if all European countries participated in the development of overseas territories, particularly in Africa, such development would be accelerated, to the great advantage of all concerned."[91] The plan was never implemented, but its aims echoed the postwar iterations of Eurafrican ideology now taking the fore. Given Britain's choice not to join little Europe (the Six), its relationship to postwar Eurafrican policy can appear divorced from that of France. However, after World War II, French and British authorities found the prospect of cooperation enticing, leading to attempts at European collaboration in the management of empire.[92] In the late 1940s, the French and British joined to introduce development projects, notably health and hygiene, agriculture, teaching, and more, in their African colonies. This did not erase tensions; the Horn of Africa remained a source of competition. These efforts at points involved other powers, notably Belgium, Portugal, and South Africa. In order to "avoid giving this work the look of a colonialist front," Liberian and Ethiopian officials were periodically invited to planning conferences as well.[93]

Shared concerns about challenges to French imperial dominance and fears of Soviet influence drove these efforts, but French willingness to collaborate only went so far. Cold War concerns about anti-imperial nationalist movements expanded in the 1940s and 1950s and French authorities were aware of the United States' interest in keeping the Soviet Union out of Africa. As one US State Department official told the French embassy in Washington in 1949, "Africa today is (one of) the borders of the West."[94] While working with Britain was a logical way to pursue that goal, by late 1949, the French began to push back against their would-be partners, wary when the British suggested that an intergovernmental committee of imperial powers (Belgium, Portugal, South Africa, South Rhodesia) be headquartered in London.[95] As the

French withdrew from their collaborative efforts for technical work in Africa, France's ambassador in London, René Massigli, expressed alarm, worrying that his fellow French "so quickly took such a categorical position" against what amounted to "a French initiative."[96] In what would be a constant of the postwar period, French officials were not shy about alienating their European allies when it came to imperial affairs, even as some French ministries bemoaned the actions taken by other French officials.

By the founding of the ECSC, French officials realized that they were on shaky ground when it came to the confluence of France's self-appointed roles as both imperial power and European leader. In late 1952, a foreign affairs official produced a seven-page memo on "the position of overseas French territories in the question of European integration." Days earlier, a letter out of Louis Jacquinot's Ministry of Overseas France had declared the urgency of looking into whether the French Union states could or should be involved with that integration process. The unnamed memo author weighed the benefits and drawbacks. On the one hand, "juridically, the overseas territories belong to the 'Republic,' just like the metropole. Therefore, if the integration of metropolitan France to a European political community occurs, it must ipso facto be the same for the overseas territories." Even more pragmatically, "the weight that France will have in a European system will be greater if it brings with it its colonial territories." On the other hand, among the issues would be the potential exclusion of Morocco and Tunisia because of their associated status, and Cameroon and Togo because of their trusteeship status. Overseas populations' opinions would also need to be accounted for. Yet France "is not a uniquely European power. It is a global power. Its interests, aspirations, and destiny have long exceeded the bounds of the continent." He concluded that France should proceed with caution, carving out a position in Europe that "accounts for the existence of the extra-metropolitan territories in which France still largely places its reasons for hope in the future."[97] This official's analysis displays the ambivalence that would characterize French attitudes toward European integration's potential impact on the French Union. It was an ambiguity invited by pragmatic French reasoning about economic need and political exigency, rendered more complicated by the open-endedness of how French officials understood the juridical nature of the French Union itself.

2

Reforming Empire, Forming Europe

When the Council of the Republic convened on April 1, 1952 to debate whether President Vincent Auriol should ratify the Treaty of Paris, creating the European Coal and Steel Community (ECSC), the French Union barely garnered mention. In sharp contrast, speakers repeatedly raised questions about West Germany.[1] Beyond a doubt, the perceived menace of West German rearmament remained of paramount concern seven years after the end of World War II, even if warnings about ascendant Germany were at points tempered by expressions of hope that the ECSC would usher in a new period of peace in Europe.[2] Although often unspoken, French officials' fears of resurgent Germany—and a loss of French power in Europe and beyond—were compounded by concerns about the maintenance of the empire. Those twinned apprehensions shaped French attitudes toward European integration and the future of the French Union.

During the ECSC debates, there was one major exception to the relative silence about the French Union. Algiers senator Abdennour Tamzali called Algeria's absence from the ECSC treaty a new form of "economic *indigénat*," harkening to the now-defunct regime of legal discrimination propagated by the French in Algeria and elsewhere. This accusation accentuated the inequality in Algeria's day-to-day operations and now in its relationship to not only the rest of the French Republic but to Europe as well. A medical doctor, Tamzali had been one of twenty-eight elected Muslim officials to sign Ferhat Abbas's 1943 "Manifesto of the Algerian People," which called for the equality of all peoples in Algeria to be constitutionally guaranteed.[3] His remarks made little impact on the day's discussions and his Rassemblement des gauches républicaines coalition is sometimes remembered as a do-nothing organization.[4] Yet his assessment of the ECSC and its exclusion of Algeria foreshadowed the debates that would soon plague the Six, as the French mounted diplomatic efforts to insist in some venues that Algeria was a constitutive part of France and simultaneously to maintain in others that Algeria—and all of the French Union— had no place within a European institution. Tamzali pointed to the fundamental issue built into the Treaty of Paris: the excision of Algeria from the French Republic. What did it mean that while French officials touted, in Tamzali's words, "the juridical and economic credo of the intangibility and indivisibility of our economic union with the metropole," the Treaty of Paris made the departments of Algeria the "subject of an arbitrary discrimination"?[5]

Despite appearing untouched by the earliest iterations of integration, the French Union was already deeply embroiled in the project, as the reactions of Tamzali and others first to the ECSC and then to the abortive European Defense and Political Communities attest. The first half of the 1950s marked the final years in which French officials considered it possible and desirable to manage the problems of empire internally, without the material or moral backing of their European partners. They also believed that the empire positioned France to maintain a place of authority in Europe and beyond. As metropolitan officials emphasized the importance of drawing a line between continental Europe and the French Union, French Union representatives and anti-colonial activists alike leveled challenges to such a Eurocentric view of the world. Their dissent heralded the issues that French officials would soon face as they pursued European integration in the midst of growing colonial crises. When agitation and outright rebellion in Algeria became impossible to brush off, European venues became key sites for French claims making about their imperial sovereignty in Algeria. But in the years just after World War II, confident in their assumptions about grandeur, global relevance, and the singular place of continental France within the French Union and Western Europe, most French officials insisted that European and imperial affairs were mutually exclusive.

Tamzali was not a mere foil to French officials. He *was* a French official, as were numerous other representatives from the French Union who forced their counterparts from the Bouches-du-Rhône, the Marne, and elsewhere to confront the pitfalls and hypocrisies that attended the exclusion of the empire from newly integrated European institutions. Léopold Senghor, then a deputy for Senegal in the National Assembly, saw European negotiations as a forum in which to agitate for more overseas representation. Business leaders with ties to the imperial economy fretted over the risk to their coffers were France forced to "share" its markets. Military officers locked heads over whether a pooled defense scheme would protect or endanger their ability to defend the French Union—from enemies without or, more likely, within.

This chapter focuses on French discussions of European integration, directing little attention to the opinions of other European states because at this point in time, officials in France framed imperial questions as merely domestic. This was a deliberate choice meant to emphasize the indissolubility of the French Union and to allow Paris to position itself as an imperial and a global power. From French leaders' vantage, the empire secured France's economic and political might on the global stage and no prospective European partner had the right to dip its hands into that source of dominance.

In the first half of the 1950s, European officials pursued successful and failed schemes to pool their countries' economies, military resources, and more. Whether the empire would be a part of these integrations was subject to extensive debate, not least because after World War II, officials felt pulled in a number of directions, all purportedly with the same goal: France's defense. Just what needed defending was not clear. The ECSC, meant to fortify Europe's economy and tie together the war industries of France and the Federal Republic of Germany, came into being with the signing of the Treaty of Paris in 1951. The European Defense Community (EDC), meant to intertwine the Six's security, failed in 1954. The negotiations for and reactions to both treaties featured passionate pleas about the need to defend France's empire. Whether the empire needed defending by or from the rest of Europe was less clear, but the question lingered as French officials pursued colonial administrative reform such as the 1956 *loi-cadre Defferre* and prepared for further steps in integration after the release of the Spaak Report, which laid the groundwork for the European Economic Community (EEC).

Although the 1950s in France are often celebrated as the heady years of the *trente glorieuses,* this era hummed with anxiety. War was on the minds of French officials, with memories of World War II fresh and the First Indochina War raging since late 1946. French worries about actual war were compounded by their deep-seated mistrust of Germans, whom the United States government—driven by Cold War concerns—was eager to rearm. At the same time, France became one of the founding signatories of the North Atlantic Treaty Organization (NATO) in 1949 and thus committed to seeking military solutions to maintain peace and sovereignty in its fellow member states and beyond. The pressure to reconcile with West Germany, not yet a part of NATO, was intense, and European integration provided an avenue for satisfying this demand while also maintaining France's international relevance.

Given this new Cold War reality, French officials struggled to make sense of what they owed to various international communities and how that might impact the French Union. The decision to bar Algeria from the ECSC typified French practices of colonialism; in this case, despite official assertions that the Republic included Algeria, foreign affairs bureaucrats denied Algeria's status as French when the question of European membership arose. Only when it appeared to be a retort to anti-colonial activism across the French Union did those same functionaries push for Eurafrican-inspired policies within integrated Europe. For now, French officials maintained the need to hold the empire close, away from the prying hands of their would-be European partners.

Wedding Bells of Coal and Steel

On May 9, 1950, now commemorated as Europe Day, French minister of foreign affairs Robert Schuman delivered an address that jump-started European integration. The Schuman Declaration laid out a plan for "pooling basic production" of West German and French coal and steel, which would build "the first concrete foundation of a European federation indispensable to the preservation of peace." Based on a plan written by Jean Monnet, the influential statesman credited as the father of Europe, the declaration led directly to the launch of negotiations for what would become the ECSC. Schuman spent much of his brief oration extolling how the plan served the greater good by making inseparable France and West Germany's war industries, eliminating deadly competition. In what would turn out to be a highly consequential remark, he also invoked a shared European responsibility to develop Africa.[6] No longer couched in overtly exploitative language, Schuman's emphasis on development fit the postwar narrative of the modernizing mission.[7] Whatever sort of brotherhood Eurafrica's French proponents envisioned, they had not shed their basic beliefs about who needed whom. Schuman's decision to bring up Africa during a speech about European integration spawned a flurry of reactions demonstrating that regardless of some officials' best efforts to keep separate France's self-imposed duties in Europe and Africa, those functions were already intertwined.

Two weeks after Schuman announced the plan the issue came to a head when he infamously declared that France would bring "as a dowry" both its industry and Africa's market.[8] Schuman, a member of the Mouvement républicain populaire (MRP), made this statement in a speech at a party convention in Nantes. The offer to share Africa in a European marriage echoed Eurafrican ideology dating to the interwar period. In this line of thought, European peace and prosperity would be forged jointly in Africa, through the communal effort to exploit the latter's resources and, in some versions, also to assist its populations.[9] Little wonder, perhaps, that two years later Tamzali would rail against the "concubinage" in which Algerians found themselves now that France entered a "marriage of convenience" with the other members of the Six.[10] With Schuman's comment, the possibility that the French Union might be a part of an integrated Europe had been raised and this avenue toward future partnership remained open, and contested, for years to come.

Schuman's apparent magnanimity alarmed French representatives who bristled at this promise to share. The range of parties reacting to the "dowry" idea calls attention to the multiple actors with a stake in this question and the volume of opinions toward the French Union and a united Europe alike. The Parti communiste français (PCF) held the project of European integration generally in contempt, given the implications of rearming what it cast as an unrepentant West Germany and of luring France away from the Soviet Union and into the arms of American capitalism. PCF representatives in the French Union Assembly called for the end of negotiations, warning that the government was dealing in the "fate of African peoples, without asking their opinion," diverting them from "their legitimate aspirations for liberty and independence."[11] In the PCF representatives' view, the promise of a dowry was but one of a series of contestable French actions taken in the wake of World War II. Linking Africa to an integrated Europe would facilitate an unholy union and perpetuate the imperialism that the PCF purportedly disavowed.[12]

Senegalese senator Ousmane Socé Diop (Section française de l'Internationale ouvrière, SFIO) addressed Schuman's comments at the Council of Europe in Strasbourg. Socé Diop argued that Schuman alienated Africans at the precise moment that Europeans needed them most. Europeans, he argued, should focus on constructing "an economic house, habitable for" Africans, otherwise, the criticism of the "extreme left press" would be justified—criticism claiming that "in the execution of the Schuman Plan, France will bring Africa as a marriage gift to Germany." Socé Diop stoked Cold War fears about France becoming irrelevant in the face of two powerhouses. Africa's "148 million consumers and producers" had already drawn the attention of the United States, he warned, and "maybe tomorrow, the USSR." If Europe as a whole did not reevaluate its integration scheme, "its influence in Africa could completely disappear," and Africans, like Southeast Asians, might take arms to rid themselves of European influence. He called for "a political and economic construction that has the revolutionary ambition of creating a third continent." Africa, with this course of action, would not be the "wedding gift, but the best man who will have his place at the banquet table."[13] In Socé Diop's version of Eurafrica ("a third continent"), European officials would be obligated to recognize Africans as equal partners in the endeavor. The issue was not that a marriage would take place but rather, how.

Meanwhile, French officials warned about the prospects for Africa—and therefore France—of European integration, tying it to the dangers of reconciling with Germany. The economic journal *Marchés coloniaux* ran an article by Raphaël Saller, senator of Guinea and a member of the Groupe des Indépendants d'outre-mer, in which he criticized rhetoric in the West German press, including statements by Chancellor Konrad Adenauer, about "developing Africa together." This was another way of saying "France would cede to Germany the African market to gain or maintain other European markets." For Saller, a Martinique-born *évolué* and recipient of the Medaille de la Résistance, the thought of collaborating with Germans in Africa was abhorrent.[14] Not only was it "surprising" that French officials "sincerely believe one could make African development an international task," but it was "even more shocking" that Germans could be part of that project considering it was "this Germany that left such a bad memory in Africa" so recently. Although Saller's criticism might be read as a rejection of European integration plans inclusive of Africa, in reality he was fighting for integration that would put Europeans and Africans on equal footing, seeking the advice and participation of the latter.[15] Officials worried that the economy would be imperiled if the French Union's resources became European property. Former prime minister Georges Bidault (MRP) declared in 1951 that the French Overseas Territories (TOM) were "one of the principal assets of France. Putting them at Europe's disposition before it has been truly unified leads to nothing but a loss without compensation."[16] French officials saw European greed—except their own—everywhere.

While Socé Diop, Saller, Bidault, and others were talking about the whole of the French Union, concerns about the impact of European integration on Algeria were particularly pointed. This was in part because of its mineral resources, with their attendant powerful business lobby, and in part because of the distinct political and psychological links forged by French legislation and mythmaking that bound Algeria to the metropole. During the negotiations for the Treaty of Paris, French observers noted that there would be no "juridical difficulty" in including Algeria in the ECSC as a part of France.[17] Although most historians of Eurafrican thinking have emphasized ideology's preoccupation with sub-Saharan Africa—itself a geographic imaginary that divides the continent along perceived racial lines—the vision was never complete without Algeria.[18] French officials understood Algeria as both a profitable element in the scheme and a bridge between Europe and so-called "Black Africa." It was not the law, but French economic and political imperatives, that would keep Algeria outside of integrated Europe.

In the eyes of Parisian bureaucrats and European business leaders in Algeria, Algeria's mines, especially the coke mine of Kenadsa, needed special protection from the grasping designs of Italian steelmakers.[19] Unlike later negotiations for the EEC in which Italian representatives balked at the extension of integrated European regulations to Algeria, while in talks for the ECSC, the Italian delegation was eager to recognize France's southernmost Saharan border as long as it meant they could access Algerian iron.[20] This did not sit well with French representatives in Paris or Algiers. If included within the European pool, Algeria's resources would become common to all six member states in the sense that they would be exportable without the tariffs typically associated with foreign trade. France, in this vision, would share Algeria's bounty with Italy, encouraging peace and industriousness. Members of the Algerian Chamber of Commerce—a body that upheld French and settler interests—strenuously objected, contending that the pricing demands of the ECSC would have disastrous results for Algeria. Further, they argued, Algeria's mining industry was inextricably linked to Morocco's and Tunisia's. A rupture of this harmony would be economically and politically devastating for the region.[21] The Chambre syndicale des mines d'Algérie, an organization that defended mining interests, implored René Mayer, then a National Assembly deputy for Constantine, to intervene and sway the minister of foreign affairs to back off from any plan to include Algerian mines in the ECSC, blocking Italy from gaining unfettered access.[22]

Fears about Italian pretensions toward Algerian resources spilled out beyond closed discussions and into the public eye. A reporter in the *Dépêche quotidienne d'Algérie* asked, "What will the French Parliament say when it realizes that Mr. Pleven and Mr. Schuman have ceded a part of France's riches and a portion of its public power to Mr. de Gasperi and Mr. Sforza?" referring to René Pleven, then-president of the French Council of Ministers, and Italy's prime minister and minister of foreign affairs. Algeria, the reporter concluded, "already crippled by its taxation and social costs, energetically refuses to pay the cost of the pool."[23] Months later and only days after the April 18, 1951 signing of the Treaty of Paris, *L'Écho d'Oran,* perhaps with some relief, quoted Schuman declaring that "France maintains its total, exclusive sovereignty over mineral mining."[24]

There were also emotional, even existential, reasons behind the uproar. French national identity had long relied on its self-conception as an imperial power, benevolent civilizer, and global leader. During World War II, the colonies—in the form of legions of soldiers, republican African leaders, and resources—helped to liberate the occupied metropole and maintain some degree of dignity for France despite the shameful Vichy regime.[25] Although France's relationship with its colonies might look different after the war, with the transition to the French Union, officials' belief that this relationship was imperative to France's very existence remained as steady as ever. This conviction only amplified in the case of Algeria. Algeria's settler identity was virulently defended in the legislature, as the debates surrounding the 1947 *statut organique* made clear. Faith in Algeria's inherent Frenchness was widespread and routine. Following the National Liberation Front's (FLN) coordinated November 1, 1954 attacks, which officially launched the Algerian War of Independence, Minister of the Interior François

Mitterrand declared, "l'Algérie, c'est la France," a phrase soon repeated by Pierre Mendès France.[26] Unlike elsewhere in the French Union, where officials gradually supported an associational relationship between colony and metropole, in Algeria integrationist practice remained standard. Integration, in this sense, did not hold the federative quality of European unity; instead, it implied the subsuming by the metropole of Algerian governance and interests. In spite of this, officials still balked at allowing Algeria to be considered "la France" on the international stage, jealously guarding its resources and believing that including Algeria in the European arena would threaten French sovereignty there.

When the European wedding day arrived, France's equivocating on empire showed. Article 79 of the Treaty of Paris, establishing the ECSC, specified that "the present Treaty is applicable to the European territories of the member States." It went on to stipulate that each member state would be responsible for "extend[ing] to the other member states the preferential measures which it enjoys with respect to coal and steel in the non-European territories subject to its jurisdiction."[27] Although this might sound as if the French Union's economy was fully included in the ECSC, in practice it represented a most favored nations clause which applied to the Six's exports to the French Union but not vice versa.[28] It also stopped short of extending to overseas holdings the ECSC's promise of protecting immigrant (European) laborers with the same rights as national laborers in the coal and steel industries. While officials remained fond of celebrating a France that stretched "from Dunkirk to Tamanrasset," Article 79 appeared to sever this expanse, drawing a clear divide between continental France and the Algerian departments. This juridical split worried some officials, who saw the parceling of the French Republic as imperiling its economic and political harmony. But more administrators viewed integrated Europe as the potential threat to a harmonious French Union. That danger only increased as the Six embarked on their next major unification scheme: the creation of a European army and a common defense community.

Defending Empire from the Defense Community

The early years of the Cold War witnessed a flurry of diplomatic efforts—some successful, others not—meant to combat the menace of the opposing bloc. In 1948, Belgium, France, Luxembourg, the Netherlands, and the United Kingdom signed the Treaty of Brussels, creating a collective security body known as the Western Union. The Western Union's military function was soon subsumed by NATO, one of the most consequential postwar institutions, formed in 1949 by twelve so-called Western powers, including France. One year later, with the outbreak of the Korean War, NATO officials—particularly American—sought assurances that Western Europe could defend itself. Without the rearmament of West Germany, such a task appeared impossible. But with the bitter memory of World War II still fresh in French officials' minds, the notion of a German army appeared deeply unpalatable.

The solution to this conundrum—the "German question" versus security—came in the form of the Pleven Plan. Monnet approached Pleven, an ardent supporter of the Schuman Plan, with a scheme to unite a European army under the auspices of NATO. In presenting the proposal to the National Assembly, Pleven celebrated France's participation in both NATO and the soon-to-be ECSC while laying out specifics about the bureaucratic apparatus of the EDC. Its foundation, he proclaimed, must not allow Europeans to "forget the lessons of two world wars" and should ensure that the new military force would "never be used for anything except the defense of international security and peace."[29] The Pleven Plan appeased France's nervous politicians, and in February 1951, EDC negotiations, and the push to rearm the Federal Republic of Germany, began in earnest.

French efforts to maintain imperial order complicated any dream of a European army. In Indochina, the French army continued to wage a war against the Viet Minh that had formally begun in December 1946. NATO's treaty formally recognized Algeria as within the zone of its defense pact—and continued to do so until January 1963—but no such guarantees existed for France's holdings in Southeast Asia or elsewhere.[30] French military and civilian authorities worried that the demands of a European army would divert troops from the Indochinese theater. When they were more realistic, however, they acknowledged that it was smaller states, such as Belgium, that would send disproportionally high numbers of troops to serve Europe.[31] Dutch officials argued that rather than France suffering from a diversion of troops, it would be so tied up in Indochina that it would not even have a sufficient number of divisions to send to the new force.[32] Thus, concerns about empire dogged the EDC's proponents.

Despite such concerns, after months of negotiations the Six agreed to the EDC treaty, signing it on May 27, 1952. Yet it would never come to be. The treaty resolved to establish the EDC, "supranational in character, consisting of common institutions, common armed forces and a common budget."[33] Adoption of the treaty was subject to its ratification by the Six's national bodies. The ensuing French debates about whether to approve the EDC exposed further concerns about its impact on France's imperial sovereignty. Although a Frenchman—Pleven—introduced the plan and the treaty was signed in Paris, ultimately the French National Assembly ended the dream of a European army when it rejected the treaty on August 30, 1954. That the French at once championed and killed the EDC is indicative of ideological divisions within the halls of power. Generally at odds, the PCF and the Gaullist Rassemblement du peuple français (RPF) could still agree that the EDC was dangerous. The PCF, expressing its general skepticism toward European integration, disdained the EDC's connection to the United States. The RPF, eager to see France retain national sovereignty in all forums, raised the concern that the EDC would cause the secession of African countries from the French Union.[34] In the face of this opposition, members of Schuman's MRP offered only uneven support. Little wonder, perhaps, that it failed.

As with the ECSC, in the years between the initial signature and the National Assembly's vote, a range of actors voiced a host of ideas about the EDC's potential impact on France. A pro-con feature in the monthly journal *Fédération* included among others General Maxime Weygand arguing *contre* and Generals François Georges-Picot (of Sykes-Picot fame) and Antoine Béthouart *pour*.[35] An officer in both world wars, Weygand—with a certain flair for words—declared he was "for a European confederation of strong and lively nations, and not for an arbitrary community of emasculated peoples ready to submit to stronger domination." He claimed that the treaty violated the constitution and would "dismember" the French army. An "integrated army" would be "impracticable" within the framework of "complicated and expensive supranational organisms." He foresaw and decried the blow to French sovereignty that the EDC would cause. Even in his support for the plan, Georges-Picot lamented the "insufficiency" of the 1948 Brussels Accord and the subsequent Americanization of European defense, the latter underscored by plans to have the EDC operate under the aegis of NATO. Still, he insisted, the EDC was a necessary bulwark against the Soviet Union.

Béthouart, who would soon serve as a senator for French citizens in Morocco, offered that France's "cultural capital and traditions" afforded it an authority that would allow it to stand up to a West German challenge for superiority, as would "our 80 thousand French and overseas residents, our African territories without which European defense would be impossible." Although supportive of the EDC, Béthouart, a member of the MRP, acknowledged that without some clarification that he believed had already been provided, it could appear that the treaty invited "dangers to the unity of the army and the French Union."[36] Concern about such an impact hung over these discussions. A report by the Institut des hautes études de défense nationale posited that to secure France's sovereignty overseas, the European Political Community (EPC), a supranational legislative body meant to be paired with the EDC, needed to include the "French Union at the heart of a European Community," with "relations between the members states of the community and the TOM formed through the intermediary of French political institutions."[37] French officials bristled at the thought of losing their privileged position in the French Union, even, or especially, as they pursued avenues for European unity.

In the same era that an American official worried the Soviet Union would "shake and if possible destroy the positions of the Western powers in the Middle East, Asia, and Africa," some French officials argued that were they to sign the EDC treaty, they themselves would be responsible for the destruction.[38] Jean Iehlé, a civil servant in the Ministry of Overseas France, argued that the treaty endangered French Algeria because by limiting its scope to "the European territories" of the member states, the would-be institution curtailed Algeria's guaranteed protection under NATO. Like Weygand, he warned that the EDC treaty directly contradicted the constitution because it could reduce Paris's role as coordinator of the entire French Union.[39] Elsewhere, Iehlé argued that "the treaty project does not seem adaptable to a policy that attempts to consolidate both Europe and the French Union."[40] If the war had taught these officials anything, it was that Germany could not be counted on, while the French Union was dependable, necessary, and vital to France's future.

Just as the question of Algerian mines raised hackles in discussions about the ECSC, the EDC also inspired fear in France's business community. At a 1953 meeting of the Comité d'études et de liaison du patronat de l'Union Française (CELPUF), an employers' lobby, founder Paul Bernard complained that between the ECSC and the upcoming EDC treaty, "the break between France and the rest of the French Union will be complete." CELPUF's secretary intoned that "the French Union is a reality while Europe is but a potentiality." If France did not assert itself as the sole leader in the French Union, these territories would soon become a "common European good." Jean Blanchard of Algeria echoed these sentiments but nonetheless insisted that "the future of Algeria, like all the rest of North Africa, is North-South and not East-West," a reference to the danger of the Maghreb falling under Soviet influence. Indeed, another attendee warned that Europe should remember that it would need economic support from the United States for a long while and that it would be a mistake to give the US government the impression that the Six "wish to en-circle" their new economic union "in a 'bamboo curtain' that will prevent all external exchange."[41] French businesspeople, it appeared, dreamed of maintaining their exclusive access to overseas markets but were at least as anxious about Soviet encroachment as they were about European competition. In reality, as Todd Shepard argues, "the most direct challenges to French colonialism came not from the two superpowers but from colonized peoples themselves," which can go a long way in explaining why French officials changed their European integration tactics only in later years, with increasingly impossible-to-ignore anti-imperial activism.[42]

As the Cold War emerged, the specter of West German intrusion inspired more fear than that of the Soviet Union. Critics of the EDC lumped it in with the already-established ECSC, painting it as part of a wider German takeover and deploring its impact on France's premier position leading the French Union. Minister of Overseas France Louis Jacquinot opined at a banquet of the Cercle de la France d'outre-mer that "France, which has made so many great sacrifices, truly deserves to keep its overseas territories."[43] Such a sentiment marks the intermingling of economic interests with an existential belief in France's imperial vocation. A two-page illustrated spread in L'Express titled "The German Plan for the Conquest of Europe" included cartoons depicting five risks to France were it to integrate with West Germany. The first four threats were unemployment, salary reduction, shrinking investments, and competition in the dairy, auto, and textile industries. The fifth was represented by the image of a mighty, barrel-chested German shoving aside a small, shocked Frenchman, both standing on the African continent. The caption read, "The substitution of the French effort by a foreign effort."[44] The danger of Germans

Fig. 2.1   "Le plan allemand pour la conquête de l'Europe," *L'Express*,
November 14, 1953, 7.

muscling onto French African territory—so literally illustrated in
L'Express—was by the 1950s a well-worn trope. That both a high-
ranking minister and a popular publication expressed the same
dread over German intrusion in French imperial affairs should give
us pause. For all the rhetoric hailing the construction of postwar
peace, anxieties over the emergence of the Federal Republic as a

potential rival to French power were vividly expressed in pro-
nouncements about the special relationship between the metropole and the whole of the French Union.

Outside and within France, European federalists tried to in-
still confidence in the EDC. In a challenge to anti-German fears,
lobbying groups distributed tracts in France emphasizing the
EDC's peacemaking potential and suggesting that had it existed
earlier, the Franco-Prussian War and both World Wars would
never have occurred.[45] Luxembourg's minister of foreign affairs,
Joseph Bech, went lengths to promise that regarding "North Africa, the six countries of the European Defense Community have
now surpassed the stage of envy or jealousy . . . and consider that
France's difficulties are in reality Europe's. . . . Nobody, not even
Germany or Italy, would think of paralyzing France in an undertaking of common interests."[46] Despite calling France's Maghreb
issues "Europe's," Bech signaled that the Six understood that this
remained France's arena. Faith in the EDC—or at least the desire
to take European integration a step further—resonated beyond
France. Bech's compatriots ratified the EDC treaty in April 1954,
on the tails of Belgium, the Netherlands, and West Germany. Italy
awaited France's decision before proceeding. With French support,
the EDC would all but certainly become the latest unified institution of the postwar era. Instead, in late August, the French National Assembly killed the dream conceived of by France's own
Monnet and Pleven.

The EDC died at the hands of the rules of order when deputies voted 319 to 264, with 12 abstentions, to approve a "preliminary
question" (*question préalable*) demanding that they cease debate on
the subject. In accordance with French parliamentary proce-
dure, the preliminary question would need to be settled before

the actual topic—the EDC treaty's approval—could be addressed. By voting not to talk about the treaty, the National Assembly rejected the EDC without casting a direct vote against it. In what might generally appear to be a footnote of history, the deputy who posed the question was none other than Algiers Républicain indépendent deputy General Adolphe Aumeran, one of the most outspoken participants in the 1947 *statut organique* debates, with Radical Republican and former prime minister Édouard Herriot cosigning the question at the last moment. In making the case for his preliminary question the day before the vote, Aumeran appealed to the deputies' distaste for West Germany and their fear of rearming it. He also implied that the EDC would please the United States greatly and suggested that the Soviet Union would feel dangerously threatened by it. In Aumeran's view, appeasing the Americans and alienating the Soviets would be missteps. France, he argued, should embrace the role of the "mediator, a role for which it is destined," between the superpowers. This destiny meant that France was "something other than a neighbor and traditional target of Germany, it is the harmonious whole where all of the races and religions of the earth come together."[47] His argument elevated France beyond just being a magnanimous imperial motherland; here, France became the very embodiment of universalism.

The debate remained fraught. Deputies alternatively lamented the breakdown of decorum and mocked those who supported the EDC as being unrepentant collaborators, if not German Nazis. Before the vote, Résistant and Buchenwald deportee Christian Pineau (SFIO) spoke out emphatically against the question's adoption—and thus in favor of the EDC's passage—asking, "Do you think me crazy enough to not be thinking of how we suffered because

of Germany?"[48] When the results of the vote were announced,
some deputies stood up to sing "La Marseillaise," with one shouting
"Down with the Wehrmacht" as leftist deputies took up a rendi-
tion of "l'Internationale." As socialist André Le Troquer, the National Assembly's president, called for order over cries of "Vive la
République" and "Vive la France," Jean Nocher (RPF), who spent
much of the war incarcerated for his Resistance activities, declared,
"Now we'll have the supporters of the EDC sing us 'Deutschland
über alles'!"[49] This chaotic, ebullient response to the EDC's foreclosure is a testament to just how strongly many French politicians
loathed the idea of rearming West Germany.

Examining only this celebratory scene, it might appear that disdain for *les boches* alone drove the French decision to kill the
EDC. The debates leading up to the vote show that fear of losing
control over the French Union also drove deputies' opinion. They
rejected the EDC because both German rearmament and the community's projected impact on the French Union would undermine French sovereignty. That the ECSC succeeded where the
EDC failed does not make an examination of the latter any less
crucial to understanding French approaches to the question of empire and European integration. In French officials' eyes, those
risks were intertwined, not least because of the armed conflict in
Indochina. That the EDC, according to its proponents, would
guard against unfettered German militarism and protect European
sovereignty in what they argued was becoming a bipolar world
mattered little. Nevertheless, the normalization of West Germany
continued at a fast clip. West Germany, along with Italy, signed
the Treaty of Brussels in October 1954. It joined NATO several
months after that and ceased to be occupied by Britain, France,
and the United States. Regardless of French maneuvering, the

Federal Republic was now a definitive part of the security scheme for Western Europe and beyond.

Just as French conversations about Algeria, the French Union, and the ECSC demonstrate ambiguity—and at times outright hostility—about how officials understood Algeria's relationship to integrated Europe, the debates about how these failed projects would engage France's empire are instructive. Their failures, in part a result of Europe's inability to convince French officials that integration offered better solutions for the French Union than a jealous guarding of imperial interests, offer insight into how the French perceived foreign interference in the empire as a threat to French sovereignty overseas. It would take the intensification of the Algerian War in the second half of the 1950s to disabuse the majority of French bureaucrats of this notion.

Repeating Napoleon's Mistakes

Debates about European integration were never just about export markets or military organization. Rather, they reveal a curious interplay of pragmatism and ideology. French industrialists, settler lobbyists, and elected officials all viewed the French Union as vital to France's economic and political might. French Union countries imported metropolitan products almost exclusively and Algerian iron was but one of many resources on which the French market depended. The wine industry relied on Algeria for its table wine, for example, a reality that would come back to haunt France after Algeria's independence.[50] Such supposedly clear-headed economic reasoning for why France must maintain its empire was accompanied by emotional claims that underlined French officials' near-psychic belief that France both deserved its colonies (a right) and would wither away without them (a matter of survival). Indeed, at the CELPUF meeting, Paul Bernard stated, "France created North Africa. Without France, there would be no Algeria, no Tunisia, no Morocco."[51] Frantz Fanon skewered this familiar line of argumentation in *The Wretched of the Earth,* writing, "Thus the history which [the settler] writes is not the history of the country which he plunders but the history of his own nation in regard to all that she skims off, all that she violates and starves."[52] Underneath Bernard's bravado ran an anxious current: without North Africa, what was France?

In the 1950s, between the ambiguous promise of the "quality of citizenship" for people living in the French Union and newly acute concerns about what resurgent West Germany might do to France's global status, the empire appeared more important, but also more complicated, than ever. Celebrations of *la plus grande France* were nothing new, but now greater France comprised individuals whose rights—perhaps as French citizens—had to be acknowledged, often for the first time.[53] In that vein, in a debate about the EPC, Léopold Senghor argued that in the proposed Chambre des peuples, which would be elected by universal suffrage, France should receive extra seats to account for its overseas residents, seating eighty-three representatives in total, twenty more than was allotted to West Germany or Italy. During this speech, delivered before the Assemblée consultative de l'Europe, the parliamentary arm of the Council of Europe, Senghor harnessed Schuman's "dowry" promise, delivering what may be its best known rebuttal. Claiming to speak for most of the National Assembly's African deputies, Senghor declared, "We are for the European Community and, beyond that, for the Eurafrican Community. We are for Franco-German reconciliation." Africans' involvement in this "marriage of convenience [*mariage de raison*]" would not be as "wedding gifts or the dishes that bear the brunt during household spats, or dolls to entertain the children of the estate." Instead, they wanted to be the "pages who carry the bride's veil." The extra seats would allow Africans to take an active role in Europe, rather than serve as an offering to a continental European project. Senghor commended his own restraint in demanding only twenty extra seats, saying, "I am not suggesting to you sixty-three additional seats for the 40 million overseas French citizens."[54] But the mere thought of extending even underproportional representation to people with "the quality of" French citizenship appeared a bridge too far, not unlike during the *statut organique* debates for Algeria. A legal advisor in the Ministry of Overseas France warned that "such a representation, [if] considered as special for the overseas [holdings], will be dangerous for national unity."[55] The assertion that equality would trample unity appears near comical until we recall the importance to empire of inequality and difference.[56] Senghor's suggestion was ignored, and the Chambre des peuples, along with the rest of the EPC, never came to be.

In his proposal, Senghor offered a history lesson and harnessed the French self-conception as an imperial force to sway his listeners. First, he invoked the National Convention's abolition of slavery in 1794 (Year II), which he called a "deed [*geste*] of generosity, which was also a deed of political intelligence." This decision, he declared, "is why today, I am a deputy in the National Assembly." Next, he pointed to Napoleon's rejection of Toussaint Louverture and the disastrous Leclerc expedition, which ultimately led to France's loss of Saint-Domingue. Senghor did not mention Charles Leclerc arresting Louverture, the latter's death in prison, or the independence of Haiti, but he did note that Napoleon on his own deathbed regretted the expedition, with the implication that this was the result of the French state working against, rather than with, its empire. Senghor left no room for interpretation of these examples as he concluded his speech with a prediction: "If you do not follow my propositions, which are moderate, in twenty years you will regret today's deed."[57] Warnings like this came not just from Senghor and the Algerian senator Tamzali but from a range of metropolitan actors as well, demonstrating the growing fear that anti-imperial movements in the French Union and beyond represented a menace to France. They forecast the reversal in France's approach to European integration that was to come only a few years later, in direct reaction to internal threats to French imperial sovereignty.

In March 1954, one day after the Belgian Senate voted to ratify the EDC treaty, French forces in Indochina launched the disastrous assault on Dien Bien Phu that would finally end their attempt to retain the colony. The French signed the Geneva Accords, abandoning their claim on Indochina, just weeks before the EDC's failure. By that time, French confidence in their imperial strength was shaken. Beyond the Indochinese theater of war, French officials had witnessed challenges to their authority since the very day World War II ended, with the Algerian protests in Sétif and elsewhere, followed shortly by a multiyear uprising in Madagascar. Georges Le Brun Kéris (MRP) of the French Union Assembly warned that if France proved unable to reconcile its European aspirations and its empire, his "North African friends"—with whom he did "not share, I must say, political opinions"—would tell him, "This is perfect; you, France, adhere to the European Union; us, we'll adhere to the Arab League."[58] In the National Assembly, Jean-Jacques Juglas (MRP) similarly warned that any exclusion of the overseas from European integration schemes would have "repercussions on the unity of the French Union."[59]

Beyond a fear of anti-imperial nationalism, there remained the question of France's sizable settler population, particularly in Algeria. Writing critically about European integration in 1952, then-senator Michel Debré argued that European integration would reduce France's role as the key power in Africa. Officials would do well to remember that "the French, on the whole, feel more solidarity with the French of North Africa or of the French Union than with the Germans or Italians. . . . Cutting the links of the French Union will not result in the creation of a European union but will reinforce anti-European nationalisms."[60] For Debré, the real risk of a poorly planned European policy would be the impact on settler communities. Anti-European nationalism, a reference to the destructive nationalisms of World War II, stood to damage France itself. As with the Franco-Italian issue about Algerian mine access—and in common fashion over decades of colonialism—when discussing European integration, an overseas holding could be reduced to its resources and the Europeans "developing" the land. The opinions or outlook of Indigenous populations remained invisible or unimportant to decision makers in metropole and colony alike. Yet the fear of losing face in front of, or control over, these peoples and places inspired tremendous anxiety in French officials who were convinced that France's future still lay with a strong and closely guarded French Union.

Third World Internationalism in Defiance of Empire

Although French officials worried that newly integrated European institutions would undermine their unique position in the French Union, European internationalism did not undercut basic assumptions about the justness and legality of empire. In sharp contrast, as the Six prepared to elaborate their union, leaders from the Global South pursued their own form of internationalism. The results would disconcert European officials and make French administrators more eager than ever to seek out European venues to secure the French Union. Delegates from twenty-nine independent Asian and African states convened in Bandung, Indonesia, in April 1955 to forge their own way in the international order. Participants called for self-determination in still-colonized lands and railed against racism. Although perhaps most famous for helping to lay the groundwork for the Non-Aligned Movement, Bandung Conference participants discussed the potential for economic cooperation and technical assistance (both among themselves and from other states), common oil policy, and cultural and educational exchange.[61] They also proclaimed support for self-determination, drawing attention to the promises of the Charter of the United Nations (UN) and the Universal Declaration of Human Rights.[62]

One of the precursors of Bandung, the Congress of the Peoples of Europe, Asia, and Africa, held in Puteaux, France in 1948, drew participants from the Netherlands, Britain, India, Indonesia, the French Union, and more, opening the door to a wider solidarity network than South-South relations alone. Organized in part by the Movement for the United Socialist States of Europe, its attendees included Senghor and the Algerian socialist Mohand Saïd Lechani. Anne-Isabelle Richard demonstrates that there existed a possibility for anti-colonial advocacy and European integration to operate together in the postwar era but that ultimately those interests drew the movement into opposing directions. Although "the common story unraveled," one legacy was Third World solidarity, of which Bandung is a particularly salient example.[63] Internationalism outside of European venues was on the rise, provoking scrutiny and fear from powers accustomed to being in charge of diplomacy and geopolitical affairs.

The participant nations at Bandung were diverse—including both the People's Republic of China and Turkey, a member of NATO since 1952. But the message of anti-imperialism was clear in the rhetoric of its speakers. In his welcome address, Indonesian president Sukarno celebrated that "hurricanes of national awakening and reawakening have swept over the land, shaking it, changing it, changing it for the better."[64] European observers took note. French commissioner general in Indochina General Paul Ély brushed off the conference as ineffective and lacking in unity. He could not fully mask his underlying concerns, grousing that the South Vietnamese delegation did nothing when one of their ranks, General Trình Minh Thế, "circulated an insulting diatribe attacking the attitude of the French colonialists in Cambodia."[65] A retired French general and Eurafrica lobbyist warned that the congress should "enlighten our leaders" because its mission "is to 'drive us out of Africa,' as they have nearly done in Asia."[66] Among his creative solutions to anti-imperial nationalism was a car race celebrating Eurafrica, which ran five times from 1951 to 1961.[67] One of the outcomes of Bandung, during which FLN representatives addressed the congress, was a statement supporting Algerian independence in the final joint communiqué of the conference.[68]

From Senghor's invocation of Toussaint Louverture to Sukarno's celebration of the hurricanes of national awakening, observant Europeans should have been well aware that change had come to the imperial order. The same year as the Bandung Conference, the UN General Assembly voted to debate the Algerian problem, although this did not actually come to pass.[69] Challenges from anti-imperial activists, armed and otherwise, and the expanding electorate in the French Union both stood to topple French officials' assumptions about how to do empire. Even as they attempted to cast European integration as purely pragmatic and focused on trade or security, the archives make clear that the economic and psychological drive to maintain the empire helped to shape debates about whether France should join Europe with its empire. In the early 1950s, the answer was always no, and French officials worked hard to keep domestic questions of empire separate from the international sphere of integrating Europe. It was a policy that would die as the Algerian War raged on and voices from beyond Europe grew impossible to ignore.

What Rights for the French Union?

In 1956, Minister of Overseas France Gaston Defferre (SFIO) shepherded in his eponymous framework law, or *loi-cadre,* which extended significant autonomy to African authorities and created Conseils de gouvernement to be elected by universal suffrage. He had received input from Félix Houphouët-Boigny, an Ivorian and minister in Guy Mollet's government. Defferre declared the law to be a salve for "the malaise" felt by Africans who believed that France had not kept its promises and by French people who "have the impression that the government has the intention of abandoning its territories."[70] Defferre's words refute the sometimes backwardly read claim that the *loi-cadre* was a deliberate step toward inevitable decolonization. As Martin Shipway notes, "It would be somewhat strange . . . if the *intention* behind Defferre's law had been to bring about the rapid end of French rule . . . of a France extending . . . 'from Flanders to the Congo.'"[71] The law came about only months after the publication of the Spaak Report, whose arrival marked a new phase in negotiations, resulting in 1957 in the EEC. The lessons of the ECSC exclusion and the EDC failure would be instructive to this next stage of integration. Notably, under pressure from Defferre, the French delegation took a new, hardline position mandating the inclusion of the French Union within any resulting integrated body. Just as administrators and business leaders spent countless hours debating what it meant to exclude the French Union from the ECSC and the EDC, officials also puzzled over other forms of integration and the possibility that those bodies' regulations might touch the French Union.

The growth of integrated Europe, among other international projects, and the internal reforms that expanded French citizenship rights, raised questions about whether laws applicable to France could be limited to the metropole. Such lines of questioning intensified and only became harder to answer as reforms to French imperial law expanded sovereignty to and representation of populations overseas. These reforms were attempts to counter anti-imperial movements across the French Union but might be regarded as having the opposite effect, both because more African populations used their voices to press for change and because the cost of equality appeared too great for metropolitan authorities. As Frederick Cooper argued, when the French "rather belatedly got serious about using colonization as a tool of social transformation, they very quickly backed off."[72] In other words, the expense and effort of resources concomitant with citizenship in Africa made the notion of colonial reform unappealing, even untenable. But in the mid-1950s, French authorities had yet to adopt such a belief and far from viewing decolonization as necessary or normal, they fought doggedly to slow its arrival.[73]

In the years prior to the EEC negotiations, Quai d'Orsay efforts to delineate clearly the scope of integrated Europe were confounded by the existence of international accords affirming Algeria as constitutive of the French Republic. Clarifying this mattered because it would indicate the reach of laws and also determine to what extent French officials had to account for Algerian people and resources as they headed to negotiations. In 1952, a French representative to the ECSC's Common Assembly, Paul-Henri Teitgen (MRP), proclaimed that the overseas territories were a part of the Republic and therefore "must enter into the future European Union."[74] Teitgen did not name Algeria, but the demand tacitly included Algeria, grouped without distinction with the rest of the French Union. As the Council of Europe prepared for what would be the 1955 European Convention on Establishment, providing reciprocal treatment for member state nationals residing in other member states, French officials debated if it should apply to all Algerians or only those already residing in the metropole. At a Quai d'Orsay meeting between French ministerial officials attended by public health, labor, interior, agriculture, and commerce administrators, one foreign affairs official warned that "the proposed wording for the definition of 'nationals' [*ressortissants*] is unacceptable to the French government. It would in essence contradict the spirit of the Constitution of 1946 and be politically unthinkable to allow wording that does not enshrine the principle of the indivisibility of French nationality [*nationalité française*]." Further, attempts by some council member states to exclude the non-European nationals of other states "poorly conceal the anxieties that lean towards racial discrimination." France, if it were to see all nationals benefit from the convention, would have to allow for concessions, namely that the convention extend into French Union territory.[75] The official put a name to the accusations by the likes of Tamzali and Senghor—racial discrimination—but highlighted one of the reasons for this possible unequal treatment. The French state was reluctant to apply European policy in the French Union, inviting racial discrimination by drawing a line between two Frances, one continental, the other imperial.

The final version of the treaty specified that no state "shall be obliged to grant the benefits of this Convention to nationals of another Contracting Party ordinarily resident in a non-metropolitan territory of the latter Party to which the Convention does not apply."[76] In other words, Algerians living in Algeria could be denied protection under council law. That same year, French officials argued that the in-progress drafting of the European Convention on the Social Security of Migrant Workers by the International Labour Organization (ILO) must account for Algerian laborers in Europe, an important claim given that roughly 5,000 Algerians already worked in Belgian mines alone.[77] These inconsistencies in protection, in which an Algerian's address determined their access to rights and potentially upheld selective racial discrimination, are evidence of the piecemeal nature of European policies meant to appease continental interests rather than tackle systemic issues facing constituents deemed lesser.

The interplay of regulations pertaining to the Six and wider regional institutional decision making reveals that French policy determining Algeria's place within or with Europe was not fixed. Rather, French officials pursued the policies that they believed best served their commercial profit (excluding Algerian mines) or material interests (requiring another state to support Algerian migrants' families). Opening overseas holdings to the other member states risked reducing France's ability to benefit from its long-held economic privileges in Algeria and beyond. But as the examples of the Council of Europe and ILO discussions make clear, maintaining exclusive sovereignty over Algeria appeared increasingly tenuous, or potentially unsavory, and the draw of integrated European assistance seemed to offer benefits for France.

Uniting with "Our Enemies of Yesterday"

When Tamzali stood up before the French Union Assembly to decry Algeria's exclusion from the ECSC, he pointed to some of the fundamental contradictions of France's pretension to maintain separate sovereignty in Europe and in the French Union. He warned, "Our constituents will not easily understand why their territory is placed outside of the [coal and steel] pool like a poor, second-rate relation."[78] Neither would they understand why they were integrated into NATO, with its attendant demands, but not Europe. Tamzali emphasized the shameful past of European plans to share Africa, saying that "the concept of Eurafrica, which already got bad press during the era of dictators, has made its reappearance." Now France was poised to make available to its "enemies of yesterday" colonized territory where those states would "find an outlet for their excess population."[79] By lambasting Eurafrica, Tamzali forced his audience to recall the past and present of European attempts to dominate African land and peoples. In his view, Eurafrican policy directly translated into Algerian exclusion and disenfranchisement, to the benefit of non-French European peoples.

Tamzali's reticence to allow West Germans or Italians to profit in and from Algeria fit easily within the broader Germanophobia of the EDC debates but added a little-repeated clause that the real and likely insurmountable issue was the exclusion of Algerians from the benefits of European membership. His concern about the latter would prove prescient as the French began to pursue policies that would bind Algeria to the EEC and in doing so open the possibility of free movement of Algerian laborers to the Six and the guarantee of social security protections for their families. European integration occurred not in signing ceremonies but in the debates and decisions made even before the creation and (sometimes) implementation of treaties. The France—or French Union, to be more precise—that approached the EEC negotiating table was not the same one that had joined the ECSC.

Belgian stateman Paul-Henri Spaak presented his committee's report on April 21, 1956, a month and one day after Tunisia celebrated its independence from France. Morocco had marked its independence just weeks before Tunisia. Between the two independence days, the French National Assembly granted special powers to the government in their war against Algerian nationalists. Notably, this extended more authority to the military, opening the door for intensified violence and torture. In the face of growing challenges from North Africa, officials in the Ministries of Overseas France and Foreign Affairs turned to a tool they had not previously thought necessary to secure their imperial sovereignty: European integration. With a push from Defferre, the EEC's treaty would allow French officials to make a diplomatic claim on Algeria, simultaneously securing material benefits for these departments and forcing the Six to confirm publicly that Algeria was a constitutive part of France. Discussing plans for a European common market, Defferre insisted that it include the whole of the French Union, creating "the Eurafrican Common Market."[80] It was a bold demand, one that changed the course of European integration, and Algeria's relationship with integrated Europe, for decades to come.

3

The Ultimatum for the Treaty of Rome

In the third week of February 1957, the French government harnessed a new tactic in its war against Algerian nationalists. It was not the *ratonnades* or torture; the army had already unleashed these weapons. It was the in-progress treaty for a European common market. Algeria, French officials in Brussels declared, needed to be named in the treaty, or else France would withhold its signature. Including Algerian territory in the Treaty of Rome would not win the actual war in Algeria. French government officials trusted the military's might. Rather, the treaty afforded French administrators the chance to showcase the fact that other European states *agreed* that Algeria was a constitutive part of France, undercutting the Algerian nationalists' claims. As negotiations for the Treaty of Rome unfolded, so too did the Algerian War, whose violence and scale amplified in the latter half of the 1950s. In response to the ongoing war, French officials swiftly reconfigured their demands on their European partners, successfully committing the Six to naming Algeria as a constitutive part of the nascent European Economic Community (EEC).

The history of this critical stage of European integration, which began in earnest with negotiations launched in 1956 and ended with the Treaty of Rome's signing in 1957, cannot be disentangled from the history of empire. France's tactic of naming Algeria in a European document emerged as a direct response to the Algerian War.[1] In leveraging the weight of their signature, French officials correctly banked on the other members of the Six privileging French demands despite intense resistance to the policy.[2] Although the final result shows six European states collectively implementing a treaty influenced by Eurafrican ideology, in reality it was French pressure that led them to this wording. Even Belgian officials, who most closely collaborated with French representatives on this effort, were not fully a part of the planning process for linking Algeria and, in a different manner, the whole of the French Union, to the EEC.

The distinct place of Algeria in these treaty negotiations exposed Algeria's tenuous legal status and underscored the precarity of French claims that it was indeed an integrated part of the Republic. The primacy of geopolitical or geostrategic decision making in the crafting of the Treaty of Rome demonstrates that political exigency drove European administrators, who saw strategy, not "culture" or "identity," to be the oil greasing integrated Europe's wheels. Rather than formulate a Europe based on racial or religious identity, they constructed an institution based on economic and political rationale. Nevertheless, racism permeated the decision-making process, with French officials reluctant to demand the same rights for Algerians as they would expect for white metropolitan citizens. Thus, the Six constructed the EEC on a foundation of what appeared to be commonsense self-preservation of individual states' best interests. For the French, this now necessitated an expansive version of the ends to which Europe might stretch, inclusive of Algerian land and, possibly, people. Contrary to the continentally bound borders of Europe established in the European Coal and Steel Community's (ECSC's) treaty, the EEC treaty negotiations reflect that the French had come to believe that inserting the empire in integrated Europe was the best way to preserve their overseas sovereignty and remain relevant in Europe and the world.

These negotiations culminated in the March 1957 signing of the treaties establishing the EEC and European Atomic Energy Community (Euratom), typically referred to collectively as the Treaty of Rome despite their plural nature.[3] Focusing on the seemingly repetitive and mundane negotiations reveals a decidedly unmundane outcome: Algeria would be included in integrated Europe, thereby made eligible, in theory, to benefit from the trade preferences, free circulation of labor, and promise of aid that would also apply to the continental territory of the Six. This only came about due to two French sine qua non, or nonnegotiable demands that they made on their partners. The first, in 1956, insinuated—contrary to the French constitution—that Algeria was an overseas territory (TOM). Although legally inaccurate, it allowed French officials to demand a limited range of EEC protections for the French Union en bloc. The second demand, made in 1957, reversed this strategy and—leveled only weeks before the treaty was finalized—explicitly named Algeria as a constituent part of the Common Market. With the Six acknowledging that Algeria was French, the French could showcase their legitimate legal claim on Algeria, regardless of the calls for independence emanating from Algeria and beyond. Naming Algeria was the French goal; whether or how the treaty's regulations would be implemented across the Mediterranean was, for the moment, at best a secondary concern.

The explicit naming of Algeria, first in French demands and then in the Treaty of Rome itself, signaled a turning point in European negotiations. Earlier discussions witnessed French officials making little effort to mention Algeria—indeed, silence remained a key diplomatic strategy—and they commonly grouped Algeria with the rest of the French Union despite its administrative distinction. This French-led version of Eurafrica elided the juridical status that made French Algeria so peculiar. By the second half of the 1950s, the war became impossible to ignore and French authorities scrambled for weapons to wield against the National Liberation Front (FLN) and other nationalist groups. Now they saw the utility of highlighting Algeria's legal difference and its departmental status as one method of claiming their right to maintain sovereignty in the region.

The two best-known figures involved in this decision were Minister of Overseas France Gaston Defferre and Minister of Foreign Affairs Christian Pineau, but they were supported by the French diplomatic corps and the legions of civil servants who wrote most of the memos that forwarded the plan. It was Defferre who brought the tactic to the attention of Pineau. Although he held his ministerial position only for little over one year (February 1, 1956–May 21, 1957), he left an indelible mark on the French Union. In 1956, after championing the framework law bearing his name, he introduced to Pineau the initial TOM-European integration scheme. Pineau, whose ministry oversaw the signing of the Treaty of Rome, relied heavily on reports from Raymond Bousquet, a career diplomat who served as France's ambassador to Belgium from 1956 to 1962. They, along with the mid-level bureaucrats who go unnamed in the archival record, shaped much of the negotiation process. Serving French interests above European goals, they forged a plan to ensure that the Six would guarantee support for the French Union and, eventually, affirm that Algeria was indeed inseparable from the rest of France. Regardless of the vocal support of European integration and Eurafrica by Léopold Senghor and others since the late 1940s, the actual negotiations for the Treaty of Rome largely excluded representatives from France's overseas departments and territories. In this new stage of negotiations, imperial inclusion in European institutions stood not as a potential conduit of equality but as a cudgel against decolonization. As anthropologist Sally Engle Merry wrote, "Colonial authorities did not accept failures without making efforts to buttress their control in new ways or strengthen the old ones."[4]

Algerian nationalists, for their part, largely ignored the ongoing process in Brussels. Rather, the FLN launched a highly visible and eventually successful campaign in a different venue—the United Nations (UN).[5] On February 13, 1957, the UN General Assembly held its first discussion of the conflict, "placing the Algerian drama at the heart of the discussion at the United Nations," as FLN combatant Zohra Drif recalled it.[6] Five days later, on February 18, Defferre and Pineau implemented their second sine qua non, calling for Algeria to be named in the EEC treaty. The timing makes clear that for French officials, the menace to Algérie française in one international venue appeared answerable through another. The Six's assent would legitimate France's territorial claims. In particular, the French feared the influence the FLN might have on the US delegation, which in turn could sway other countries against the cause of French Algeria.[7] The perceived hostility of the UN, coupled with the US government's lack of enthusiasm and

French fears about Soviet encroachment on the political leanings of the French Union as a whole, drove French authorities to insist that Algeria be written into integrated Europe, an arena where they were confident they still held considerable sway.[8] In negotiations for the EEC, then, we locate a transformation in France's tactics against Algerian nationalists, partly in reaction to the FLN's increasingly savvy foray into the global arena and the changing tide of opinion from powerful would-be allies like the United States. Unlike in the UN, where the Algerian cause eventually won the diplomatic revolution, in Brussels France scored a temporary victory for Algérie française.

Pivoting toward Europe?

There is no shortage of pithy quips about who is responsible for Europe's integration. A 1949 British political cartoon jokingly celebrated Joseph Stalin as its unwitting instigator.[9] Following the signing of the Treaty of Rome, the head of the newly established Euratom anointed Egyptian statesman Gamal Abdel Nasser "the federator of Europe."[10] Both imply the significance of an external force to European integration: the threat of the Soviet Union to Western Europe's security and economy, the danger of Nasser's clout in the Global South. These concerns dovetailed with a broader European fear building in the 1950s: what appeared to be a tide of anti-imperial activism and decolonization. In under a decade following the signing of the Treaty of Paris, France and its empire witnessed enormous change and the European project forged ahead. By thinking these timelines together and considering the interplay of ministries concerned with both phenomena, it becomes apparent that empire impacted the construction of Europe and that fears about the changing imperial order would shape the very borders of the emergent Common Market.

In October 1956, French, British, and Israeli forces launched a fruitless and ultimately embarrassing attack on Egypt at the Suez Canal. It left an indelible mark on French administrative attitudes toward empire, and these, in turn, influenced new French approaches toward integrated Europe. Following the humiliation of Suez, West German chancellor Konrad Adenauer told Prime Minister Guy Mollet, "France and England will never be comparable to the United States and the Soviet Union. Nor Germany either. There remains to them only one way of playing a decisive role in the world: that is to unite to make Europe. . . . Europe shall be your revenge."[11] Historians of European integration have typically interpreted this (possibly apocryphal) promise as marking the moment when French elites understood that the era of empire was over, now pivoting France toward the continent. Here, Nasser instigated the change; France's own empire had nothing to do with it. In reality, although Suez inspired in other leaders in the Global South the confidence to pursue anti-imperial activism, it fostered in French administrative circles the conviction that France's future grandeur would be dependent on protecting the remainder of its empire. European integration offered a pathway toward that protection. The vigor with which French officials pursued the association of the French Union and then the integration of Algeria into the Common Market is evidence of just that.

Like the labor stipulations that plagued European debates, Euratom also emerged out of colonial crisis and its foundations would rely on colonial resources. The Six's motivation to establish Euratom lay in their concern over American, British, and Soviet nuclear capacity and the belief that, in the words of the Euratom

Commission's second president, Étienne Hirsch, "nuclear power can be developed most efficiently only at a larger scale than that of the nation-state."[12] Ahead of Suez, the French government favored nuclear collaboration with Europe and appeared less interested in the economic union of Europe, in contrast to West Germany. Unlike the Common Market, whose rules on labor, social security, and development aid might all directly impact people living outside of continental Europe, the significance of Euratom to the overseas territories and vice versa appeared limited in the eyes of many of its proponents and detractors. As one French official wrote, Euratom "only concerned the Overseas Territories in an indirect fashion."[13] This conviction overlooked the influence of imperial anxiety on European integration. It also failed to account for the French nuclear program's future reliance on overseas resources and test sites.

Suez catalyzed Euratom's establishment by leading French officials to be more amenable to the Common Market plan, which in turn could convince West Germans to back atomic cooperation. This appeared urgent now that, as one European federalist group noted, "the insecurity of extra-European energy sources" had left the French on edge.[14] Henri Rieben, a Swiss lawyer and close collaborator of Jean Monnet, argued, "After Suez, Euratom appears as the only way out of a situation that without it would be hopeless." In clear Cold War tones, he argued that "the greatest influence that a technologically advanced country can exercise on an underdeveloped country comes from . . . energy equipment. For giving new energy gives more than technology, it gives hope."[15] Euratom fit within a Eurafricanist discourse of using unified Europe to uplift and maintain control of overseas populations. Indeed, the influential Eurafrican ideologue Eugène Guernier declared in January 1957, "If Euratom must make Europe, Eurafricatom could make Africa."[16]

Euratom would also rely on colonial resources, namely uranium from the Belgian Congo. This was not without issue for the Belgians themselves, who had already entered into bilateral accords with both the United States and the United Kingdom. Indeed, integration architect Paul-Henri Spaak garnered criticism in some Belgian circles that felt he had ceded the Belgian Congo's resources to the Common Market.[17] In an opposite critique, a handful of European representatives questioned their compatriots' motives in pursuing nuclear might. Henri Rolin, a Belgian socialist, warned that France would be able to use uranium for "military needs," declaring that "Suez came from France [*Suez est bien venu de la France*]."[18] By and large, however, European representatives embraced or, at the least, tolerated, Eurafrican impulses in both the Common Market and Euratom.

Even before Suez brought Euratom's urgency into stark relief, French and European wariness of Nasser influenced integration planning. When the Six adopted the Spaak Report at the Venice Conference of May 29–30, 1956, French administrators had already leveled a challenge to the report by raising the issue of the TOM. Organisation for European Economic Co-operation (OEEC) official Raymond Bertrand favorably judged that the French position "would leave more freedom to the overseas areas, would be less tainted with colonialism, and would bring greater economic benefits." It also could "discourage" "Nasser-like habits" in Morocco and Tunisia and what Europeans perceived as the trickle-down effect of anti-Western behavior in the rest of Africa. Further still, it was "bold new policy" that could avert situations like the one that led "Algeria into rebellion."[19] In other words,

Bertrand contended that incorporating the TOM into integrated Europe would assuage anti-imperial sentiment and allow for the continued presence of European powers across the whole of Africa.

The push for an integrated Europe inclusive of its empire came from Defferre, who found a willing ally in Pineau.[20] Joining the TOM to Europe via development aid and the encouragement of trade, they believed, would offer the French a means of maintaining influence throughout the French Union, a notion also supported by key French business leaders with overseas interests.[21] A memo out of Pineau's ministry pointedly asked, "If Europe became disinterested in [overseas holdings], would it be possible to keep these countries in the Western orbit for much longer?"[22] The French used such language to encourage the other members of the Six, particularly West Germany, as well as the United States, to promote their version of Eurafrica in the late 1950s. Yet the real purpose of this push would be for French authorities to continue to exert near-exclusive control over the French Union. The Treaty of Rome would be more than a weapon in the Cold War. It would block the process of decolonization itself.

Empire of the Common Market

In 1956, Mollet declared before the French Parliament, "because it contains 8 million unassimilated Muslims, Algeria is not a French province like any other, Artois or Normandy for example. At the same time, because it contains 1 million Frenchmen who run everything, neither can it be a Muslim nation-state. We reject absolutely the idea of an Algerian nation-state that bears no relation to any historic or ethnic reality."[23] This strange tension—Algerians as unassimilable; Algeria as anything but a Muslim nation-state—impacted European integration negotiations precisely because French officials pushed the legal fiction of Algérie française until the final months of the war and because they erroneously believed that even in the event of Algerian independence, the settler population would remain. The Treaty of Rome would quell the so-called events that France's elites were confident would end in French victory. In the aftermath, it would be imperative to bind Algeria's economic future to France and to Europe as a whole. The government saw the conflict as one that intimately involved French citizens and business interests, not least because of the large settler population living in Algeria ("1 million Frenchmen who run everything") at the outbreak of the war of independence.

Negotiating the Common Market demanded a consideration of the European "quality" of Algeria. Yet most early French communiqués about treaty negotiations emphasized TOM association writ large. Locating Algeria in this history demands a reading of the spoken and the unspoken. Algeria was present, even in its absence, in the Brussels negotiations. This was true because France's constitution cemented Algeria's legal status as a part of France, despite Algerian nationalists battling against such "facts." It was also true because the negotiators sent by their governments to bind together Europe shared an imperial common sense, whose logics and assumptions could go unsaid. They were woven into the very fabric of European administration itself.[24]

As the Six's representatives readied themselves for treaty negotiations, Defferre insisted that French colonial concerns should fall within the purview of united Europe. France, he declared, "cannot sacrifice its African vocation for its European vocation." This would cause a rapid "rupture of economic ties with the metropole, and then . . . political secession." In arguing that France was on the verge of imperial crisis, Defferre implied that it could avert the worst—independence across Africa—only by adhering to a European common market with the TOM associated. This demand sharply diverged from the explicit exclusion of the TOM from the ECSC. As part of the TOM's association with the Common Market, Defferre envisioned a European-wide equivalent of the Economic and Social Development Investment Fund (FIDES), the French organism aimed at funding development projects in the French Union.[25] He alerted Pineau to the need to include the TOM in the Treaty of Rome out of a fear that if France devoted itself to only European cooperation, it would lose sight of its priorities in the French Union. Indeed, his *loi-cadre,* although it loosened ties and decentralized governance in Africa, did so in order to strengthen bonds and maintain unity in a federalized future. Defferre's Europe-TOM plan would further reinforce the indivisibility of the French Union.

Defferre's demands elicited varied reactions from French ministries, reflecting concerns about both France's postwar economy and its chances to enhance its alliances with the Six or within the French Union. Quai d'Orsay officials feared that it would be politically difficult to maintain separate *zone franc* (French Union and former protectorates) and Common Market economic spheres without alienating the members of one or both of those units. The General Planning Commission argued that preferential trade outlets would suffice as a counterbalance to competition from the Six, something that Defferre's ministry and the secretary of state for industry both contested. Secretary of State for Moroccan and Tunisian Affairs Alain Savary, who had opposed the European Defense Community (EDC) earlier in the decade, expressed reservations because of the "consequences for the future of our relations with the former protectorates."[26] An official in the Ministry of Foreign Affairs' Service for Economic Cooperation (DE-CE) attributed Defferre's strong push for the TOM's association to his ministry's tendency "to show itself to be more attached to the maintenance of existing political and administrative forms than to economic positions." The DE-CE official worried that association would prove unpopular at home, leading to hostility toward the entire EEC plan and weakening French Union bonds. Worse, the other members of the Six, by virtue of their financial contributions, would invariably come to share France's "political responsibilities" overseas.[27]

In different ways, these officials expressed worry over any risk of France showing divided loyalties, which might alienate the Six or, perhaps more dangerously, the populations of the French Union. It could also invite European meddling in French overseas affairs, jeopardizing French authority across Africa. Even Defferre appeared ambivalent at points, telling Pineau that the French Union would require protections in the agricultural sector and arguing that local—meaning African—authorities should be involved in the project. He warned of the danger to the French Union's labor market if the free movement of labor envisioned within the Common Market were fully opened to European-TOM circuits.[28] Defferre's fear that a relationship with integrated Europe would simultaneously protect and menace the French Union exemplified the tension of the varied priorities that concerned, and sometimes divided, French and other European ministries throughout the negotiation period.

On May 29, the Six's ministers of foreign affairs gathered in Venice. By the morning, Pineau made known that it would be "impossible" not to associate the TOM in the Common Market and proposed a future conference to examine the issue.[29] France had announced its first sine qua non of the negotiation. The other members of the Six had not anticipated this demand.[30] Beyond surprise, the French demand garnered a variety of reactions.[31] As we will see shortly, the Belgians would prove to be France's allies in this policy push. Belgian officials saw its utility, although they had to contend with private business interests fearful in particular of sharing access to Congolese uranium. Other delegations were more suspicious. The Luxembourgers feared the financial burden of the funds. The Dutch, Italian, and West German delegations worried about how the inclusion might impact their relations with newly independent states, including recently forged trade connections. The Italian delegation also worried that European funding would be diverted to Africa from the Mezzogiorno, the impoverished southern region that would draw comparisons to Algeria in the months and years ahead. The Dutch found it to be, in the words of two Dutch scholars, an "utterly unattractive" proposal that came as a "nasty surprise."[32] Along with the West Germans, the Dutch envisioned African development to fall under the purview of the United Nations. An administrator in the Federal Republic's Ministry of Foreign Affairs worried that "the inclusion of African territories in the Common Market would be fraught with danger if it were used by France to prevent organic political developments in these areas." This would imperil "the maintenance of the colonial status quo . . . no longer in the name of France, but in the name of Europe."[33] Put differently, a common market inclusive of the TOM would implicate all of the Six in French imperial affairs. For French officials, that was the point.

Given that Defferre's own ministerial mandate did not extend to Algeria, Algeria's presence in Defferre's plan for TOM–Common Market association introduced a reading of Algeria as something other than French departments. This was inaccurate in light of the 1946 constitution. As such, from 1955 until early 1957, the word *Algeria* rarely arose in Treaty of Rome negotiations. Yet administrators acknowledged that Algeria's juridical status complicated negotiations. A DE–CE administrator speculated in August 1956 that were France to demand for Algeria the types of European measures targeting underdeveloped regions, "it would be hard to imagine that the European partners could validly justify a refusal of admission to Algeria" and would have to "recognize easily that Algeria would be an underdeveloped region in the European Community." The goal for Algeria must be "the accession to a standard of living '*à la française.*'" This administrator argued that "a new notion" should be added to the treaty, "for example of 'economically delayed region' accompanied by measures of aid and exception to push even further than for the underdeveloped regions of Europe." This was a thinly veiled reference to Italy's Mezzogiorno. For those states interested in "the construction of a Eurafrica . . . Algeria must necessarily compose the most important African element."[34] This version of Eurafrica would, he argued, be founded on economic assistance for Algeria. The participation of the Six in the investment funds open to Algeria would enhance economic and social development, and their assistance would be rewarded by the improved commercial prospects they would find in Algeria. Such claims masked but did not erase the paternalism inherited from Eurafrica's interwar proponents.

A Franco-Belgian Plan

After the Venice Conference, the question turned to how the TOM would be associated to the Common Market. When the Intergovernmental Committee of the Six met from June 1956 to

March 1957 at the Val Duchesse château near Brussels, this issue arose, along with myriad other discussions about trade, "social" questions (such as equitable wages for women), and Euratom. The French spent these months attempting to hone their position and win allies. The most logical, and willing, ally was Belgium, given its own presence in Africa. The Franco-Belgian proposal that emerged in this period bolstered France's previous calls for African-European partnership. It also drew criticism. Detractors operated at the highest level of European negotiation, notably in the Dutch delegation, but some French officials not present in Brussels also voiced concern, particularly in the halls of the French Union Assembly. Support for and opposition to the Franco-Belgian plan and the more general scheme of associating the overseas territories with the Common Market demonstrated that while some representatives of France and Europe could envision a harmonious Eurafrican future, others saw such ploys as risky to France or as stifling to overseas populations. The lesson of the EDC's failure nevertheless encouraged the Six to accept France's terms, even if they did not approve.

In the fall of 1956, French and Belgian officials joined to put forth a proposal for how their overseas territories—with Algeria—would be associated with the Common Market. The plan involved resource sharing, aid funding, and investment in industry. In return, the Six would enjoy a preferential tariff regime with these overseas territories, effectively "buy[ing], in a way, the advantages from which [they] will benefit."[35] Crucially, the Franco-Belgian plan envisioned TOM funding that would apply to Algeria and that would be "completely distinct" from the European investment fund.[36] This meant that projects in the TOM would tap a different pool of money than those development schemes aimed at the Six, notably Italy. For the French, demanding European assistance in the development of the TOM was a savvy way of securing more funding for the French Union. Journalist Raymond Cartier's 1956 admonition in *Paris Match* popularized the contention that the colonies cost France more than they benefited it. *Cartiérisme* could be answered by an influx of non-French money into the French Union.[37]

The projected financial demands were considerable. Based on the 1955 figures from France and Belgium, a European effort to support overseas development would require at least 179 million French francs for the French Union (60 million for Algeria alone), 5 million Belgian francs to the Belgian Congo, and 400,000 Belgian francs to Ruanda-Urundi. The final tally put annual European investment in empire at over 1 million European Payments Union units of account.[38] Bousquet, France's ambassador to Belgium, predicted that this proposal would draw opposition from the remainder of the Six, given the amount of money they would be expected to contribute to the investment fund.[39] He was right.

When delegations from the Six met in November, representatives from the Netherlands and Luxembourg criticized the scale of the investments being demanded. The Dutch warned that the project was "too ambitious" because it entailed politics as well as finances. Yet they were loath to take aim explicitly at France's conflict in Algeria, given their own concerns over Indonesia's pursuit of Netherlands New Guinea at the UN.[40] The West Germans, though more amenable, cautioned that there were political ramifications to the plan, as did the Italians. The French bristled at these claims. Robert Marjolin, the former secretary general of the OEEC now serving in Pineau's ministry, insisted that France would not relinquish its "political responsibility." Rather, it would "*assume the whole of the sovereignty costs of the TOM,*" such as paying for civil servants and the army in overseas territories. He reminded the Six that Africa was "the complement to Europe, it provides: oil (in the Sahara), manganese (AEF), iron (Mauritania)." He made clear in a meeting of the Six's delegation heads that "in accepting the Common Market, France *renounces a century of protectionism;* this is a great sacrifice on her part. For anyone looking closely at France's economic and financial situation, *her entry into the Common Market represents a heroic act.*"[41] Writing in a European federalist publication, General François Georges-Picot celebrated Algeria's oil resources—the French Régie autonome des pétroles discovered oil in the Sahara in 1956—alongside the other riches of the French Union. "If Europe possessed these natural gas and petrol resources, its fate would be entirely changed," he promised.[42] The supply from Hassi Messaoud alone was deemed bountiful enough to supply three-fifths of France's petrol needs. From 1957 until partway through 1961, it would produce over 5 million tons.[43] Beyond oil, Algerian trade remained critical to the metropole. Algeria dispensed 199.7 million francs to France in 1955. Eighty-one percent of imports to Algeria originated in continental France, and in return, 71 percent of its exports went there. In their benevolence, the French could count on preserving their relationship with Algeria, the metropole's largest buyer and its third largest supplier after the United States and West Germany.[44]

The Belgian delegates joined the French in defending the proposal. Delegation head Jean-Charles Snoy et d'Oppurs insisted that the goal of the project must be to protect not only the interest of the metropoles but also "that of the *indigènes.*"[45] Spaak, apparently in order to answer any critic who would point to alternatives for African development, called the UN's investment fund "a boat" he "would not want to board."[46] The Belgian press,

Fig. 3.1   Hassi Messaoud oil field, Algeria. © CDHA–Photos de Presse
[Fi–912 PRE]

however, proved unimpressed with the Franco-Belgian push.
Flemish dailies sided with the Dutch and disdained being caught
up in France's colonial affairs. A late January 1957 editorial in *Het
Volk,* a newspaper tied to the centrist Christian People's Party,
criticized the chance the Six were taking by being bound to French

imperial policy through the Common Market. The editorialist asked if the TOM would "remain attached to *la mère patrie?* This is a matter of importance, especially for Algeria. If France fails to restore order and peace, it will be rather unpleasant for its partners to be compromised in this affair."[47] Despite growing hostility among their own population, Belgian authorities chose to privilege their relationship with France and their own imperial interests over the demands of certain sectors of the Belgian voting public.

Impressing upon their partners the importance of incorporating the TOM with Europe, the French and Belgians invoked recent history to insist on the normalcy of such a policy. Their motivation, they claimed, "could be compared to that which inspired the Marshall Plan."[48] The French, for their part, maintained that the Franco-Belgian proposition was an act of extraordinary altruism that was also politically imperative. The Ivorian deputy and minister Félix Houphouët-Boigny warned that if the Six did not associate with the TOM, "the Afro-Asian bloc, 'spearhead' of communism, will implant itself progressively in these territories," just as they had begun to do in Britain's African colonies.[49] The month after the Suez Crisis, Spaak proposed a formal group to examine the Franco-Belgian plan for the association of the TOM. The Six would have been wary of the Soviet Union, Nasser, and more. Closer integration already offered a means of staving off European irrelevance in a bipolar world. It followed that drawing Africans into such a plan would protect European power, particularly from both Soviet and American criticisms of colonialism.

The Algerian War of Independence itself garnered no mention in these discussions. It is unlikely that a French representative would have wanted to name the crisis during meetings and perhaps out of diplomatic decorum, no other European negotiator did either. Silence dominated the early years of the war, as historians of the use of torture in Algeria have demonstrated.[50] It follows that French authorities, in their capacity as negotiators with the Six, would have little desire to bring up the "events," as they called the war, risking censure from European officials whose own national press and electorates were skeptical of the cause of French Algeria. The obstinate silence in these diplomatic circles indicates not a lack of awareness about the ongoing war on the part of French or other European officials.[51] Rather, the silence allowed them to continue pursing European integration without introducing uncomfortable and potentially difficult-to-navigate questions. The Six's representatives knew what might happen were European integration discussed in tandem with colonial conflict; the EDC's failure was tied intimately with a French concern for defending their overseas holdings.

In Paris, ambivalence, even dread, reigned. Administrators struggled to make sense of how the French Union's attachment to a European institution might impact France's privileged role overseas. In early January 1957, a mid-level Banque de France administrator wrote a dire letter to the bank's governor, Wilfrid Baumgartner. Questioning the wisdom of the Six spending money on territories whose "political evolution is uncertain," he echoed Defferre's earlier concerns by asking if France could "claim to maintain sole political sovereignty" in the French Union while demanding that the Six share the costs. Doing so would invite other states to have a say in the French Union's "management and control. . . . *It is certain that the political links that unite France with the Union will loosen by the very fact of the multiplication of interests at hand.*" He wondered how Africans themselves would view the "presence on [their] soil of new arrivals more concerned with business than fraternal assistance?" Unusual for this milieu, the bank administrator acknowledged Africans' right to approve or disapprove of the movement of Europeans in their countries. But ultimately, in his view, the stakes were highest for France and the choices were unforgiving. Were the Six to provide much-needed funds, the French would extend to the Six a role in French Union affairs. Without those funds and at the risk of appearing to have chosen Europe over established African ties, the political damage would be at least as great.[52]

Unified European engagement in French Union affairs loomed as an unknown and raised concerns about both French sovereignty and the potential risk Europeans posed to African peoples. This is most evident in the discussions at the High Council of the French Union, a body comprising government representatives from each associated state as well as representatives of the French government. The council's general secretary was the Constantine-born Chérif Mécheri, who following World War II became the first French Muslim prefect. Mécheri's career spanned the Third to Fifth Republics, inclusive of the Vichy era. During his tenure as a *haut fonctionnaire* after the war, he frequently intervened on topics related to "Muslim" questions and the colonies. His career path was atypical for men of his generation born to Muslim households in Algeria. Even during the Algerian War, when a desperate French state attempted to "integrate" more Algerians into its public sector, Mécheri's trajectory remained singular in many respects.[53]

In his role as general secretary, Mécheri reported to President René Coty the concerns he and other council members shared. Overseas representatives feared potentially uneven investment by France's partners, who might refuse to make investments that were not "directly productive," neglecting key sites such as schools and hospitals in favor of mining and oil interests. If such projects were "to continue to be assured only by France, [the Common Market] would proceed as a true 'fool's bargain' as Mr. Mendès France pointed out." Mécheri was unequivocal: "the inclusion of the TOM in the European Common Market would virtually abolish the *zone franc* and crumble the cement that bonds the pieces of the French Union's edifice." Mécheri alerted Coty to rebukes from African representatives, such as Senghor's prediction that the free movement of labor would lead to "massive German and Italian immigration to Black Africa." Although some technicians and skilled laborers would be welcome, Mécheri reported that Senghor "fears the increase of the number of '*petits blancs*' who clutter the streets of African ports."[54] Even a Eurafrican proponent like Senghor feared that the TOM-Europe bond would remain one-sided and undermine African peoples' autonomy and economic prospects. Only a day after Mécheri wrote to Coty, Bousquet observed in a letter to Pineau that "there is no point in authorizing Italian and other *petits commerçants* to set up in French and Belgian African territories if they bring no riches but their presence."[55]

Metropolitan members of the French Union Assembly also expressed skepticism about the French Union's connection to new European institutions but ultimately cast it as necessary for France's very survival in the face of Soviet power and the emergent postwar order. This assembly, half of whose members represented the metropole, the other half the remainder of the French Union, was a non-lawmaking institution that could forward propositions to the National Assembly. Political parties and coalitions like the Rassemblement des gauches républicaines and the Centre républicain d'action paysanne et sociale demanded safeguards for the French

Union and its economic ties to the metropole. Socialist Georges Monnet, a member of the former and president of the assembly's agricultural commission, depicted the Six as caught between the United States and the USSR. Unless Europeans and Africans cooperated, he implied, the two blocs would entirely subsume Europe. Here, Africans meant people living in what the French dubbed Black Africa, a categorization that divided the continent through simplified racialized lines and administrative organization. In the nondiscussion of Algerians at this stage, those living in the Maghreb should be understood as having been implicitly grouped into this mission to rescue Europe via the French Empire.

In Monnet's vision, integration between the Six and beyond the metropoles would allow Europe to escape the menace of Cold War obsolescence. The France in the "new Europe" would be "the France of the Brazzaville Conference," or else France would not be a part of this Europe at all. Monnet offered a dire vision of what would occur if the French Union did not entirely integrate with Europe: Europe centered on the Rhine, meaning West Germany at its heart. The only solution was France joining Europe with the entirety of its overseas possessions, "an *ensemble* entirely open toward a continent that needs it." At the same French Union Assembly meeting, the Gaullist Marcel Léger promised, "Eurafrica will be humane; it will be built with Africa and for Africa or it will not be built. . . . What would become of Africa without Europe? Delivered to internal disorder . . . , it would be divided against itself and risk perishing. What a temptation for the Asian masses!"[56] Again, the imperatives were mixed. Africa could not survive without Europe; Africa faced falling to communism, which (unspoken) would bring Europe to its knees.

The weight these officials put on Africa can be read as two-fold. On the one hand, the "France of the Brazzaville Conference" meant a France devoted to imperial reform, allowing for the "humane" Eurafrica that Léger envisioned. This forward-looking France, working in concert with its empire, would lead Europe through its moral right and by safeguarding it against an Eastern menace. On the other hand, the France of Brazzaville was the France that stood up to Nazi rule, a heroic narrative that obscured the embarrassing capitulation and collaboration in the metropole. As historian Eric Jennings asked, "Without the support of these colonial holdings, what credibility, what international recognition, what counterweight to Vichy's legitimacy could a maverick general in London have mustered?"[57] This France of Brazzaville was the France of active Resistance, and in continuing with its fight against (West) Germany's overtaking of Europe, it would center power in a France supported by its brave and, even more importantly, loyal African peoples.

The Parti communiste français (PCF) held a different attitude toward the construction of Europe and its link to Africa. Although the PCF's record of anti-imperialism was anything but solid, by the mid-1950s its members increasingly mobilized critiques of French empire. The Corsican communist Arthur Giovoni, a Résistant who had served on the Provisional Consultative Assembly when it was based in Algeria from 1943 to 1944, took the floor of the National Assembly to tear down arguments for TOM-European association at the same meeting where Monnet and Léger spoke.[58] He questioned the promise of the Common Market ("according to its propagandists, the Common Market will be a life preserver for France and Europe"), derided Eurafrica ("cherished idea for German geopoliticians for over 50 years"), and alluded to forced population relocations in Algeria. Giovoni's view of the Common Market was stark: "This project is nothing but an enterprise of colonial pillage; dominated by America, it will not bring well-being but heightened misery. . . . It will not be the road to liberty, but the stumbling block in the movement toward the national independence of colonized countries."[59] His assertions challenged those of his fellow assembly members but by 1957 were more mainstream than in prior years, given that the metropolitan French public had begun, slowly, to renounce French Algeria. Growing dissention may have further fueled French negotiators in Brussels, who sought the approval of the Six both to respond to international pressure from the United Nations and to answer domestic opponents skeptical of France's position as an imperial power.

France's colonial ventures invited attacks from the Six as well. The Dutch led the charge, and the West German press added to the criticism. Already by 1956, Dutch officials expressed distaste about "launching [themselves] into an adventure."[60] This disagreement indicates that the incorporation of colonial and European economies did not appeal to all imperial capitals. The Dutch had recently solidified a commonwealth arrangement in the Caribbean and they would not withdraw from New Guinea until 1962, but Dutch officials sought to keep these affairs outside the confines of integrated Europe. By the mid-1950s, public opinion, particularly in the Federal Republic and the Netherlands, had turned firmly against French colonial policy in North Africa.[61] This meant that although the French could count on West German political support, given its leaders' focus on rapprochement with the French, they could not be sure of their popularity. In an article in *Die Welt* titled "Should We Return to Africa[?]," the author opined that West Germany should not accept the Franco-Belgian proposal, given that it would contribute more than it would gain from the deal. Further still, the article cast the German people as "victim . . . to Soviet colonialism" and warned that Africans would view Germany as "participat[ing] in dying colonialism." The article claimed that Minister of Economics Ludwig Erhard "exploded like a rocket" when he learned of France's plan.[62] Meanwhile, Lodovico Benvenuti, head of the Italian delegation, told the Six that Italy would require $150 to $200 million a year, in particular for the Mezzogiorno, and that these funds should be available during the first five years of the EEC's existence, rather than on the type of delay that so many regulations entailed.[63] This privileged European assistance for Italy over aid to the French Union. Further, Italians leveled accusations of dangerous competition between their own citrus-growing industry and those in the TOM.[64]

Even some in Belgian political circles challenged France's imperial policies. On March 21, 1957, four days before the Six signed the Treaty of Rome, the Belgian socialist Rolin announced that he would submit a proposition to the Council of Europe that questioned whether France's army respected the European Convention on Human Rights, whose Article 3 prohibited torture. Rolin, president of the Juridical and Administrative Commission of the council, was a veteran of World War I, lost three brothers in that conflict, and became drawn to pacifism while still in the trenches.[65] Perhaps little wonder, then, that he would demand an inquiry by the Council of Europe's Commission of the Rights of Man to investigate "abuses and torture." Although all members of the Council of Europe signed the Convention of the Rights of Man in Rome in 1950, France alone had not yet ratified the convention.

Quai d'Orsay officials hoped that they could convince Spaak and others to intervene and convince Rolin that "an initiative of this sort would be inopportune."[66]

The Franco-Belgian proposal and the general French push to associate its TOM to the Common Market and Euratom never convinced their detractors, yet the Six begrudgingly accepted this as a precondition to the launch of the treaty. In economic historian Catherine Hodeir's words, for French business lobbyists and politicians, now "the European dream and the overseas dream seemed to walk hand in hand."[67] French negotiators in Brussels and their colleagues in Paris understood their clout well. By February 1957, they amplified their demands by calling for a special policy for Algeria. This new demand would serve to combat the FLN at the UN General Assembly with a supranational agreement naming Algeria as a constitutive part of Europe. It would push against Giovoni, Rolin, and others who questioned what France was doing in Algeria. And it would draw a map of Europe with a southern border well below the Mediterranean. To say the least, this perturbed even France's most willing partners.

Weaponizing the Common Market

In February 1957, the Six still appeared to be debating the same issue, with the Dutch and even West Germans criticizing the amount of aid that the French demanded for the TOM ($209 million). Yet something was different. The French had issued a new demand at a conference of the Six's foreign ministers on February 18: the "inclusion" of Algeria and the overseas departments (DOM) in the Common Market. For the second time in just over a year, the French in Brussels introduced a major change to European integration policy. In 1956, the change was the demand to associate the TOM, used as a blanket term for the entire French Union regardless of juridical intricacies. In 1957, the change proved even more consequential: Algeria itself would be named as a region intrinsic to integrated Europe. French representatives argued that "Algeria and the overseas French departments . . . must be included in the Common Market as constitutive parts of the national territory."[68] The timing was not incidental.[69] Only five days prior, the UN had opened debates on the Algerian question.

The French decision to shift the discussion from the TOM, implicitly comprising Algeria although this was juridically inaccurate, to a separately named and regulated Algeria emerged from economic need and political exigency. Economically, the French feared that their European partners were not inclined to provide sufficient funds to Algeria via communal development aid. Politically, the lack of funds, to say nothing of Algerian nationalists' rejection of Algérie française, rendered the French position in Algeria precarious. The treaty could secure monetary appeasement, the French believed, and achieve European consensus in support of France's continued presence in Algeria. Naming Algeria in the treaty would create a supranational document affirming France's claim on Algeria. Securing protections through the treaty would harness new funds as Algeria became increasingly expensive to maintain, due to both the cost of the war and the price tag of the modernizing projects officials promised as a remedy to underdevelopment. As we will see, the economic benefits were less certain or imperative than the political ones. After nearly a decade of unevenly defining Algeria's place within the French Union, in the final weeks of the negotiations for the EEC, Algeria's peculiar juridical status as an integral part of the French metropole would now take center stage.

This change in policy direction emerged only with the intensification, in terms of violence and international attention, of the Algerian War in the months prior. The FLN launched the Battle of Algiers in late 1956. France arrested FLN leaders including Hocine Aït Ahmed, Ahmed Ben Bella, and Mohammed Boudiaf that same year and Generals Raoul Salan and Jacques Massu rose in power and responsibility under Governor General Robert Lacoste's orders. Beyond the growing military crisis, French officials faced the international challenge of the UN General Assembly's choice to discuss, and thus acknowledge, the Algerian crisis. If Algeria *was* France, French administrators needed to prove to the Six why that should remain the case. This, in turn, might allow them to reaffirm Algeria's status in the eyes of the international community and metropolitan French citizens themselves.

The new sine qua non mattered because of what it symbolized politically. If Algeria appeared in the Common Market treaty, the French could answer anti-colonial voices in the UN and elsewhere with the affirmation of five European states who acknowledged Algeria's relationship with France. This would potentially do little to change, let alone improve, Algeria's actual economic situation or upend France's outsized role there. Indeed, the final result was anything but economically secure for Algeria, given that Algeria would only be granted loans from the European Bank with the unanimous approval of its board of governors. Its agricultural products—notably wine and citrus—would continue to be excluded from the new preferential regime. Algerian laborers were unlikely to be allowed to take part in the movement of European laborers given that few French administrators were eager to alienate their partners to such a degree in favor of people whom at best they viewed as second-class French citizens.

Officials characterized these agricultural restrictions and the limits on free movement as sacrifices made by France, not Algeria. One DE-CE official warned that France would experience a two-fold influx of laborers: Algerians denied access to the rest of the Six would flood metropolitan France's labor market at the same time that laborers from the Six also sought employment there. The official argued that France's financial contributions to Algeria would far outstrip those coming from their European partners. The average yearly total contribution to the Overseas Investment Fund, $102 million per year, $40 million of which came from France, would also represent a paltry sum given the amount France dispensed in Algeria already. France would continue to make these contributions "to ensure the rapid development of Algeria, after the pacification of the latter and even as the French economy begins to face the increased competition resulting from the progressive establishment of the Common Market."[70] France, it appeared, would potentially gain little financially in the immediate extension of the Common Market to Algeria. French officials signaled that Algeria's fuller incorporation would operate on a delay, further underscoring that the optics of Algeria's inclusion mattered at least as much as any actual financial support.

The French attempted to appear conciliatory, implying that were Algeria to be inserted in the treaty, the French "would content themselves to the *application, to the benefit of Algeria, only of certain chapters of the Treaty*," leading all delegations, save the Italians ("even the Dutch") to a more amenable position.[71] By limiting themselves to select provisions, the French signaled that Algeria would not accede to the same privileges as the metropolitan territory of the Six, except for a handful of pertinent regulations related to trade, agriculture, and labor. Denying Algeria full benefits through the Common Market, the French reaffirmed Algeria's inferior status and positioned Algerian workers as people unworthy of full European rights. Indeed, the French raised no objections when the Six sidestepped entirely the question of nationality as they drafted the treaty chapter on the free movement of labor.[72] Given that at this point in time, Algerians did not enjoy equal treatment to their French "fellow citizens," with social benefits such as family allotments applying unevenly to Algerian laborers and government representation still nonrepresentative, little wonder that French authorities did not hesitate to promise that the European regime Algerians might experience would be a curtailed version of the one enjoyed by continental Europeans.

Even with the concessions, the demand nonetheless drew ire, particularly from the Italian delegation. Naming Algeria exacerbated tensions between France and Italy in large part because by naming Algeria as a site of application, the distinction between Algeria and the continental territory of the Six risked being flattened. For the first time, it appeared that Algerians might be poised to partake in the benefits of EEC membership, notwithstanding the clear lack of enthusiasm for such an extension on the part of the French delegation. The Italian delegation feared Algerian labor nonetheless, as well as Algerian agricultural products, which were direct competitors with Italian ones and could "benefit from the same advantages as those of Italy on the metropolitan market of the

Six." Finally, the Italians were upset to think that Algeria's under-developed regions would benefit from the European Investment Bank, which they had understood as principally structured to help disadvantaged Italian regions.[73]

Italian hesitation did have its limits. At a prime minsters' conference in Brussels in February 1957, Spaak argued that although Italy's prime minister "seemed to have a consistently negative attitude," he had not "been able to find any valid arguments to defend the position of his government, . . . notably concerning the inclusion of Algeria in the European Common Market."[74] The Italians were unable to reject the French demand out of hand precisely because they, like the other members of the Six, continued to accept the imperial logic that drove Europe's assumptions and self-image. Indeed, just prior to this conference, the Italian and Dutch delegations indicated interest in associating Somalia and Libya at Italy's behest, and New Guinea at the Netherlands' behest, indicating that European empire remained the order of the day, even for those who opposed French demands.[75]

When Italian officials attempted to capitalize on France's vulnerability during negotiations, they appeared obstructionist in the eyes of European integration's greatest advocates. Bousquet reported to the Quai d'Orsay that Italian demands at the prime minsters' conference put Spaak in a "justifiably bad mood." The Italians argued that the inclusion of Algeria in the upcoming treaty and the earlier exclusion of Algeria from the ECSC created a "void" between the two treaties. Given the Italian interest in accessing Algerian iron deposits in the early 1950s, this observation suggests that the Italians still hoped to secure material benefits from European integration's imperial policy or, in the eyes of the French, simply hoped to provoke. Although the French delegation appeared ready to concede somewhat, Spaak became so enraged by the Italian challenge that he left the meeting. Notably, it was the Dutch and West German delegations who attempted to coax him back into the room.[76] Despite their own hesitations regarding Algeria, the Common Market was simply too important to be killed by squabbling.

The reaction to the French policy change evinces the uneven quality of European integration. The case of Algeria makes this especially clear. Excluded at one point and then included when politically and economically exigent, Algeria had an inchoate relationship to (or in) Europe. The French, meanwhile, used integrated Europe as a tool to justify and normalize their ongoing presence in Algeria in the face of an ongoing war and pressure from the UN. Realizing they were on thin ice, the Italians submitted a proposition that simply requested that the issue be resolved "in a spirit of reciprocal collaboration" when the ECSC treaty was reviewed as scheduled in the future.[77]

Spaak held a key position in the overall negotiations for the EEC and his focus on achieving European unity demanded a French signature on the treaty. In his 1969 memoir, Spaak proudly recalled his support of France during the Algerian War, which he considered a French domestic issue.[78] More than most negotiation participants, Spaak appeared to serve "European" goals even above the needs of his native Belgium. Indeed, some of his own countrymen questioned his ability to speak for them. A month before the meeting during which the Italians antagonized Spaak, the Christian Democrat *La Libre Belgique* published an editorial asking if he "still possesses the full moral freedom desirable (we may even say required) . . . at a time when it falls upon him to defend fundamentally the interests of Belgium." The front-page editorial was titled "Shouldn't M. Spaak Recuse Himself?" Bousquet called it "perfidious."[79] A month after the meeting, the right-wing Belgian Catholic Parti social chrétien accused Spaak of acting against Belgium's interests in the Congo as he pursued wider TOM–Common Market association.[80] That same month, *La Libre Belgique* again questioned if Spaak had the "état d'esprit" necessary to defend Belgium in European negotiations, fearing that "Eurafrican" policy could jeopardize its colonial interests.[81] This would not be the last time a European administrator would be accused of shirking national duty.

As the signing date approached, the heads of the European delegations attempted to settle questions regarding how Algeria might fit within the Common Market. Conciliation and compromise reigned, with the Six focused now on securing a treaty, not dwelling on differences. The Italian delegation joined the French and Belgians in supporting the application of the whole of the Treaty of Rome's agricultural regime in both Algeria and the DOM.[82] The West Germans, although fearful of hurting their burgeoning trade ties with countries like Brazil, retracted their concerns about the agricultural regime.[83] All members of the Six agreed that the labor circulation stipulations should not automatically apply to Algeria or the DOM. They recognized the inconsistency: "the inhabitants of these territories possess French nationality," thus fitting the "necessary conditions to benefit from the application of the rules relative to free circulation."[84] Rather than address this dissonance, the Six adopted a deliberately obfuscatory tactic.

In the final weeks ahead of the treaty's signature, the Six's representatives adopted a policy so novel and so strange it merits being quoted at length, as outlined by Bousquet:

> The free movement of French nationals from Algeria and the French overseas departments in the Europe of the Six will, in the opinion of all Heads of Delegation, be subject to the procedures laid down in the Treaty.
>
> No chapter or article relating to Algeria or the French Overseas Departments will mention it. It was understood that the national administrations of the member states could, in this respect, apply the safeguard measures requested by all our partners. This formula obviously has drawbacks in the sense that French nationals from Algeria and the French Overseas Departments, who would have complaints about such safeguarding measures, would be likely to challenge them in the Court of Justice of the Common Market.[85]

The policy seemingly invited serious legal challenges to integration policy, particularly from overseas citizens. In the vague and tenuous language that was a hallmark of many high-level discussions of the Common Market, the Six effectively left open the possibility to discriminate against Algerian and DOM citizens who would seek the benefits of EEC membership to which they were entitled by virtue of those places being both juridical parts of the French Republic and named in the Common Market treaty. The first part ("the free movement . . . be subject") indicated an alignment between the rights of an Algerian (and therefore French citizen) and the rights of a Dutch or Italian person. The follow-up ("No chapter . . ."), however, foreclosed this possibility. Knowing that this exclusion opened integrated Europe to legal action, the French chanced such a development as an easier solution than the wholesale extension of European rights to noncontinental French nationals. This indicates that the French anticipated that this circulation might be negligible, but it also suggests that they were willing to force DOM and Algerian residents to *prove* that they were French and therefore deserving of equal treatment under European law. The racism undergirding this choice is apparent. It is unclear whether the Six envisioned the European settler communities when they enacted such language or if those people's race would protect them from this slapdash solution.

Disagreements in the realm of labor, agriculture, and nuclear cooperation all hinged on French officials' insistence on the importance of empire to the European project. Despite serious reservations from their partners, let alone the views of Algerians and other Africans that went largely ignored, the integration project trundled on. On March 25, 1957, representatives of the Six signed the Treaty of Rome. They agreed to stipulations that would explicitly name the French Union, along with other colonial holdings. Article 227 delineated where the Treaty of Rome would be applicable. Section 1 named the Six's continental territory, while Section 2 declared that "general and particular provisions," such as some agricultural regulations, the liberalization of services, and the movement of goods, would apply "to Algeria and the French overseas departments" once "this Treaty enters into force." Section 3 guaranteed "special arrangements for association" that would apply to overseas countries and territories. This would include French, Belgian, Italian, and Dutch holdings. A fourth section addressed the Saar.[86]

When the French named the DOM alongside Algeria in their European strategy, the choice appeared to be made largely out of the logic that all were *départements,* and thus a special part of the French Union, distinguishable from the TOM and Associated

States. The "old colonies" of French Guiana, Guadeloupe, Réunion, and Martinique had become DOM in 1946. Like the Algerian departments, this status suggested close administrative ties but hid distinctions in treatment that, though not expressed aloud, fell along racial lines. In practice, although Article 227 comprised Algeria and the DOM alike, Algeria was the focal point in the debates ahead of the Treaty of Rome and in the years to follow. Only after Algeria's independence would these policies' impact on the remaining DOM be viewed in its own right. In the late 1950s, the point of the "inclusion" demand was to solve a political and diplomatic quandary; officials felt no such imperative in the case of the other departments.

Far from quieting criticism, the association of the TOM and the integration of the DOM only invited further challenges, particularly from newly independent states. The UN was not the only emergent forum in which the French and their European partners feared challenges from the emboldened Third World. By 1957, a decade after its inception, the General Agreement on Tariffs and Trade (GATT) offered independent states openings to challenge European power. The Treaty of Rome stipulations for the TOM caused concern among GATT members. Notably, Latin American countries, as well as some members of the British Commonwealth, argued that the Treaty of Rome would have negative repercussions on international trade.[87] On a trip to South America in 1957, Pineau fielded local concerns about European capital destined for South America being redirected to profit Africa. He apparently calmed the situation enough to come away with a favorable opinion of Latin America, where he found an economic and cultural "affinity" for Europe. This would have been a relief given European, and also American, fears of losing sway to communism in the

Global South.[88] Pineau noted approvingly, "This state of mind is encouraging and deserves all the more attention, as everyone knows the sadly very different one which drives the countries of the Afro-Asian group."[89] Pineau had reason to be concerned and the GATT would prove both a friendly and a dangerous forum. The Indian delegation in Geneva, for example, introduced questions about whether the EEC's relations with overseas countries and territories could be reconciled with GATT regulations.[90] Five years later, the inception of the UN Conference for Trade and Development (UNCTAD) would cause further consternation in France and the EEC, whose members feared that the forum would allow for criticism of the Common Market. The Six, with the exception of the Netherlands, voted against UNCTAD's convening. Its first conference would be held in Geneva in 1964.[91] The signing of the Treaty of Rome did not cement on the global stage the logic of empire; it invited conversations and challenges from within the European continent and, more troublingly for EEC administrators, from without.

An Empty Treaty?

The question of Algeria reveals internal and external strife as French and European officials tried to understand exactly where the limits of the EEC were located and in whose interest those borders were created and maintained. Although the EEC and Euratom formally launched on January 1, 1958, this day held little import for French Algeria, juridically a part of the mother country, yet excluded from immediate application of the treaty's provisions. Five months later, the May 13 coup mounted by military authorities in Algeria precipitated the fall of the Fourth Republic and the return of Charles de Gaulle. He visited Algeria shortly thereafter, delivering his now (in)famous promise in Algiers, *"Je vous ai compris,"* or "I have understood you." Settlers took this to mean that he understood their plight and would restore French order in Algeria. They would be bitterly disappointed.

Defferre, Pineau, and countless unnamed bureaucrats in Paris and Brussels pushed first for the TOM, implicitly comprising Algeria, and then explicitly for Algeria to be associated with or integrated within the Treaty of Rome because the treaty could serve as a weapon in the war against anti-imperialists. The French ultimatums demonstrate these officials' willingness to antagonize their European counterparts. As the apparent emptiness of their demands—all of which were delayed and characterized by loopholes—attest, Algeria's *name* mattered more than actual guarantees or rights for Algeria. The concessions of the other members of the Six suggest that France's signature was more significant than any frustration arising from French demands of aid and trade benefits for the French Union. The treaty for the Common Market did not stem anti-colonial action in Algeria or elsewhere. That was not its intent. Despite securing development aid that could, French officials believed, quiet discontent, the purpose of the treaty language was principally to legitimize France's continued presence there. In the hands of the French and with the signatures of its five European partners, the Treaty of Rome became a means to combat calls for an independent Algeria and to affirm on an international stage the legitimacy of French Algeria.

While the French attempted to implement this plan, they also negotiated in Brussels how the Treaty of Rome would actually be applied in Algeria. Thus, in considering March 25, 1957 and its place in the histories of France, Algeria, or European integration, the signature was not as a full stop but a jumping-off point for tense future negotiations. It represents only one date in the much larger constellation of the histories of the Algerian War of Independence and the unification of Europe. Indeed, although special provisions for Algeria and the French Union were prerequisites for France even agreeing to sign the treaty, such provisions were slated for realization at a later date. When the Treaty of Rome came into effect at the turn of 1958, administrators in Paris and Brussels were at a loss for how its regulations might apply in Algeria. For the next five years, until Algeria's independence in July 1962, representatives of the Six contended with the legal reality that Algeria was in Europe—in the sense of an integrated institution—but remained uncertain about if they would be forced to allow its residents to enjoy any of the benefits promised by European citizenship.

4

Algérie Européenne

It is easy to read Charles de Gaulle's call for Algerian self-determination, leveled in September 1959, as the signal moment when French officials acknowledged that Algérie française would come to an end. Yet the war raged on, as it had in the months and years prior, notably with a new counterinsurgent push. In the diplomatic sphere, administrators were no more poised to release the French hold on Algeria, and they continued to prepare for a future where Algeria remained deeply entrenched in French and European affairs. Indeed, since the European Economic Community (EEC) came into effect in January 1958, Algeria was an integrated part of the European Common Market. A year and a half later, the journal *France Outremer* treated its readers to a geography lesson: "The distance is not further between Luxembourg and Algeria than between Naples and Amsterdam." The trope of France from Dunkirk to Tamanrasset is familiar. But what about Europe, from Hamburg to Adrar? The Algerian Economic Affairs official who wrote this claim warned, "In any event, it is important not to commit the error of considering Algeria as a far-off overseas territory, merely associated with the EEC. . . . Algeria must be considered the youngest of these adolescent regions of the Community, whose member states are committed to facilitating economic and social development."[1] So close to de Gaulle's appeal for self-determination, this claim, and the work of French bureaucrats in Brussels to tie Algeria even closer to European institutions, seems to suggest a willfully blind optimism or a deeply confused atmosphere among those French administrators. In fact, a third reading of their actions and rhetoric is in order: for French officials, it still appeared advantageous to insist that Algeria benefit from EEC membership.

For nearly five years, the EEC stretched across the Mediterranean, with concrete ramifications for Algeria, France, and the Six that extended beyond that half decade. The application of the Treaty of Rome in Algeria stood to alter trade practices, offer monetary aid, and open labor circulation between Europe and Algeria. This served French interests in two key ways. First, it allowed officials to maintain that Algeria was a juridical part of France. Second, although a lesser concern during the treaty's negotiations, it opened an avenue for French officials to demand EEC financial support for costly Algerian development projects, which they understood in part as remedies for the ills that instigated the war in the first place. In the immediate, Algeria's integration under Article 227 guaranteed favorable tariffs in trade with the Six and obligated the Six to support development projects there. French officials' continued insistence that Algeria was a part of integrated Europe invited a new round of criticism from their partners. This was exacerbated when the French insisted that Algerian projects be supported by funding sources once earmarked for other regions. Dutch and West German officials recoiled at the price tag of development aid; Italians balked at the risk of competition from Algerian exports, agricultural and human. The French, for their part, remained willing, and unafraid, to antagonize their partners in order to secure material support for French projects in Algeria. The convergence of new international law and old notions of the validity of colonialism led to tense debates not about *whether* Europe would be involved in Africa but how.

French officials attempted to assert or maintain their supremacy in integrated Europe even as they themselves demonstrated an evolving understanding of where France might be sovereign and where such a status was diminished or terminated. They planned for an evolution in trade relations with Algeria that they believed would be realized. In doing so, they laid the groundwork for how future commercial and development aid treaties would be implemented in the overseas departments and across the French Community. In claiming Algerian territory, they also attempted to cast France as the center—literally, the capital—of future European-African relations. Indeed, Michel Debré insisted that Brussels must *not* be understood as the capital of such a world, telling European Commission president Walter Hallstein "there must not even be feeling that Brussels may be a recourse against Paris."[2] This unsubtle remark emphasized the importance French officials placed on being in charge of any form of European-African collaboration. With the whole of the French Community integrated or associated with the EEC, France would remain the largest economy of Europe, even next to West Germany.[3]

Read together, the episodes of the years in which Algeria was part of both France and the EEC reveal the difficulty of implementing French notions of territory and trade zones and also point to Europe's future development aid and labor migration structures.

The year 1960 marked the end point of the mandated two-year delay on the application of Article 227, the section of the Treaty of Rome that delineated what EEC regulations would operate in Algeria, and whose implications especially alarmed Italian officials. That same year, most countries in the French Community gained their independence in what is known as the Year of Africa. France's map had changed profoundly, but in the eyes of the officials now demanding EEC funding for Algeria, at least it still stretched to the southern shores of the Mediterranean.

A close analysis of the years when Algeria was a juridical part of integrated Europe reveals the stakes for French officials—Muslim Algerians remained excluded—as they attempted to shape a Europe whose institutional goals would buoy France's status as an imperial power. It demonstrates that after the treaty was signed, the real work of parsing out its meaning—and its potential to bolster French sovereignty—began. In particular, the administrators representing France at the EEC in Brussels, notably the permanent representatives Éric de Carbonnel (April 1958–November 1959) and Georges Gorse (November 1959–June 1961) and their staffs, went to great lengths to ensure that their counterparts among the Six would support France's imperial endeavors. They and other French officials received encouragement from memos coming from the General Secretariat of the Interministerial Committee Responsible for Questions of European Economic Cooperation (SGCI), France's European affairs department.[4] SGCI authorities, often unnamed bureaucrats, sent missives that laid out what kinds of Algerian-focused benefits the French might extract from the EEC. Even ostensibly European officials—meaning French administrators serving the EEC as a whole, not representing their home country—fought to maintain a French preeminence in African and Algerian affairs, as one particularly contentious diplomatic clash with a West German official makes clear.

The French in Brussels and the SGCI pushed continuity in European relations with Algeria while their colleagues in other French ministries or offices began officially to pursue channels for a cease-fire and to acknowledge publicly the potential of an independent Algeria. Indeed, even with de Gaulle's return and the establishment of the Fifth Republic, France's approach to Algeria as a constitutive part of Europe remained remarkably steady.[5] Thus, the period 1958–1962 reveals not only that France's imperial interests interacted with and influenced its European integration policy; it demonstrates how long the life of such interests would be. France, even when stripped of nearly all of its former colonies, grasped to maintain a position of dominance in Europe via what was left of its imperial grandeur.

Europe's Southern Border

Jacques Pélissier, director of agriculture and forests in Algeria, was flummoxed in May 1958. The litany of legal definitions seemingly applicable to Algeria had muddled discussions of French agricultural policy within EEC policy. Some reports, Pélissier fretted, labeled Algeria "an overseas territory, which causes confusion, as overseas territories are associated with the Common Market, while Algeria is integrated into it." Algeria was at other points treated "as a foreign country, meaning a third-party state."[6] Failing to establish a consistent version of how Algeria related to France, it could appear that French officials undermined their own chance at advancing their goals in Brussels, potentially opening loopholes undercutting Algerian trade. Yet such ambiguity could prove useful, as the lack of a firm approach allowed them to make claims that would support labor rights and economic aid funneled toward Algeria without taking a firm stand about its position vis-à-vis Europe.

The Council of the Republic adopted the Treaties of Rome in July 1957, following debate and approval by the French Union Assembly and the National Assembly. The council's Commission on Overseas France supported the ratification, despite concerns that the overseas departments, given their economic similarity to the overseas territories, might suffer from the swift application of EEC regulations, "but here the fiction of juridical assimilation to the Metropole has won."[7] Algeria's *patronat*—an association of employers and business people—meanwhile spoke out against the "rupture of economic unity" that would arise from a free trade zone that excluded the French Overseas Departments (DOM).[8] One threat to Algeria's agricultural exports came from the potential of non-European products to receive "EEC provenance" certification if they were processed in Europe.[9] Algerians' political status within and outside France complicated this further. Fears of trade competition were exacerbated as Belgian, Dutch, and Italian representatives in Brussels all made clear that they would oppose attempts to extend the EEC social security regime to Algerian laborers.[10] Yet in West Germany, officials deemed it impossible to grant political asylum to Algerians because they were French.[11] The question of where and when the Treaty of Rome would apply in Algeria and whether Algeria and its population merited special treatment relative to the rest of the French Union remained unanswered.

In the years after World War II, legal maneuvers such as the *statut organique de l'Algérie* and the *loi-cadre Defferre* and gradual moves to extend voting rights to people in Algeria and the overseas departments and territories all fell short of creating a single French citizenship that guaranteed equality across the empire. French officials told a different story in Brussels in order to make the case that Algerian workers in Europe should be treated equally to metropolitan workers. During the Treaty of Rome's drafting, then–cabinet member in the Ministry of Foreign Affairs Robert Marjolin argued that "there was no distinction of nationality between a Frenchman born in France and a Frenchman born in Algeria, whether he was a Muslim or not."[12] One official in the SGCI asked rhetorically, "How can an 'Algerian worker' be defined? The national identity card is the same for all French nationals [*ressortissants*] no matter their department of origin and it is difficult to conceive of our partners wanting to establish racial discrimination in the name of the European Community regarding the free circulation of labor."[13] In making this observation, the SGCI official implied that the other members of the Six hoped to enact racist labor policy, while the French made no such distinctions between its citizens. As Amelia Lyons has shown, the "drive to save French Algeria required the metropolitan government to highlight Algerian migrants' rights and eligibility for all the benefits of the French welfare state." At the same time, Fifth Republic officials attempted to curb the risk of "excessive" Algerian family settlement in the metropole.[14] In the European context, this translated into French attempts to seek financial security and work opportunities for Algeria's underemployed and restive laboring class, compelling the Six to comply under threat of being labeled as discriminatory racists, while maintaining a settler-hierarchical French Algeria and continuing to wage war against Algerian nationalists.

The earliest months of the EEC's existence coincided with the fall of the Fourth Republic and de Gaulle's return to French po-

litical life, precipitated by a coup led by Generals Jacques Massu and
Raoul Salan, among others. In October, the National Assembly
approved the constitution of the Fifth Republic, the French Union
was reconfigured as the French Community, and de Gaulle, now
president, introduced the Constantine Plan. The plan was meant,
in Muriam Haleh Davis's words, "not merely to perpetuate a
French Algeria, but to make Muslim Algerians compatible with
the dictates of European integration."[15] De Gaulle announced that
"all of Algeria must have its share in what modern civilization
can and must bring to men." The Constantine Plan, via industri-
alization and development, would make it possible. Among the
modernizing practices that Fifth Republic officials claimed the
plan would usher in were new housing initiatives, agricultural
reform, industrial growth, and job creation. These changes were
unsuccessful and, at times, destructive. But as Davis argues, as late
as 1958, development "helped institute a geographic imaginary
that would merge Algeria and France in a common framework
known as EurAfrica."[16] Reform, not independence, remained the
goal of French administrators. The EEC could underwrite the costs
of these wide-ranging changes.

The rebranding of the empire from the French Union to the
French Community under the Fifth Republic's constitution did
not resolve Algeria's status under French law. This ambiguity appeared more unwieldy now that officials in Brussels had turned to
questions of treaty implementation. Pierre-François Gonidec, a
law professor in Rennes who had worked at the Dakar law faculty
in the early 1950s, argued that the DOM were "*in* the Common
Market and not *associated* with the Common Market." He cited
an interwar appeals court decision that "qualified the Algerian departments as 'trans-Mediterranean' to make clear that they were
simply the prolongation of French territory beyond the sea."[17]

Although Gonidec's opinion aligned with the French delegation's own contentions at the still-recent Val Duchesse negotiations, not all Fifth Republic representatives or the other members of the Six wholeheartedly shared his confidence that the DOM were in the Common Market and that Algeria was a mere prolongation of France. Rather, these European officials continued to struggle to define the position of Overseas France in the EEC. Algeria, unsurprisingly, was the greatest source of consternation.

From the treaty's ratification until Algeria's independence, the actual implementation of its rules remained a constant source of concern for French officials. Salah Bouakouir, a high-ranking, Algeria-born economic affairs official, warned of the "very serious drawbacks" of excluding Algerian products from regulations related to the Common Agricultural Policy.[18] In other words, if France pursued European trade policy absent Algeria, it was Algerian trade that would suffer most. Gilles Warnier de Wailly of the Secrétariat général of Algeria complained in 1959 that the "implementation of the Treaty of Rome in fact still poses for Algeria a series of very poorly managed problems, in my opinion." He cautioned, "It is difficult to imagine that the Algerian market will be open to European products, but that the European labor market is not open to Algerian workers."[19] His invocation of Algerian labor represented a rare acknowledgment of the attendant human cost of such policies.

France's representative to the EEC in Brussels, Éric de Carbonnel, offered a novel solution for circumventing the pitfalls of how to label Algeria. De Carbonnel suggested that the "problem of this regulation's application domain as it concerns Algeria can be treated by preterition."[20] Preterition is the rhetorical device of omission, or of feigning omission, an argumentative logic perhaps inspired by *lycée* public speaking, or, *exposé,* strategy.[21] De Carbonnel implied that by *not* addressing Algeria outright—or by insisting that Algeria, as a part of the French Republic, need not be explicitly addressed—the French could tacitly create a legal environment in which their partners would accept their contested claim to the territory's Frenchness. Algeria ipso facto would be integrated into the EEC. Although they never implemented this tactic, the argumentative style of absence appealed to French officials in Brussels because it enabled them to sidestep challenging questions about Algeria's status. As the negotiations for the Treaty of Rome in the mid-1950s showed, silence was an enduringly useful tactic for diplomats. In the act of deliberately not talking about Algeria, French officials hoped to usher the benefits of EEC statutes into the region. The same silence could potentially serve the interests of their European partners, who would wish neither to raise awkward topics that could alienate the French nor to go on the record appearing supportive of French Algeria, given their own populations' opinion of the war. The other members of the Six became more emboldened by the mere fact that the Treaty of Rome had already been ratified, meaning that they no longer had to appease the French as they did when they needed to secure a signature. The French soon found themselves facing overt criticism from the Dutch and Italian delegations in particular. Preterition may have seemed appealing, but silence gradually became untenable.

French officials examining treaty application procedures became stymied by the costs of insisting that Algeria be accounted for in these stipulations. Free circulation of labor questions proved fraught. The Italians suggested delaying the application of labor circulation rights in Algeria until 1965, with wording that risked excluding French citizens of the settler population from enjoying the benefits of EEC membership. Such a decision would be at odds with over a century of assimilationist policy in Algeria and threatened to introduce yet another form of second-class citizenship in the French Community. Indeed, it appeared that by virtue of insisting on Algeria's assimilation to the EEC, the French had opened the possibility not that Algerian Muslims would enjoy European rights but that European settlers in Algeria would be denied them. The question of labor circulation and Algeria invited the peril of unskilled Europeans competing for jobs on Algerian soil and the generalized fear that the French would inspire "apprehension" in their European partners, mainly about Algerians moving to their states.[22] Conversely, not recognizing Algeria stood to reduce even settlers' rights in Europe and chipped away at assertions of Algeria's Frenchness, the latter of which was precisely how officials pushed for Algeria's naming in the Treaty of Rome in the first place.

This was not the first time that French officials struggled with the application of rights outside of the continent. In 1789, a white colonist in Saint-Domingue mused, "One of the mistakes of our deputies was to have asked to be assimilated to the provinces of France. A trap was set for them in the National Assembly by treating the rights of man in general." The *colons* themselves had demanded representation when the Estates General gathered in Paris at the dawn of the French Revolution. That invited a dangerous flip side: the unintended extension of rights to those deemed unworthy—in this case, meaning free people of color and, as would transpire in the years to come, enslaved people.[23] In the 1950s, French officials in Paris had also set a trap for themselves. In order to defend the settlers' rights within the EEC, would they have to insist on Muslims' rights as well? A version of de Carbonnel's preterition arose, with an SGCI official floating the possibility that Algeria could simply be regulated like the metropole.[24] Examining the question of free circulation of labor, French officials came the closest to advocating on behalf of Algerian rights in Europe, rather than enjoying Algeria's inclusion in name only. An SGCI official deemed it "unfortunate that Algeria's position . . . continues to be indeterminate." A new draft proposal about labor mobility "provides a typical illustration of the abnormal nature of this situation."[25] This abnormality, which in fact was fairly representative of Algeria's ambiguous relationship to both the metropole and Brussels, was not resolved ahead of its independence.

Although French ministerial sources said little about whether Algerians knew or cared that their home was tied up in the Common Market, it is clear that North Africans were well aware of the efforts. An editorial in the first issue of the Messalist *Réalités algériennes* declared that the end of the war was the only way to achieve "the economic and cultural flourishing of the underdeveloped countries of the Franco-African Community and to see the birth and materialization of the Euro-African *grand ensemble*."[26] Days after the editorial's publication, the Moroccan Berber hero of the Rif War Abd El-Krim told a German newspaper that "the Common Market results in a new exploitation. If the people of Europe really wish for sincere economic cooperation with North Africa, they must start by giving sovereignty to these people and by helping them to develop their economic potential."[27] Provisional Government of the Algerian Republic (GPRA) officials in Bonn told West Germans that they were pro-Western but would recognize East Germany if they did not receive promises of economic cooperation.[28] Although they were excluded from negotiations and still subject to French rule, they understood what the

EEC could mean for their future—in terms of both economic assistance and the continuation of inequality.

After the Treaty of Rome's signing and its ratification by the Six, French officials mobilized multiple tactics to insist that Algeria be subject to its regulations. Ambiguity not unlike what Pélissier lamented could be useful for leveraging claims, despite the distaste expressed by West German and Dutch representatives especially. At the same time, French officials struggled to find convincing language to defend their position. In one SGCI official's words, the delay in resolving Algeria's status "left hanging a question of capital interest that merits being the subject of a thorough examination."[29] As they eyed the risk posed to Franco-Algerian and Euro-Algerian trade by Italy, or potentially Greece, Portugal, or Turkey after future EEC expansions, French officials emphasized Algeria's underdevelopment without acknowledging that over 130 years of colonial rule undermined its economic growth, necessitating European aid. Rather, French officials drew comparisons between Italian north-south disparities and the poverty that divided the metropole from Algeria. Algeria's economic and social situation, they argued, was no different from southern Italy's. In this line of argumentation, Algeria's inclusion in the EEC was not just normal but imperative for its future success.

A Maghrebi Mezzogiorno

Jean Pouderoux, director of the Maison de l'agriculture algérienne, wondered in 1959 if the harmonization "of social legislation [would] be so much more difficult between the Algerian departments . . . and the European economy than the harmonization of the standard living between a Sicilian or southern Italian peasant and a cereal farmer from the north of France?"[30] Pouderoux drew an equivalency, quite popular among French officials, between the Italian Mezzogiorno and French Algeria. In this line of argumentation, the two regions were alike in poverty and underdevelopment. Following this logic, the extension of the Treaty of Rome, and particularly European aid schemes, to Algeria was as natural as the EEC's presence in the Italian Midi.

This argument conflicted with distinctions French officials often insisted on between Algerian *fellah* and French peasants but fit within a long history of asserting that southern Europe was not unlike North Africa.[31] French officials did not have to look far to find ways of equating Algeria with Italy. Scholars and political figures, including in Italy itself, had long portrayed its southern regions as benighted.[32] Just as Europeans viewed their colonies as spaces of experimentation, deviance, or conquest, so too did they understand the Mezzogiorno as both destitute and exotic.[33] This long-lived stereotype held that southern Italians were in need of civilizing to escape, in the words of nineteenth-century British reformers, their "semi-Oriental" lifestyle, along with their "backward" economy and the social conditions that made them "a mean and idle race."[34] The comparison to the Mezzogiorno allowed the French simultaneously to cast Algeria as a part of Europe while also explaining why it was not like prosperous parts of the continent. Like the Mezzogiorno, Algeria needed time and resources to catch up to its supposedly more advanced kin elsewhere in Europe. Italian officials, for their part, bristled at the notion that Algerian laborers could compete for European jobs with their citizens. Unspoken, they likely also fretted over being associated with Africans in terms of their own populations' civility, given that their country's forays into colonialism under Benito Mussolini had only recently afforded Italians a new narrative in which their citizens were "whitened" in contrast to the Africans they attempted to conquer.[35]

French officials openly antagonized their Italian counterparts as they argued for the application of Treaty of Rome rights in Algeria. Now that the Six had signed the treaty, French officials acted to claim financial benefits that they previously indicated were far from the top of their agenda. They appeared to follow through on Pouderoux's insistence, echoing Defferre, that France maintain both its "African vocation" and its "European vocation."[36] Now cast as a question of economic need rather than racist differentiation between Algeria and Europe, the French could normalize the racialized treatment of Algerians while demanding EEC benefits for the region. Here, the blurring of civilizational and racial arguments implicit in their invocation of the Mezzogiorno allowed the French to call for Algeria's inclusion while depicting its economic and social conditions as inherent to the region rather than a product of French colonial policy. Italy, with its poverty-stricken southern regions and prosperous, relatively industrialized north, they claimed, was not unlike France, with its flourishing metropole and the undeveloped Algerian expanse. In this light, Algeria was, in the words of French agriculture officials, "not a 'poor country,' but an insufficiently developed province" of France.[37] If underdeveloped Italy could be a part of the Common Market, they contended, why not the neediest region of France?

For the French, the Mezzogiorno's economic plight offered a method of justifying the presence of a poor, seemingly unruly region within the EEC. For Italian officials, the very fact that Algeria could be linked to the Mezzogiorno threatened Italian trade, labor migration opportunities, and access to development aid. Italians, of course, were an important guest worker population, notably in West Germany, where officials coded Italian arrivals as "Southern" or "Mediterranean," another indication of the slippage of identities between the Maghreb and southern Europe.[38] Historian Rita Chin argues that policies regarding guest workers cannot be treated as "tangential." Rather, "these migrants occupied a central place in the most important and enduring question of the postwar period: How would West German national identity be reconstituted after the Third Reich?"[39] The furor over the right of movement for Italians to West Germany *and* Algerians to continental Europe forces us to expand this question. We can ask not only how the presence of European migrants might help to form postwar European identities, but also how the possibility of other migrant groups claiming the same rights further challenged European identity in this period. Indeed, the meaning of "European" had been in flux for decades. If southern Italians themselves were long considered a different race of peoples from northern Europe's population, how would the ability of Algerians to access European rights further threaten the notion of a European identity based on race or religion?

French officials, who had their own domestic record of sidelining Algerian rights, saw value in harnessing European benefits for Algeria. They fought for a European rights regime based on the geography cemented by Article 227 and not on the racialized notions of citizenship that they themselves upheld at home. French officials began to argue that the European Social Fund should be accessible to Algerian laborers in the Six's metropoles and Algeria itself and that the European Investment Bank should fund Algerian projects. Development, officials in Brussels and Paris alike believed, would pacify Algerians who were frustrated with their low standard of living, thereby crushing anti-imperial nationalism. Like decades-earlier campaigns to "civilize" the Mezzogiorno, now it was Algeria's turn to experience Europe's civilizing light.

Italian officials, outraged by this diversion of funds, pushed back. Giovanni Falchi, Italy's representative in Brussels, pointedly reminded his homologue Georges Gorse, de Carbonnel's successor, that the European Social Fund was "conceived to help Italy in its fight against unemployment and is thus an important element in the political equilibrium of the Common Market." Were Algerians to access the fund, it would "reduce the expected advantages" for Italians. For the sake of "certain appeasement to the Italians," Gorse suggested that the French delegation could negotiate a two-year delay, with some components of the fund not accessible to Algeria during the first stage of the treaty's implementation.[40] Months later, the issue remained unresolved. Falchi warned that Italy's minister of labor was "concerned about the extension of the free circulation of labor regulations to Algeria and to Algerians. The evolution of events makes him fear the arrival in Europe of many Muslim individuals who can compete with the Italian workforce even in Northern Italy." Gorse mused in his report of this meeting that the Italians "fear, in fact, that too much haste on our part will arouse in the other delegations concerns that will . . . further compromise the slight advantages that the Italian government expects from the execution of the treaty in this area."[41] Italian concerns did little to stop French officials from pushing for more concessions for Algeria, given the potential for the French to access useful financial assistance to support development in Algeria.

French officials cast themselves as victims of Italy's paralyzing opposition to the correct application of EEC social policy. Yves Roland-Billecart in the Ministry of Algerian Affairs warned that although the free circulation of labor within the Six was an

"important theoretical guarantee" for Algerians, in reality metropolitan France would remain "the essential outlet" for those
workers, and worse, the guarantee "will not bring any new good
to Algeria." Rather, it would open the Algerian labor market to
"unqualified Italian laborers." His solution was to push for the
French to settle the extension of social regulations to Algeria "at
the same time as that of the member states for their European territory."[42] Christian Delaballe, the Algerian Affairs minister, however, caved to Italian pressure and recommended delaying the extension of free labor movement and the applicability of the social
fund to Algeria until the end of 1963.[43]

Pouderoux's contention that the Treaty of Rome's social regulation would be as easily applicable to the Sicilian peasant, the
northern French cereal farmer, and the Algerian laborer did not
bear out in European negotiations. Italian officials fought the lik-
ening of the Mezzogiorno to Algeria and challenged French claims
that the benefits of the EEC might be evenly distributed between
the two regions. French officials, in spite of their rhetorical celebration of Algeria's potential to thrive along with Europe's other
"least developed regions," ultimately bowed to Italian demands
and acknowledged that they could not obtain all of the European
rights for Algeria that they initially hoped. Their willingness to
abandon these claims speaks once again to the ambiguity surrounding Algeria's place within integrated Europe: was it just another Mezzogiorno, or was it a territory easily shed when it caused
too much strife between would-be allies?

Testing the Franco-German Friendship

In a 1959, Ferhat Abbas told *Der Spiegel*, "Nobody wants to stop
you from being good friends with France. But that does not mean

you have to marry France's mistakes, support its colonial rule." He was responding to his interviewer's assertion that the Federal Republic was not financing France's war in Algeria. Abbas contended that through EEC funds, Bonn was doing just that.[44] Ahead of the interview's publication, French officials worried about reports that West German officials were angered by France's divergence to Algeria of common EEC funds meant to develop the French Overseas Territories (TOM), of which the Federal Republic had contributed some $200 million.[45] West German skepticism of French intentions had arisen earlier, during Treaty of Rome negotiations. A 1957 political cartoon published in the *Frankfurter Allgemeine Zeitung* depicted the French Marianne encouraging Der Deutsche Michel—a national personification not unlike England's John Bull—to "close [his] eyes and think of Europe" as he dumped countless 100 DM bills into a flaming pyre labeled "North Africa."[46] The meaning was clear: Paris was coercing Bonn to throw its money at an unmitigated disaster. The West German delegation had signed the treaty nevertheless. After the treaty's ratification, French officials risked exacerbating tensions with West Germany, in many ways their most important ally among the Six, in order to secure greater amounts of aid for Algeria. The French embassy in Bonn warned that some West Germans felt France was attempting to use "an international label" to maintain its position in Algeria.[47] Indeed, in their quest to secure more European funds for Algeria, French officials antagonized their EEC counterparts, backing away from earlier promises and seeking more and more money for projects in the warring region.

The Treaty of Rome's Convention of Application stated that the French would not "request the intervention of the development fund outlined in Article 1 of the Convention except for the

Fig. 4.1   Hanns Erich Köhler, "Gemeinsamer Markt," *Frankfurter Allgemeine Zeitung*, October 19, 1957. Wilhelm-Busch-Gesellschaft e. V. Inv. No. KKG 03278 / 70

overseas countries and territories under the purview of the Minister of Overseas France." In a change from the earlier flattening of Algeria under the TOM label, that terminology now explicitly meant "not Algeria." In late 1959, Prime Ministry officials reached out to the Quai d'Orsay, aiming to reverse this and list Algeria among the beneficiaries of the EEC Development Fund. The drawbacks might prove considerable, notably losing aid that had been earmarked for French West and Equatorial Africa and Madagascar and cutting off from Algeria the European Investment Bank funds aimed at continental European territory.

The French rejected out of hand any West German accusation of the unacceptable nature of France's about-face regarding fund beneficiaries. If Bundestag members during its ratification debates had assured other German authorities of the French intention not to extend the funds to Algeria, that was not France's problem but rather of an "internal order."[48] The French were unafraid to invoke the Constantine Plan and to suggest that their reversal on the funding question was imperative to its success.[49] An unsigned memo likely written by Michel Debré proclaimed that "the problem of aid to Algeria takes a scandalous appearance" due to the attitude of France's partners. It continued, "I believe it necessary to recall to what degree this policy of supranationality is at once unrealistic and dangerous. . . . France drowned in the European Communities can no longer be at the head of the [French] Community. The union of France and Algeria is in itself compromised."[50] In this way, French officials worked to cast their policy shift as a natural part of peacekeeping in Algeria, all while attempting to maintain metropolitan supremacy there and in the entirety of the French Community. For the most Eurosceptic among French administrators, like Debré, the EEC both offered opportunity and posed a real danger to France's global position.

Fantasies of Eurafrica, although generally less overt by the late 1950s, continued to influence people in France and beyond. Some pro-Europeanists harnessed the ideal of federalism in order to push for French Algeria. For example, in 1958, the French-based organization Fédération, which survived its Vichyist associations of the war years, invited thirty European mayors to spend a week in Algeria, presumably as a public relations campaign to showcase France's achievements there.[51] More radically, a group calling itself the Premier comité européen de salut public, a clear nod to the coup of 1958, published a screed celebrating French Algeria and Eurafrica. "Thus Algeria," it read, a "French province *integrated* since 1830, must be the sumptuous dowry that France brings tomorrow to the wedding basket of Europe. After this 'marriage,' each nation [of the Six] will have the right to consider this province as its own and contribute to its prosperity equally to us."[52] This nuptial language, more common in the early 1950s, served to remind Europeans of the imperial bounty that awaited an EEC oriented toward Africa.

Other European federalists used their platform to condemn France's empire, although they themselves did not fully shed their Eurocentric assumptions about how the world should instead be organized. As early as 1956, a communiqué likely written by a member of the Congrès du people européen criticized the French Union, calling it a "false federation that is nothing but a hoax." Algeria should be independent, but this independence in national affairs would go hand in hand with Algeria's federation "into the community of the United States of Europe or of Europe and Africa on equal footing with all other member states." This would both uphold Algerian independence and help craft a truly democratic future. Although demanding Algerian independence, the memo emphasized the evils of nationalism, concluding with a call for African "nationalists of today [to] be the federalists of tomorrow."[53] That Africans, and especially Algerians, should shun nationalism for the sake of peace and humanity fit an older discomfort that European internationalists felt for incorporating former colonial subjects into their organizations. During the interwar period, for example, tensions arose in transnational women's pacifist circles when the Egyptian delegation was forced to support either their country's full independence, inclusive of a national army, or its occupation by the British.[54] Goals of federalism and international cooperation, as the Egyptian case and the 1956 memo make clear, operated differently for peoples depending on whether they had previously been allowed to enjoy sovereignty, although anti-imperial thinkers and activists also called for political futures rooted in internationalism and federation, rather than the nation-state.[55]

Notwithstanding a perhaps naïve view of the meaning of nationalism as a response to colonialism, some European federalist groups did offer full-throated support for the cause of Algerian independence. The Turin section of the Mouvement fédéraliste européen (MFE) screened a film on the Algerian War in early April 1962, to be followed by a debate on "the crisis of French democracy."[56] The very day of the event, however, the MFE in France released a statement telling its members to cast white ballots, meaning abstentions, for the April 8, 1962 referendum on Algerian independence.[57] The year before, the MFE declared that Algeria should be granted independence but warned that the only real solution would be through "an association of a federated Europe and an Africa free of nationalism."[58] Such a desire reflected an assumption that European settlers and business interests would remain present and powerful in Algeria and elsewhere in Africa, a belief strengthened by the discovery of oil in the Algerian Sahara.

Saharan oil made the maintenance of French Algeria that much more important to the metropole and offered the French heightened bargaining power in Brussels as the promise of access to this rich new source wooed the Six and other partners. In 1957, just a year after the first discovery, the daily newspaper *L'Echo d'Alger* declared, "And if the forecast for 1960 bears out—a few million tons of hydrocarbon—the Sahara will be the great opportunity for France in the new Europe."[59] Indeed, in 1960, the same year that the Organization of Petroleum Exporting Countries (OPEC) formed, the Compagnie française des pétroles invited West German journalists to visit the oil field of Hassi Messaoud.[60] French ambassador to Italy Gaston Palewski declared on Italian television that iron deposits in Algeria, the largest "in the Eurafrican *ensemble*," would offer Italians opportunities for investments.[61] As they had done before the Treaty of Rome's signing, French officials continued to frame the inclusion of Algeria as a net gain for the whole of Europe. Oil could sweeten the promise of ongoing EEC cooperation in French Algeria. Unsurprisingly, Algerians felt differently. Ferhat Abbas intoned that "when the French speak of petrol in the Sahara, it is not French petrol, but Algerian petrol." He asked German and American investors to wait until they could reach agreements with an independent Algerian government, but the promise of access to the oil proved too tempting.[62] The Six paid little attention, with "European" oil sources representing an appealing version of reality.

Experts in the Ministry of Economics and Finances agreed that because more oil had been discovered in what they judiciously labeled the *zone franc,* the question of oil products would be raised during tariff negotiations. The restriction of the overseas development funds to Algeria was therefore "no longer justified" and these experts declared their intention to pursue the first series of projects, amounting to 8 billion francs, aimed at expenditures for hospitals, schools, and other works of a "social character."[63] Proposed Algerian European Development Fund (FED) projects were not insubstantial. The French requested 186 tractors be purchased. One irrigation project around Bône (Annaba) was estimated at 58.5 million NF. Six hospitals were estimated to cost 2.7 million NF each.[64] The first FED project actually approved to go to a DOM did not in fact benefit Algeria but Réunion. In 1961, a clean water project in Saint-Denis received the go-ahead, at a cost of 172 million francs CFA.[65] Clearly, pursuing European support for overseas development could be lucrative.

In one of the only instances I found in the archives on European integration that overtly acknowledged the existence of a war in Algeria, French officials admitted that their reversal would strengthen criticisms within West Germany that Bonn was "indirectly financ[ing] the Algerian War."[66] Antagonizing the Germans was worth it, however, because of "the political benefit that the French government can expect to draw from the support that the European Economic Community will give [France] in the Algerian departments."[67] The Delegate General of Algeria estimated that roughly a fifth of the FED (62 billion francs, a quarter of the credits "returning to France") could be funneled to Algerian projects.[68] This came at the same time that West German officials attempted to strengthen their own relations with the Arab world, such as Minister of Economics Ludwig Erhard's visit to Cairo in 1960. German motivations may have been muddled by their own involvement in Algerian industry: German investments and manufacturing outfits in Algeria included Hoechst petrochemicals and Salamander shoes.[69] The presence of West German firms highlights the economic possibilities for France's partners, as trade and industry opened between the EEC and France's empire. Nevertheless, tensions flared as French officials pursued self-serving policies and expected Bonn to fall in lockstep behind them.

The question of European aid to Algeria dogged French–West German relations and bled into personal disputes between leaders of the two countries. On June 7, 1960, Bonn announced that it would recall Helmut Allardt, second-in-command at the EEC Commission's Directorate General VIII, overseeing FEDOM (DG VIII).[70] Allardt had reportedly clashed with the French director of the commission, Robert Lemaignen, over future relations between the EEC and independent African states. Allardt, a long-time civil servant, had previously served as German ambassador in Jakarta and as head of the Auswärtiges Amt's Near, Middle, and Far-East Department. The French-published *Marchés tropicaux et méditerranéens* applauded his service and his ambition but claimed he "kn[ew] more the Asian mentality than the African mentality" and that he and his African contacts did not enjoy mutual goodwill.[71] The last straw came when Allardt addressed a letter to Lemaignen in which he wrote, according to Lemaignen's chief of staff, Jacques Ferrandi, "Obviously, one can see that given your origins, your background, the business world, etc., and given that I myself, I am of a *corps noble,* I am from Foreign Affairs, from diplomacy, there are profound differences between us." Lemaignen was "naturally distraught" and demanded Allardt's resignation.[72]

The Allardt affair, as Véronique Dimier has demonstrated, is an example of the French "colonizing" Brussels as European officials "recycled their imperial experience and *esprit de corps*" in emergent European institutions.[73] It also illustrates the struggle for supremacy and control within the Six. The West German press portrayed the affair as an example of both French and German managerial missteps in Brussels. The Deutsche Press-Agentur reported that Allardt could not abide the commission "becoming the executive organ of a single member," meaning France.[74] Another newspaper reported that "Mr. Allardt recently declared in private that we are making fools of ourselves regarding the current evolution in Africa, in seeking to apply the letter of the EEC Treaty."[75] For Germans, the affair also led to introspection regarding their role in Brussels. The *Neue Rhein Zeitung* slammed EEC president Walter Hallstein for "very simply refusing to back Allardt," claiming that Hallstein "is German. But in reality, European." This was troubling because "the French members of the EEC remain French above all," meaning that they put French national (thus imperial) interests ahead of communal European need. Allardt and Lemaignen perfectly illustrated this contrast. The newspaper warned that the Germans in Brussels had "become superfluous."[76] Such analyses underscored the human, and sometimes clan-like, nature of European diplomacy. French officials closed ranks when African policy was at stake and used their influence to secure ongoing European-African relations on their terms.

Allardt's replacement, Heinrich Hendus, transferred from his post as West German consul general in Algiers, where he was reported to have had "excellent relations" with French authorities.[77] News of his appointment was met with overt pleasure by the French, and the knowledge that he had joined the Nazi Party in 1933 caused little concern.[78] In Ferrandi's recollection, "They say that a thin pope is always replaced by a fat pope, a difficult man by a charming man." Hendus, was just such a man, charismatic and "Francophile, Francophone, literally seduced by France."[79] Only a few weeks after Allardt's ouster, Bonn informed Paris that it would lift its opposition to financing Algerian projects through the FED.[80] Projects would include soil restoration, the improvement of 55,000 hectares in "sheep country," the purchase of 186 tractors for agricultural insurance companies, a 400-bed hospital in Guelma, and the construction of some 60,000 rural dwellings across Algeria.[81] The boxing out of Allardt demonstrates that the French were set on maintaining control over such institutions. That Bonn would send a man like Hendus marked the West German desire to conciliate France and participate in integrated European affairs, even under a degree of French influence.

Independent Algeria at Europe's Door

Around the March 18, 1962 signing of the Evian Accords, France's assistant permanent representative in Brussels, Jean-Pierre Brunet, commented that the cease-fire would advance the French goal of linking Africa with Europe. With France having demonstrated "that our decolonization policy is, in the whole of Africa, a success," the other members of the Six would now be amenable to ensuring the association of those newly independent states with the EEC. He also predicted that French officials might in "the coming months" take up "a great effort" to see the Maghreb states associate with the Common Market as well.[82] Ahead of the referendum that decided Algeria's fate, an SGCI official insisted that as the EEC reassessed the development fund, it must protect Algeria's status. He declared that any decision made should not impact Algeria's ability to benefit from the fund, "whatever its political status in January 1963." He also warned that the French should be cautious, lest their European partners use development discussions as a springboard for "a reexamination of the whole of Algeria's place in regard to the Common Market," something that "should be avoided at the present time."[83] As we will see, Brunet and the unnamed official's predictions were largely borne out, although perhaps not exactly as they had expected.

By pushing against their Italian and West German allies, French officials shunted aside diplomatic niceties in favor of tightening their grasp on Algeria. In pursuit of a policy that accommodated Algeria's position within the EEC—dubbed "a bit hybrid" by the agricultural official Pouderoux—French officials made clear their goal of maintaining French predominance in Algerian affairs.[84] To an almost shocking degree, thanks in no small part to the lack of foresight regarding the eventual departure of the vast majority of settlers from Algeria to France in 1962, these administrators continued to insist that Algeria enjoy a privileged status with the Treaty of Rome, even as the Evian Accord negotiations were under way. In the end, it was not Dutch pressure, Italian complaints, or German worries that would halt the implementation of the treaty in the Algerian territories. Rather, when Algerians celebrated their independence on July 5, 1962, the future of France's Algerian-focused Eurafrican policy was radically changed.

A year after the Treaty of Rome went into effect, *Le Monde* trumpeted that "the affiliation of Algeria to the Common Market decides in a definitive way the choice of the orientation of [Algeria's] economy, meaning its complete fusion with the metropolitan economy."[85] For nearly five years, Algeria was fitfully fused both to France and to the EEC, rendering it a part of integrated Europe. This sparked tension and confusion in Paris and Brussels as administrators debated how to implement the EEC in Algeria. Most questions of the actual application of regulations would come only after Algeria's independence, making the already difficult question of Algeria's status within Europe that much more fraught. At the same time, the new Fifth Republic, in striking continuity with the defunct Fourth Republic, attempted to cement the ties between the EEC and the French Community. While vocalizing some resistance, France's European partners accepted on the whole that Europe's boundaries expanded to Algeria. European officials were at a loss to justify an exclusion of the Algerian economy and workforce from the benefits of European membership. This rendered European institutions potentially egalitarian. At the same time, it also underlined the assumptions of difference European officials held toward Algeria. Although named in the treaty, its residents remained unimaginable as fellow Europeans.

What happened after the international community, including France, acknowledged the new sets of borders carved out of France's former boundaries, now delineating independent nation-states like Algeria? French administrators ceased to defend the geography that *France Outremer* asserted in 1959. Yet because that geography was once taken as a reality, French and independent Algerian officials could still make political and economic claims that held potentially wide-ranging consequences. These consequences had the power to upend European definitions of authority and sovereignty even into the 1970s. Algeria might be independent, but that did not mean its European past was behind it.

5

French Supremacy in Europe after Algerian Independence

In late December 1962, the Algerian head of state Ahmed Ben Bella alerted the members of the European Economic Community (EEC) that his "government intend[ed] to inquire . . . what the possible future relations between Algeria and the Community will be."[1] Despite Algeria's independence, achieved in July, Ben Bella signaled that the Algerian government was poised to claim a privileged economic and political position vis-à-vis Europe. This would be possible because of French officials' 1957 insistence that Algeria be named in Article 227 of the Treaty of Rome, the foundational document of the foremost European institution of the postwar era. Ben Bella's query sent waves of concern through the Six. It particularly complicated matters for French authorities who, since July, had been working to establish what they believed were appropriate relations between France and Algeria and, in turn, between Algeria and Europe. The move by Algerians to insert themselves into a state of affairs from which the French summarily excluded them for half a decade threatened France's privileged place presiding over European–African affairs. It also meant that when the French tried to exploit Algeria's unclear EEC status to their own material benefit, they had to answer not just to the other members of the Six but to the Algerian government itself.

From Algeria's independence until the coup that ousted Ben Bella in 1965, officials in Paris, Brussels, and Algiers attempted to establish new relations or to secure those they already had. In the process, they also drew a new map of Europe. Historians have already demonstrated that after independence, African states continued to have deep connections with former imperial metropoles and European institutions, thanks to trade accords and developmentalist ties.[2] The term *Françafrique,* for one, denotes neocolonial ties and cronyism between France and independent African states.[3] An account of Algeria's place in the EEC pushes past the scope of those relations because beyond a history of influence or cooperation, it is a chronicle of the different spatial-administrative boundaries integrated Europe once held. Named in the Treaty of Rome, independent Algeria stood to be a part of integrated Europe. This was an ambiguous position, in that Algeria never benefited from full membership rights, such as family allocations for migrant workers or the entire suite of trade agreements established between the Six. Yet Algerian authorities found it possible to claim aid and tariff rates under EEC law. This possibility faded slowly and unevenly after Algeria's independence, a moment in which European institutional borders were far from cemented. If Charles de Gaulle's 1963 veto of Britain is the better-known rejection of a Europe beyond the continent, it was the plodding extraction of Algeria from Europe that revealed that the shape integrated Europe took was an invention in and of itself, though an invention that would come to be viewed as natural and evident in the decades to come.

The months between Algeria's independence in July 1962 and the coup that unseated Ben Bella in June 1965 represented a short but crucial period in which French, Algerian, and EEC diplomatic strategies coincided and clashed. After 1962, French officials attempted to regain France's global status. Their efforts of rapprochement with West Germany are one such example. Another is the 1965–1966 Empty Chair Crisis, when the French effectively froze EEC proceedings by refusing to send a representative to Brussels. These and other instances of French positioning and posturing in the early 1960s can only be understood fully if analyzed within the context of the emergence of the Algerian state. After Algerian independence, French officials launched themselves into a new diplomatic battle to maintain what they perceived as France's natural place as the most politically and economically influential member of the Six, in part by securing privileged relations with many former colonies. This strategy included demanding that the other members of the Six continue to accept Algeria's place within European regulations in order to protect French business interests in Algeria and the settler presence there, both of which the French government believed would endure after independence. The logic of the unequal citizenship regime of the colonial era, which lingered in French decision making, undermined this plan, as did the Algerian authorities' own pursuit of the status quo, meaning the continuation of their still unclear but potentially beneficial economic and labor relations with the EEC.

Under the Ben Bella administration, Algerian officials attempted to leverage their inclusion in the Treaty of Rome to secure favorable tariff agreements and to advocate for the rights of Algerian citizens working in Europe, 350,000 of whom lived in France alone by 1962, in addition to laborers in Belgium, West

Germany, and elsewhere.[4] In Brussels, Dutch and Italian officials who had long been the most skeptical of France's Algeria–Europe strategy saw independence as an opening to criticize France without jeopardizing European integration. This became particularly important during controversies such as de Gaulle's veto. Further undermining France's once-privileged position in European-African affairs, in 1963 the EEC drafted the first Yaoundé Convention—an accord largely concerning trade ties and development aid—with several independent African states, dispossessing France of its prized role as intermediary.[5]

Ben Bella's letter demonstrates one element of the new state's approach to foreign policy. Affiliation with Europe would secure economic benefits, while an embrace of the "spirit of Bandung" also allowed Algeria to engage with North African and Arab states and the Eastern bloc. Although Algerian leaders recognized that integration with a liberal body like the EEC did not match, in the words of one Quai d'Orsay official, their country's "genuinely socialist vocation," such ties answered material need and reflected the expansiveness of independent Algeria's foreign relations.[6] French officials, meanwhile, consistently undermined their own attempts to maintain Algeria's ties to integrated Europe.[7] This was due to their inability to shed their racist assumptions about the Algerian capacity for self-rule or to acknowledge that French law had extended French nationality to Algerians prior to 1962. As the young Algerian government forged relations beyond the EEC in the early 1960s, French officials grew uninterested in maintaining the established regulations between Algeria and the EEC.[8] Despite the relative brevity of the period in which the French attempted to uphold Algeria's special relationship with integrated Europe, the claims are notable nonetheless because they are evidence of the flexibility of the extension of "Europe," still based on economic self-interest, rather than geography or identity, in the early days of the EEC. The fraught debates about independent Algeria threatened to upend notions of the very Europeanness of the EEC, as the specter of Algeria loomed as a hypothetical—yet in the words of one administrator, "absurd"—seventh member state.[9]

What Divorce? French-Algerian Relations after Independence

The influential French economic historian Jacques Marseille sub-titled his best-known work "history of a divorce." According to Marseille, after decolonization, French capitalism could at last modernize and grow. With de Gaulle at the helm of the Fifth Republic, French officials adopted a new attitude based on the conviction that "France could not belong simultaneously to two common markets, one with Europe, the other with the overseas states." Such claims echoed journalist Raymond Cartier's argument that the expenses of maintaining France's colonies far outweighed the benefits. Indeed, Marseille concluded his book with de Gaulle himself declaring in 1961, "Algeria costs us . . . more than it brings us. . . . It is a fact that decolonization is in our interests and, consequently, is our policy."[10]

It is inaccurate, however, to understand decolonization as a divorce and even more imprecise to take de Gaulle's statement as evidence that there would be a clean rupture between a European—or hexagonal—France and a now-foreign overseas entity.[11] Nineteen sixty-two was not an end point and independence did not signal the dissolution of economic ties or political relations between Algeria and Europe. The Evian Accords, signed in March, established a cease-fire and outlined future relations between France and Algeria.[12] Both the French and the Algerians had pragmatic motivations for maintaining a strong relationship after independence. This pragmatism extended into the realm of European institutions. For French officials concerned about trade practices, Algeria's independence did not preclude the continuity of Franco-Algerian economic ties. That same continuity offered Algerian officials some economic stability as their government struggled to heal the physical and psychological wounds of nearly eight years of war.

The French tactic of demanding Algeria's naming in the Treaty of Rome now appeared to be both a liability and a promise. On the one hand, as one General Secretary of the Interministerial Committee Responsible for Questions of European Economic Cooperation (SGCI) official wrote in a particularly telling memorandum, it was "obviously absurd" to suggest that Algeria might become the "seventh member of the European Community." On the other hand, considering that Algeria was explicitly named in Article 227, it was not clear just what else Algeria might be. In this state of ambiguity, the Six struggled to revoke the EEC regulations that the French had insisted would extend to Algeria. Given that many regulations had not been slated to come into effect until 1962 or later, Algeria's status in the EEC at independence was therefore both unclear, now that it was an independent state, and unfinished, given that the details of treaty application had not been settled in all cases. Two unnamed officials heavily edited the SGCI memo and in doing so, appeared to disavow past French claims of Algeria's status within the EEC. For example, they took their pen to a section on EEC labor regulation, which would "not assure

Algeria the possibility of benefitting from the free movement of its workers in the territories of our partners, ~~as the Treaty of Rome could have led it to hope~~."[13] Despite such erasure, Algerian diplomats and France's own business interests would render this disavowal incomplete. But the edit speaks to the larger question left unanswered since 1957, if not 1951: Did French officials actually ever think this had been a possibility?

Following Algeria's independence, French officials in Brussels avoided any firm declaration clarifying Algeria's relationship with the EEC. This included fighting against the notion that independence automatically spelled extraction from the institution. France's representative in Brussels, the career diplomat Jean-Marc Boegner, opined to his superiors in Paris that the "accession to independence of this country must not, it seems to me, have the effect of depriving it of the benefits of intercommunity preference."[14] In the Direction of External Economic Relations Office of the Ministry of Foreign Affairs (DREE), François Valéry concurred, telling Boegner, "If need be, . . . underline that it would be premature and hardly opportune to change anything in the current situation. . . . It would be wise to avoid engaging this subject in one manner or another."[15] Speaking to Dutch officials a few days later, Boegner reminded them that the European Commission itself had deemed it "juridically possible not to consider Algeria a third-party state."[16] In this way, French officials bought time to decide how to tackle the Algerian question without denying the new state—and the French business interests there—the potential of continued EEC membership benefits.

With Algeria's independence, the Six attempted to clarify what its relationship to Brussels would be. After July 1962, the EEC Commission first appeared willing to maintain development aid through European Development Fund (FED) credits. Indeed, the following month, the Algerian government launched a call for proposals for the construction of six hospital operating rooms, to be financed by the FED.[17] A commission member told French minister of Algerian affairs Louis Joxe that it "remained committed" to Algeria because of agreements previously signed by France, as long as Algerian officials "refrain from any action likely to complicate" the execution of the funded projects.[18] Beyond this, the member states acted independently of one another. In early 1963, West Germany subjected Algerian agricultural imports to the same tax paid by the members of the Six, which aligned with the spirit of Article 227. The Benelux states, in contrast, applied the tax charged to third-party states.[19] Rather than acting in concert, the Six pursued their own policies.

By March 1963, the Six agreed to maintain the "status quo" in which independent Algeria would continue to enjoy the same preferential tariff rates, migrant social security regime, and customs regulations that it did when it was a juridical part of metropolitan France.[20] This agreement was tenuous and subject to constant challenges from some members of the Six, particularly as the distinct regulations mentioned above contradicted some of the EEC-wide provisions that the status quo would appear to mandate. French officials in the SGCI, the Quai d'Orsay, and elsewhere discussed internally how independent Algeria's future relations with France, and then with Europe, would look. They opted for tactics of ambiguity and delay to avoid making a decision that would jeopardize access to Algerian markets or alienate their European partners. Nevertheless, the "status quo" policy secured Algeria a measure of continuity, to a degree maintaining the relationship the EEC had imposed on it in 1957.

French officials were reticent to cede important Franco-Algerian connections, not least because the Evian Accords secured their access to Saharan oil and the survival of the French military base at Mers-el-Kébir. At this point, they also did not anticipate that the departure of the settler community from Algeria to France amounted to a permanent population migration. In the summer of 1962, nearly all of Algeria's 1 million European settlers fled to France, leaving behind property and businesses. Although they, and the French government, apparently believed this move would be temporary, in October of that year the Algerian government passed two decrees regarding farmland, including the nationalization of over 150,000 hectares of land vacated by the settler population. The following year, the government nationalized all remaining land owned by "foreigners," implementing a program of self-management (*autogestion*).[21]

The settlers' arrival in the metropole served as a visual reminder of the war and of an imperialist folly by now synonymous with shame. Metropolitan citizens perceived them as being supportive of, and having actively participated in, Organisation de l'armée secrète (OAS) terrorism. In reality, although the OAS did enjoy significant support among the settler population, it was not a universally held position.[22] Memoirs by former settlers written in the years after what is sometimes dubbed the exodus are replete with stories of discrimination and mistreatment at the hands of metropolitan French people, particularly at ports of arrival. Marseille mayor and former minister of Overseas France Gaston Defferre himself, although he denied it, allegedly declared, "The *pieds noirs* must be thrown into the sea."[23]

The extension of European rights to former residents of Algeria in some ways mirrored the uneven nature of French

Algeria's citizenship regime, exposing cracks in the decades-old assertion that Algeria had been just like any other part of France. The transfer of rights to the settler population, unquestionably French in legal terms and thus European, contrasted with the murky status of people deemed "Muslim" or "Indigenous" in France's pre-independence legal landscape. The French state implemented policies somewhat belatedly, such as procuring hotel rooms for new arrivals only in early March 1962. But in spite of their poor reception, the settlers arrived in France with a distinct advantage over other migrants: citizenship. Thanks to their perceived racial kinship—and therefore assimilability—to the metropole, their power as an electoral force, and the long precedent of their citizenship, the settlers benefited from government attempts to streamline their arrival in the metropole. Absorbed as a repatriate community, they received typical social security benefits as well as special dispensations accounting for their economic welfare and the cost of relocation. Regulations stipulated leniency if a settler could not produce necessary civil documentation, provided vouchers for gas and electricity, and delayed the collection of taxes until a settler was once again able "to meet the regular needs of their family."[24] Although the majority chose to settle either in Paris or in southern France, where the climate most resembled that of Algeria, the government also organized employment opportunities for them in the industrial north.

The treatment of the settlers by the government underscored the French contention that Algeria had been an extension of France; rights moved with people throughout the Republic. The state applied such rights only to the settler population, reinforcing the hierarchies of French Algeria and cementing the racialized (white) citizenship of the post-Evian French state. The language used to describe the settlers, *rapatriés,* suggested that they were returning to France, as if they had once been outside of it or as if the metropole was their natural or ancestral home. In this way, their treatment resembled that of the Sudentenland Germans who "returned" to West Germany following World War II.[25] The French in fact looked at their German neighbors as they prepared for the arrival of French settlers from North Africa.[26] Although they suffered humiliation and discrimination at the hands of their fellow citizens, the settlers' Frenchness was never questioned in an official capacity. The French could now "invent" Algeria's decolonization and create a new narrative in which it never had truly been a part of France.[27] In this narrative, these settlers would also be subsumed by a greater white European community. The organization Jeunesse européenne fédéraliste, for example, mounted an effort for Belgian and Dutch families to take in settler children for a summer.[28]

The hardening of French citizenship along racial lines is particularly clear in the case of the *harkis,* the Algerian men who, through choice and coercion, had picked up arms for the French during the war. Viewed as traitors to the cause of independence, in Algeria they and their families became targets of violent reprisals during and particularly after the war. Despite attempts by some of their battalion chiefs to bring them to safety in France after the Evian Accords, it was not until 1965 that the French government retroactively extended repatriate status to those *harkis* who had made it to France.[29] The French government's willingness to withhold rights from Muslim Algerians was already evident in the post-1957 negotiations with Italy over whether EEC labor circulation rules applied to Indigenous Algerians. That the *harkis* would not be treated as fully French accentuates the continuity of racialized citizenship policies upheld by the French government. The French government swiftly enforced a type of "racialized ethnicity" at the end of the Algerian War, marking this era with exclusion and exception. In the months following Algeria's independence, French officials withheld Algerians' right to French nationality, flying in the face of the laws of the Fifth Republic and firmly establishing a racialized basis for citizenship.[30] This is even more notable given the rights inscribed in the Treaty of Rome. The French disavowal of such promises denied Algerians access to the European labor market and to social security protections, delineating who could count as European and who could not.

The *pieds-noirs* and *harkis* were not the only populations to have exited Algeria. By the end of the Algerian War, 350,000 Algerians, mostly laborers and their families, lived in continental France, up from 210,000 in 1954.[31] After Algeria's independence, French officials appeared poised to apply the EEC social security regime to Algerian laborers on European—or at least French—soil, and by October 1962 they had received—"in a very provisional capacity"—the agreement of their partners to maintain this status quo until the Algerian government defined its own position vis-à-vis the European social security apparatus.[32] This secured a temporary rights regime for Algerian laborers but elided the French citizenship rights this population had held, in theory if not in practice, in the years prior to independence.

Whether or how Algeria's independence might impact the rights of these laborers did not seem apparent to French administrators concerned with EEC labor regulation. This was particularly troubling in the realm of social security and migration rights. The Treaty of Rome's geographic reach complicated the question of Algerian social security rights, which would determine what country owed payment to a retired or disabled worker. In the Social Affairs Bureau of France's Ministry of Algerian Affairs, administrators argued that it was possible that "Algeria, because of independence in and of itself, considers that it is no longer covered by these regulations." Such an attitude would only require the EEC Commission to modify certain texts to end the regime. At the same time, it was possible that the "Algerian government considers that the international engagements entered into by France vis-à-vis Algeria will continue to have effect, unless expressly denounced."[33] The divorce of decolonization was anything but a given.

Quai d'Orsay officials judged that Algerian authorities would view a forced separation of the French and Algerian treasuries as "a disparaging act," which could lead to a retaliation with "unfortunate consequences for the continuation of the French presence in Algeria (end of transfers towards France)." Yet clarifying the economic situation "in this electoral period" might prove "inopportune." Too much of an effort to differentiate the economies of France and Algeria risked unmasking embarrassing truths, such as the "considerable amount of the advances that will undoubtedly never be reimbursed."[34] This left French administrators stuck between a newly independent state with which their own economy was deeply entwined and what they feared would be a small but vocal settler electorate already outraged by their loss of home.[35] Although many of these administrators were themselves civil servants not subject to election, their superiors would be susceptible to the ebbs and flows of popularity of a particular party, and thus popular opinion concerned lifelong functionaries as well as elected officials.

EEC officials looked to France to determine its own relationship to Algeria before the Six could settle on European–Algerian relations. Ahead of a planned tariff reduction between the Six, scheduled to be implemented on July 1, 1963, the French felt added pressure. If the Algerian delegation fixed higher tariffs for all members of the Six except for France, France stood to benefit from a distinctly preferential regime, which could put French officials in an uncomfortable position in Brussels.[36] Without resolving Algeria's relation to France, EEC representatives felt disinclined to settle the independent state's relation to the European economy as a whole. EEC officials increasingly suggested that French officials would need to guide EEC-Algerian regulations forward once those bilateral relations were clarified.

Despite these ambiguities, French officials continued to shoulder their often self-imposed role of mediator between the EEC and Algeria.[37] As late as 1964, two years after independence, the status quo question remained open. France's European plans still included the preservation of Algerian trade; this protection of the Algerian economy would allow France to strengthen its own trade position.[38] Algerian officials and EEC representatives turned to France to make sense of how Franco-Algerian relations could be maintained within a system of EEC-Algerian cooperation. Algerian officials presented this as a sign of respect, "insisting on the importance its government attached to accords with France and its concern not to do anything in Brussels that could upset" France. Boegner did not appear swept away by this apparent show of goodwill, arguing that "everything happens as if the Algerians used the vague possibilities of an accord with the Community instead to obtain a maintenance of the status quo of commercial exchanges. They even go so far as to demand the benefits of certain elements of the Treaty of Rome that are no longer applicable to Algeria."[39] The French, then, were cooling to Algeria's potential links to the

EEC, perhaps in response to Algeria's emergence as a vocal force in Third World affairs.[40] There was no divorce in 1962, but the years following Algeria's independence witnessed a growing cleavage between citizenship regimes and a slipping grasp on the status quo. This rendered France and the EEC's future relationship with Algeria unclear, if not deliberately obscured.

Algerian Foreign Policy and French Aspirations

For over a decade, European integration had remained a largely continental conversation, with some notable exceptions. This changed in 1962, when President Ben Bella wrote to Brussels. He did so in order to secure future relations with the EEC and to stress the Treaty of Rome's precedent for future European-Algerian relations. His letter forced the Six to face the legal reality that integrated Europe might traverse the Mediterranean into independent Algeria. It read in part, "The Treaty establishing the European Economic Community stated in its Article 227 the conditions of the Treaty's application concerning Algeria. . . . My government intends to inquire through negotiations . . . with the Community what the possible future relations between Algeria and the Community will be. While awaiting the conclusion of these negotiations, my government wishes to see maintained the benefit of the currently established regulations for Algeria."[41] The letter and the reaction it provoked in Brussels are both instructive. Ben Bella declared that until future terms could be established, independent Algeria should enjoy the continuity of EEC privileges legally guaranteed by Article 227 and other sections of the treaty. The Six would struggle to deny this assertion outright, but how the different member states responded in many ways mirrored their pre-1962 relationship with Algeria and, more critically, with France.

Even the prospect of acknowledging Ben Bella's letter sparked debate. The French recommended that the council agree to the Algerian request; the Dutch argued that Ben Bella should receive an immediate, definitive reply; and the West Germans advocated that the articles in question remain in place until future relations could be explored. This dispute extended to the form of the response as well as its content. A commission representative suggested that the initial response be "inspired by the type of letters addressed to African states after their accession to independence," meaning the European response would class Algeria's relationship to the EEC as being akin to the EEC's relations with states like Senegal.[42] When the Six finally sent a confirmation of receipt on January 24, it was only because they had not yet tackled the actual substance of the question of whether Algerian territory would indeed remain—or ever truly had been—integrated within the EEC.[43] That same month, the Algerian diplomat Ali Lakhdari arrived in Brussels to meet with European diplomats, following through on Ben Bella's promise to pursue negotiations. The Brussels-based news service Agence Europe warned that according too favorable an arrangement to Algeria would risk "creating a precedent that could be invoked by other third-party states."[44] This ignored Algeria's peculiar status before July 1962.

The impetus for Algerian officials to (re)establish or (re)affirm relations with the EEC arose at least in part because of the economic crisis in the newly formed state. The war of independence gravely impacted the Algerian economy. The settler population withdrew its liquid assets upon its departure. Foreign trade had taken a hit in the last years of the war, and unpaid taxes exacerbated the precarity of Algeria's public finances.[45] In the war's wake, 70 percent of Algeria's active population was unemployed.[46] French officials chose to interpret this crisis as a natural result of the Algerians' ill-conceived fight for independence, not an out-come of catastrophic war. A missive from Jean-Marcel Jeanneney, the French ambassador in Algeria, to the minister of Algerian affairs expounded on the "deterioration" of Algerian order, including "administrative disorganization" and "unemployment and misery," cautioning that "the further one gets from the large towns, . . . the more one finds a country progressively falling back into its ancestral anarchy."[47] Jeanneney would go on the following year to head a commission bearing his name that analyzed French devel-opment aid. The French interpreted Algeria's post-independence struggles with the characteristic racism that undergirded their skepticism about non-Europeans' ability to govern themselves. Such an attitude masked but did not erase French anxiety about preserving economic and political ties with Algeria. Nor did it stifle the new reality that representatives of independent Algeria were now speaking directly to Brussels to demand the rights they believed the Six owed to their citizens.

The Algerian administration understood the utility of pre-serving European ties. Although ongoing negotiations between former French Union states and the EEC signaled an opportunity for new connections, the case of Guinea offered a cautionary tale. Guinea rejected French Union membership in 1958, opting in-stead for independence. In retaliation, the French government re-voked its economic support, which sparked disastrous results for the new state. France's punitive action ranged from attempting to isolate Guinea diplomatically and economically to depriving it of schoolteachers.[48] After 1958, Guinean leaders did not attempt to take advantage of the trade or aid benefits that they would have potentially reaped from association with the EEC, even though they may have had the grounds to demand them. The international relations scholar I. William Zartman speculated that had Guineans attempted to claim benefits from associating with the EEC, "France doubtless would have led a bitter political fight against the legalities of association or reassociation, spokesmen for Guinea among the Six would have been hard to find, and the Europeans could have been accused of 'expelling' Guinea."[49] In this reading of the EEC's treaty, Guinea, by virtue of its former membership in the French Union, still had legal grounds to claim EEC benefits. Such a claim could only be amplified in the case of Algeria, given that its name figured into the treaty itself.

Whereas Guinea had not explored the possibility of associating with the EEC, other former colonies had. These states' experiences with the EEC, which have received more scholarly attention than Algeria's, involved many of the same European bureaucrats who engaged in negotiations about EEC–Algerian relations.[50] In 1960, the former trusteeship territories of Cameroon and Togo gained their independence and both broached the subject of remaining in the association agreement that had linked them, along with other overseas countries and territories, to the EEC.[51] Speaking in Strasbourg in June 1960 to the Joint Meeting of the Consultative Assembly and the European Parliament, EEC Commission President Walter Hallstein argued, "Any differences of opinion which exist between European nations must not be transferred to their policies vis-à-vis the African countries. On the contrary, the similarities and the inherent connection between these tasks should become a means of achieving understanding among the European countries themselves."[52] Independence may have changed the EEC's relationship with individual African states, but it would not reduce the necessity of such connections.

Hallstein portrayed Africa as a venue where Europeans could learn to cooperate, echoing long-standing beliefs about Africa's role in European integration. Africa, or a European idea of Africa, served to advance plans for European unity and although couched in goodwill and promises of aid money, appeared first and foremost to be a useful site for European decision making. The EEC Council opted to delay a firm decision, putting off a response to Cameroon and Togo and therefore inviting further talks. By August 1960, independent Congo-Brazzaville, Dahomey, and Ivory Coast requested that they be permitted to participate in EEC discussions related to their states' affairs. African and European administrators had begun to lay the groundwork for the Yaoundé Convention, signed by EEC representatives and the eighteen Associated African States and Madagascar (AASM) in Cameroon's capital in 1963. These accords effectively extended the preferential customs regulations and aid that had been established prior to these states' independence.[53] Yaoundé did not comprise Algeria because Algeria's own status was so different that EEC representatives sought an alternative to understanding future ties. Morocco and Tunisia also did not take part, their governments immersed in separate negotiations with the EEC. Nevertheless, occurring concurrently, the discussions in Brussels about Algeria would have informed EEC decision making regarding Yaoundé and vice versa.

For the Six, the Yaoundé Convention was an important diplomatic tool for securing the AASM's loyalty to Western European markets and influence. Indeed, the Federal Republic hesitated to extend aid to the AASM because some of them recognized East Germany.[54] Yaoundé, with its preferential trade regime, could make relations with the Six an appealing choice in the face of possible Soviet ties. Cold War concerns also permeated the progression of EEC-Algerian ties. In 1964, the Six planned to send Algeria 70 million DM in aid to dissuade Ben Bella from taking part in Cairo's recognition of East Germany, hoping that the country would "not fall entirely into the communist orbit."[55] The French government could thus celebrate Algerian leaders' "realism" within months of its independence, such that it "no longer figure[d] among extremist countries."[56] Yet realism for the Algerian government featured a strong anti-imperialist sentiment, combined with pragmatic decision making. Algerians embraced a role in the Non-Aligned Movement and accepted aid from the Soviet Union and the United States alike. In 1962, the USSR helped to finance Algeria's purchase of 500 million francs' worth of Soviet agricultural and industrial equipment, while the United States sent 100,000 tons of food.[57] The following year, Algeria received a 200 million franc loan from the EEC and a further 90 million from the International Bank for Reconstruction and Development (IBRD) for a gas liquefaction plant in Arzew.[58]

Although this range of aid sources suggests that Algerian officials managed to keep options open in the international arena, it also underscores their state's reliance on aid as they sought to find their footing after the war. Further, these new sources are indicative of the nascent government seeking partnerships beyond France. One such new relationship involved Great Britain. Already by the early 1960s, Britain committed to purchasing 1 billion cubic meters of Algerian crude gas, nearly double what France committed to purchasing.[59] In October 1962, Algerian minister of foreign affairs Mohamed Khemisti met with Trefor Ellis Evans, the British general consul in Algiers, and conveyed his eagerness to see an exchange of ambassadors.[60] Algeria's minister of economics, Bachir Boumaza, visited London two years later to encourage an increase in British imports of Algerian gas, iron ore, and wine. Boumaza informed his British hosts that his government hoped to establish prospecting companies, with the state holding the majority share. The United States and Italy had already thrown in their hats as minority stakeholders. He intimated that France would not "emphasize" its objections to Algeria's third pipeline, a contract that went to the British firm John Brown for 25 million pounds sterling.[61] From 1963 to mid-1965, Britain provided Algeria with 263 million dinars in aid, more than the FED, the IBRD, or West Germany, which soon became France's biggest competition within the EEC in terms of trade with Algeria.[62]

The Algerians pursued further trade partnerships with Sweden, Poland, Bulgaria, and other states, notably many members of the Warsaw Pact.[63] Their network of potential partners reflected their position within the Non-Aligned Movement and their attempts to reduce France's outsized role in Algeria's economy, particularly through expanded ties to the United States.[64] The work of unpairing Algeria's and France's economies was still under way, however, and the same unclear language that characterized many French regulations also cropped up in Algerian legislation. The independent Algerian government in 1962 demarcated some textile and coffee imports as "made in France and abroad [*réalisées de la France et de l'Étranger*]."[65] This language suggests that Algerian officials were slow to name France as wholly foreign. Separating France from "*l'étranger*," it echoed the French state's own reluctance to concede that Algeria was not an integral part of France and signaled the lingering relationship between the two states.

French officials only haltingly reconciled themselves to independent Algeria's expanding diplomatic ties, particularly with Arab states and their North African neighbors. Even in internal memos, they discounted such relations as flights of fancy or artifice. The French embassy in Algiers reported that Algerian officials fretted over the "predicament" in which they found themselves, caught between these new ties and their obligations to Europe. A conference of heads of state in Cairo had made clear that problems could arise for "Arab states" maintaining relations with countries that had ties with Israel. In April 1964, the EEC signed an accord with the latter. Now French ambassador to Algeria, Georges Gorse mused that Algerian officials would need to "compromise between [Algeria's] economic interests and its anti-Israeli displays," given that they "intend[ed] to be at the forefront of fights led by the Arab world."[66] French administrators like Gorse failed to analyze the situation in light of Algerian leaders' own political, economic, or ideological motivations for distancing themselves from France and the EEC and moving closer to other newly independent and Non-Aligned states. He barely registered Algeria's agency in determining its own foreign policy.

Gorse, a member of the Section française de l'Internationale ouvrière (SFIO) who served in de Gaulle's cabinet in Algiers during World War II, instead read the situation as a bald example of Soviet influence over Algeria. He surmised that the question of Arab-Israeli relations most likely arose when heads of state, including Nikita Khrushchev, met in May to witness the diversion of the Nile as part of the Aswan Dam project. Gorse claimed that "the advice of Mr. Khrushchev will undoubtedly determine the attitude of Colonel Nasser and of President Ben Bella." Such an assertion gave little credit to Gamal Abdel Nasser or Ben Bella. Gorse also dismissed Algerian anti-Israel attitudes as a new phenomenon, opining that the Algerian representatives would present any outcome in EEC negotiations as a victory for "the Arab

world over Zionism."[67] In practice, the Algerians left open the
door to doing business with states that recognized Israel, namely
West Germany, while simultaneously securing foreign relations
with Arab partners.[68]

In May 1964, an Algerian delegation led by Ambassador
Boualem Bessaïh called for a preferential accord between Algeria
and the EEC, excluding Morocco and Tunisia because Algeria's
status presented "particular problems that called for particular solutions."[69] Bessaïh demanded professional training for Algerian
workers in both Algeria and Europe, guarantees of technical assistance, and the continuation of financial aid. Ongoing financial
aid would allow for the completion of projects launched under the
former development fund regime. The commission argued that
preference, which raised the issue of reciprocity for Algerian exports, would be limited by General Agreement on Tariffs and
Trade (GATT) regulation and by other states' relations to the
EEC.[70] Before Algeria's independence, its workers, "considered
like French nationals [*étant considérés comme ressortissants français*],"
enjoyed advantages such as social security and family allowances,
but "the accession to independence modified this situation, thus
posing problems." In reality, prior to independence, France had
not extended such allowances to families in Algeria at the same
rate as to those that had followed a breadwinner to the metropole.[71]
EEC officials concluded that they would forge ahead with Algerian relations via bilateral negotiations between individual EEC
members and Algeria. This was similar to how the EEC already
managed relations with "certain African states." The commission
brushed off other Algerian demands, calling requests for technical
assistance and workers' training "desiderata."[72]

These Algerian demands had come closest to resembling what could be construed as the responsibilities of the EEC to its member states. Despite the apparent European amenability to such demands in the earliest months of Algerian independence, by now the EEC found a more comfortable precedent for refusing financial assistance, arguing that since the Yaoundé Convention's genesis, it was "no longer possible for the Algerian government to present new projects" to the European Overseas Development Fund (FEDOM). The Algerian delegation responded to this with a "rather intense shock," according to an EEC official, "seeming at certain moments even to speak about acquired rights in this domain." Far from settling questions, then, these talks led to the emergence of more uncertainty. Once again, the Algerian delegation declared itself unable to resolve EEC–Algerian relations until the "primordial" problem of its relations with France was clarified. The commission agreed.[73] The French, observing what they believed was an Algerian attempt "to find the advantages of EEC association without abandoning its privileged relations with France," deemed Algerian statements on the subject to be "somewhat naïve."[74] In a blatant rewriting of history, European officials acted as if Algerians had no leg to stand on when demanding rights and as if they never had. Not limiting themselves to the EEC, however, Algerian officials saw opening before them futures constructed through *grands ensembles,* growing ties in potentially federalist configurations in the Muslim or Arab world.[75]

Rather than attempting to merge partnerships between the EEC and France's former colonies, the French began to view the Six as the clear choice for political and business dealings. The benefits of the status quo now fading, bilateral settlements appeared the best way forward. As the EEC Commission puzzled over how social security regulations related to migrant workers might apply to Algerians, French secretary of state for Algerian affairs Jean de Broglie worried that the Algerian government would only try to prolong the status quo, jeopardizing bilateral Franco-Algerian negotiations. His office suggested instructing the commission to ask questions directly to the Algerian government, given that "the French government, since the independence of Algeria, is no longer in the position to supply" answers.[76] The French minister of labor proposed that the French advocate the "suppression of the mention of Algeria" in EEC social security regulations. Although François Morin of the SGCI expressed hesitation about this "break from the status quo that we ourselves had demanded," de Broglie's office surmised that "the maintenance of the status quo will present more drawbacks than advantages."[77] Although it should come as no surprise that French officials had once again opted to pursue a policy vis-à-vis Algeria that best served French national interests, this is a striking moment nonetheless. For the first time, it became clear that French officials were prepared to pursue European relations absent Algeria.

Locating French Supremacy on the European Continent

Faced with independent Algeria's clear disinterest in relying exclusively on France as its interlocutor in world affairs, French officials feared their loss of authority in Europe and Africa. This fear was exacerbated by the direction integrated Europe began to take, as supranational planners challenged de Gaulle's vision of a "union of states" and Britain waited in the wings. Embodied by the failed 1961 Fouchet Plan, the union of states was meant to secure French supremacy next to Britain and the United States, with France acting as representative of continental Europe.[78] The plan's failure and the ongoing strength of European institutions frustrated the Eurosceptic de Gaulle's designs.[79] We will now turn to French concerns about their place in Europe in the first half of the 1960s and to European attitudes toward France. The complicated nature of French-Algerian relations, muddled by the Treaty of Rome and French officials' refusal either to accept that Algeria was an autonomous state or to repudiate the promises guaranteed by the treaty, served as the backdrop to the dramatic EEC-French relations of 1962–1965.

After Ben Bella wrote to Brussels, a DREE official lamented that the French could not insist on a more "attractive" reply from their partners.[80] This was due in part to the pallor cast on Brussels by de Gaulle's veto of British membership in the EEC. On January 14, 1963, de Gaulle declared in a press conference that he opposed Britain's accession to the EEC. Two weeks later, he effectively forced the other members of the Six to halt the negotiations. The first veto—so named because of de Gaulle's second veto of UK accession in 1967—is typically understood as a signal of de Gaulle's Anglophobia, heightened by his distaste for Anglo-American relations following the Suez Crisis. Britain's initial exclusion from the EEC can in part also be explained by French administrative fears about the role the Commonwealth might play in the European trade arena or how its inclusion would impact European aid to Francophone Africa.[81] An EEC inclusive of Britain threatened de Gaulle's vision of Europe, decentering power from Paris to London and introducing a host of new overseas obligations even as the French struggled to secure their own relations with their former empire.

Britain's exclusion did not sit well with all members of the Six and opened France to criticism fueled by frustrations mounting since at least 1957. A glance at how other members of the Six viewed the Algerian question provides a sort of Rorschach test, revealing their attitudes about France itself. Dutch officials and their popular press were especially critical. Cartoonist Opland mocked the French, depicting Minister of Foreign Affairs Maurice Couve de Murville pointing to a group of smiling Africans (donning generic headgear, robes, and kente cloth) and telling the United Kingdom, personified by John Bull, "Look, they belong to Europe, but you don't!" Opland titled the cartoon "French Lessons for Industrialized Nations."[82] The joke, such as it was, implied the absurdity that France would open Europe to people whose skin color marked them as unassimilable to Europe while excluding the properly dressed, white Briton. In a Europe unsure of whether its borders traversed the Mediterranean, the cartoon sent a strong signal coding Europe as white above all. It indicated an erasure of the centuries-old presence of people of color living in continental regions of the Six and, more immediately, the unresolved language of the Treaty of Rome's Algeria section.[83] Opland's confident punchline, indicating that belonging in Europe should be determined by looking and dressing "like a European"—in other words, being white—undermined the promise of a federative Eurafrica that had inspired hope in Léopold Senghor and others.

The Dutch criticism of French attempts to merge imperial and European interests had precedent. French banker and civil servant Pierre Moussa wrote in 1957 of the *"complexe hollandaise,"* meaning the Dutch peoples' positive feelings about the loss of Indonesia, which was understood to have been an economic boon for the

Fig. 5.1   "French lessons for industrialized nations. Couve de Murville: Look, they belong to Europe, but you don't!" Rob Wout (Opland), "Franse les voor gevorderden," February 28, 1963. © 2021 Artists Rights Society (ARS), New York / c / o Pictoright Amsterdam

country.[84] This French interpretation of the Dutch attitude is striking, given the domestic anxiety such changes stirred up. Political scientist Arend Lijphart characterized the period as a "trauma" for the Netherlands.[85] Nevertheless, in the mid-1950s, Dutch officials announced that they did not want their own colonial possessions mentioned in the Treaty of Rome. This did not mean that the Dutch were anti-imperial; rather, they did not see the material or political benefit of associating their possessions with integrated Europe, unlike the French and, to a lesser extent, the

Belgians. Moussa warned against this, but the Dutch experience surely informed Raymond Cartier, whose reporting in *Paris Match* helped turn public opinion against the French colonial project. The Dutch, already opposed to the French vision of Eurafrica, harnessed the Algerian question of the early 1960s not only to register their disagreement on the issue of associated territories but also to condemn France's outsized influence on the EEC as a whole. By then, they could count on the support of Belgium, Luxembourg, and Italy. Italian leaders in particular feared trade and labor competition, priming them to oppose versions of the EEC that would uphold a special status for Algeria.

The question of EEC-Algerian relations became a tool for France's partners to attack broader French policy. Less than a year after Algeria's independence and only months after the veto, the Dutch voiced concern about the "indefinite prolongation" of a favorable regime for Algeria.[86] In June 1963, two weeks before the Six were slated to establish a set of regulations with Algeria, Dutch secretary of state for foreign affairs Hans van Houten declared that Algeria's independence had transformed it "ipso facto" into a third-party state, although he allowed that there were arguments for maintaining "a particular regime in [its] favor."[87] Dutch frustration at France's veto of UK accession led van Houten, as one Dutch daily reported, to raise the question of Algeria's status "prudently and diplomatically." His decision to bring up the Algerian issue came just before an early July meeting between de Gaulle and West German chancellor Konrad Adenauer. The newspaper argued that his choice was deliberate, meant to encourage de Gaulle to take up "a more amenable attitude toward Great Britain." Tensions about Algeria would serve "as a wake-up call" for the French president.[88] Van Houten and the Dutch instrumentalized the Algerian question to criticize the French ploy for power in Brussels.

In sharp contrast, months prior and just a week after the veto, de Gaulle and Adenauer marked Franco-German rapprochement with the Élysée Treaty. Intended to cement ongoing ties and consistent foreign policy conversations between the two, it would diminish when Ludwig Erhard took office in October 1963. Although only briefly in place, the accord matched the West German record of supporting French policy regarding Algeria and the EEC. The Franco-German friendship, a project that progressed in fits and starts from the 1950s on, had by the early 1960s become of paramount importance to both de Gaulle and Adenauer.[89] The question of Britain and its sway over Benelux in particular amplified their drive to solidify this friendship on paper. Adenauer wrote in April 1962, "Now that the British, via their Dutch and Belgian proxies, have wrecked the political union, which was the primary goal of the entire European effort from the outset, all that remains is a France-Germany bloc, perhaps with participation of Italy and Luxembourg."[90] As the West German government continued to back the French approach to European-Algerian relations, its leaders supported France's foreign policy more generally. After the breakdown of the Fouchet Plan, de Gaulle saw the nefarious hand of the Anglo-American friendship everywhere and sought to counter it with a Western Europe dominated by France and West Germany, with Germany following France's lead.

Adenauer appeared prepared to stick with de Gaulle, even at the expense of German industry. For example, prior to independence, Renault had been the only car manufacturer in Algeria; in March 1963, Algerian officials indicated they were open to talks about Peugeot's installation as well.[91] This flew in the face of French officials' touting of the "shared" Eurafrican playing field prior to the signing of the Treaty of Rome. If West Germany had hoped that the inclusion of Algeria in the Treaty of Rome would have allowed for the entry of Volkswagen or Mercedes into the region, they would be disappointed for now.[92] Meanwhile, in late 1961 de Gaulle had pressured Adenauer into accepting an agreement on cereals that threatened German wheat producers.[93] Nonetheless, West German officials continued to err on the side of the status quo, supporting Algeria's right to enjoy certain benefits of association with the EEC. This signaled their interest in appeasing France. They also banked on future EEC-Algerian ties that would allow German goods to flow into Algeria with a reduced customs duty and wanted to see Algeria remain within the sphere of the capitalist world.[94]

Despite this support from West Germany, French officials' own devotion to Algeria's status quo was fading. In Jeffrey Byrne's words, French officials "admitted behind closed doors that the supposedly pathbreaking trans-Mediterranean relationship was quickly devolving into bilateral haggling between two self-interested states."[95] As some of France's partners hardened their stances, the French appeared to soften their own. Boegner, France's representative in Brussels, wondered in June 1963 if it was wise "to do battle to get all of our partners to continue according Algeria the intra-community regime," particularly considering that the Algerian government had never asked France to intervene on its behalf.[96] A telegram sent the next day from the Ministry of Foreign Affairs to Boegner's office in Brussels instructed that France should adopt "an attitude of abstention. However, it is important to avoid our partners interpreting this as a mark of indifference."[97]

This might seem a startling about-face coming from a state that had spent a significant portion of the past decade speaking on Algeria's behalf without its permission, but Boegner appeared earnest in suggesting that France should not take up any policy position that the independent Algerian state had not explicitly requested.

France's attitude toward Algerian-EEC relations evolved concurrent to Algeria's increased presence in Brussels and its pursuit of foreign relations outside of Europe. Algeria's integration into the Third Worldist movement began before independence and only amplified after.[98] The question of Algeria's place in the EEC still demanded a resolution, but French officials had begun to distance themselves from France's past advocacy because they feared the risk of alienating the other members of the Six. The Algerian delegation in Brussels was not forthcoming with its government's position. According to the French military intelligence service, the Algerian permanent representative "implied in private that the current situation [the lack of resolution] suited his country." He also suggested that Algeria would not be open to general Maghreb-EEC negotiations, as these would threaten Algeria's privileged position.[99] In the meantime, the Algerian government had opened conversations with its neighbors, seeking Tunisian agreement about an envoy to be sent to Brussels in fall 1963.[100] French reports analyzed this Algerian diplomacy as two-faced, sly dealmaking. Yet such accounts must be read critically. After all, they were produced by career civil servants trained to distrust Algerians' capacity for self-government and likely resentful of the embarrassment of the recently ended war.

For the entirety of 1963, Algeria's status within the EEC remained technically unchanged, though generally the material benefits of that status were not scheduled to go into effect until at least 1965 and all but France and West Germany implemented restrictions that placed Algeria on the level of a third-party state. The Algerian government meanwhile instituted a new customs tariff which appeared to label the Six, with the exception of France, third-party states, a decision they defended as "simply resulting from necessities of an administrative nature."[101] Such a decision may have deepened French ambivalence, as it extended comparative benefits to France while undermining their claim to the universality of benefits that would come from Algeria's inclusion in the Treaty of Rome. By early 1964, Algerian functionaries in Brussels emphasized that talks with the EEC were "in some way [in] a 'pre-exploratory' stage," due in part to the fact that they lacked instruction from Algiers on what position to take. They did inquire about financial assistance for commercial exchanges and suggest that Algeria would be open to coordinating a single position for the three Maghrebi states in relation to the EEC.[102] Although the talks were inconclusive, a rosy EEC press release claimed that the talks had occurred "in an excellent climate of mutual understanding."[103]

The Treaty of Rome beyond Algeria

The ramifications of Algeria's inclusion in the EEC extended geographically beyond the Mediterranean, and those consequences lingered in French Guiana, Guadeloupe, Martinique, and Réunion— the remaining French Overseas Departments (DOM)—in the same years that EEC officials in Brussels attempted to untangle Algeria from its regulations. In 1965, an SGCI administrator warned that "French tactics" had created "dangerous precedents," namely that the question of applying Treaty of Rome regulations to the DOM was to be approached piecemeal. With Algeria "settled"—a dubious claim—he argued that the application of the treaty to the DOM should be tackled through bilateral accords in order to avoid "the inevitable surveillance of journalists," which could invite "questions centered on the assimilation of certain French [citizens] from across the seas to French of the European continent."[104] Although this official was overly optimistic about the conclusion of the Algerian question, his concern about potential scandal over the different types of rights regimes echoed past imperial citizenship debates and foreshadowed complex questions of European identity that were to come.

In the early 1960s, the French department of Réunion in the Indian Ocean caused a stir about the right to labor migration in the peripheries of Europe, demonstrating that although the Treaty of Rome's inclusion of the DOM was aimed at Algeria, in practice it reached France's other farthest flung departments as well. In 1962, the Réunionnais firm Maurice de la Giroday & Compagnie hired two German master mechanics to train locals to repair Volkswagen and Mercedes vehicles. They moved to Réunion with their wives.[105] By mid-1965, the prefecture of Réunion denied the men's requests for visa renewal, effectively meaning they would be required to leave the island within a few weeks. The West German embassy in Paris appealed to the Quai d'Orsay on their behalf.[106] Réunion's subprefect defended the decision, emphasizing the "very particular situation of this department," including the high birth rate and the "endemic" underemployment of the local workforce. It also seemed "hard to believe" that after three years, the Germans had not managed to train a single mechanic capable of replacing them.[107] French officials again weighed the risks of angering a European partner, as they had when they insisted Algeria be named in the Treaty of Rome. Hugues Vinel, chief of staff in the Ministry of Overseas France, worriedly wrote to the minister of labor that although he saw the necessity of "quell[ing] immigration in an already overpopulated department, I do not wish to adopt such a measure with regards to nationals of an EEC partner without having serious juridical reasons motivating it." Further, he feared that it could spark retaliatory measures against French nationals working or hoping to work in West Germany.[108] But by December, Paris came down firmly on the side of Réunion. The director general for work and employment told Vinel's office that he "entirely share[d] the point of view" of the prefect of Réunion, which was justified given the employment situation on the island. Going further, he reminded officials in Paris that the free movement of labor within the EEC did not apply to the DOM or French Overseas Territories (TOM). The mechanics and their wives would have to go.[109]

How should this decision be understood? On the one hand, it suggests the privileged place of internal affairs for France, here the protection of a department's population above citizens from the Six. On the other hand, it reinforces the contradictions in France's understandings of its own borders and, by extension, those of Europe. Similar to Algeria, Réunion would be treated like continental France only when doing so did not threaten French sovereignty, as a restive laboring class would. EEC labor regulations were subsumed by local protocol, at the risk of angering a major ally and neighbor. Treating Réunion and the other overseas departments differently from their metropolitan equivalents also had precedent. The Fourth Republic's social security regime had not been applied automatically in the DOM, for example, yet another instance of France's universalism being applied piecemeal, with racial categorizations masked by claims about development standards. When French authorities sided with Réunionnais officials, they did so in support of the local labor force. But once again, they confirmed that the parts of France outside of the continent would only count as true, European France when it was convenient for the metropole.

"The Hand of Cooperation"

On July 3, 1962, the day de Gaulle officially recognized the results of the final referendum and two days before Algerians celebrated their independence, Adenauer sat down with him in Paris to discuss European integration. Adenauer remarked that Algeria's new status "frees France . . . to devote itself more easily to its great tasks in Europe and the world."[110] The assertion that France was now "free" of Algeria glossed over the nearly eight years of protracted armed struggle during which French forces under two republics attempted to maintain control of the territory. Just as significantly, Adenauer failed to foresee that far from being "freed" from Algeria, French officials hoped to assert that independent Algeria could still be a part of Europe, even if its exact relationship was far from clear. Meanwhile, Algerian leaders did not act in accordance with French visions of their own might and France's European partners withdrew their support of such policies. In reality, the prevailing wisdom of Algeria's natural place within, or with, France and Europe only dimmed by degrees after 1962.

On June 19, 1965, the Algerian military launched a coup, ousting Ben Bella in response to frustration over his ability to lead and to fears that he might remove Minister of Foreign Affairs

Abdelaziz Bouteflika. Houari Boumediene took the reins. Three years later, Boumediene commemorated the takeover in a speech to senior officials in which he argued that Algerian policy vis-à-vis France "has been able to overcome the hazards and hatreds arising from the past, the 130 years of occupation by the French, and the seven and a half years of war. . . . Algeria has chosen the way of forgiveness and tolerance, silencing resentment, drying her tears, and extending the hand of cooperation."[111] With Boumediene's accession to power, the Algerian government maintained its realpolitik approach to foreign affairs, but it also solidified its role in Third Worldist affairs and further resisted ties to France. The power and prestige France once derived from Algeria were now distant memories. One Quai d'Orsay administrator complained that as late as June 1965, Algerian authorities still had not set a timeline for talks meant to clarify future relations with Europe. Rather, they "gave the impression of being in no rush, and on the contrary, [appeared] very 'greedy.'" The Algerians were bigheaded in this official's eyes: "Indeed, they claimed to be able to obtain, from that moment, satisfactory prospects not only from the point of view of the trade regime, but also regarding financial assistance and labor."[112] It is clear that French attitudes toward a European-Algerian partnership were already cooling significantly before 1965, impacted by the 1963 expropriation of former settler land and the 1964 introduction of the Algerian dinar, among other Algerian actions. By the middle of the decade, the French government's wariness toward Algeria steered French policy goals away from the status quo.

Reflecting in 1967 on the evolution of Algerian-EEC relations, one French administrator linked the challenges of Maghrebi-EEC diplomacy to the Empty Chair Crisis, which stemmed from French fears about the EEC's control over the budget, particularly in light of the Common Agricultural Policy (CAP).[113] On July 1, 1965, the EEC failed to agree on how to fund the CAP, which created a system of subsidies and harmonized policies related to agriculture across the Six. Although delays in decisions were typical of the EEC's functioning, this time the French took a drastic step. Less than a week later, Paris recalled Boegner from Brussels and the French announced they would not replace him.[114] Without a representative in Brussels, the French effectively boycotted the EEC and froze its activity. This would go on until January 1966. The Empty Chair Crisis represented an important moment for integrated Europe, as de Gaulle's deliberate inaction stymied the EEC's functions and demonstrated French distrust of, and distaste for, Brussels. The early years of Algeria's independence were thus marked by French attempts to assert its supremacy in Brussels as much as in its former colonies.

After 1962, French and Algerian bureaucrats alike contended that Algeria merited distinct ties with the EEC. Algerians also pursued partnerships in other parts of the world, relegating their diplomatic relations with France and Europe to positions that were distinctly less special than what the French once touted. Algerian domestic and international goals led its leaders to drift further from Brussels and toward Cairo and the Maghreb. Yet the conversations sparked by the first leaders of independent Algeria, who themselves echoed older claims by French colonial administrators, opened debates about what Algeria had ever meant to Europe and how that relationship would look as Algeria entered its second decade of independence. Far from settled in 1962 or even 1965, the question of Algeria's relationship to the EEC—or in the EEC—remained unresolved for years to come.

6

Algeria, France, and the
Europe of Nation-States

In 1959, a thirty-seven-year-old German national named Gerd
Wolfgang Fiege contracted polio and was left wheelchair-bound.
He had worked in Algeria for eight years, after two in Strasbourg,
and received his disability pension from the social security office
of Oran. Despite a decree from independent Algeria's authorities
tying his pension to his continued residency there, Fiege returned
to West Germany in 1963 and pursued his right to a pension based
on European Economic Community (EEC) regulations. His appeal bounced from courts in Berlin, to Paris, to Strasbourg, and
then to the European Court of Justice (ECJ), based in Luxembourg.
There, in 1973, the British advocate-general Jean-Pierre Warner
argued on Fiege's behalf, creating a precedent for the EEC to recognize employment in Algeria as eligible for a European pension.
Making the case for Fiege, Warner declared, "The aftermath of
Empire has brought, for those of our countries that were formerly
imperial powers, liabilities of many kinds which, whilst unwelcome,
are for one reason or another inescapable."[1]

Fiege's struggle for benefits, one of a small handful of ECJ cases that forced officials to wrestle with Article 227's legacy, demonstrates that the high-level bureaucratic debates of the previous years, even decades, had a human impact. The "aftermath of Empire" proved long and complicated, particularly because of Algeria's undefined yet powerful relationship with the EEC in terms of social security rights, trade regulation, and more. Yet a mere three years after Warner made this observation, the EEC and Algeria signed the 1976 Co-operation Agreement, clarifying future relations following well over a decade of halting negotiations. That agreement made no reference to Algeria's inclusion in the Treaty of Rome, let alone the more than 130 years that it was attached to France, first as territory in need of pacification, then as a juridical part of the Republic itself. Although the agreement ignored the past, making it seem as if Algeria had been a foreign land all along, cases like Fiege's forced European officials to admit that the EEC did indeed bear an imperial legacy. It was a reality they hoped very much to erase.

After Ahmed Ben Bella's 1965 removal as prime minister of Algeria, Algerian officials continued to pursue privileged economic and labor relations between their state and the EEC. They found themselves in a position to make demands on Europe, even as European officials hoped to curtail the legacy of having named Algeria in the Treaty of Rome. At the same time, they pursued other foreign relations that made close ties to the EEC appear less imperative.[2] The EEC, for its part, gradually came to shed its imperial identity and become a community of nation-states. This development was helped along by their frustration with Algerian leaders over foreign affairs such as the issue of Israel and economic competition related to wine, the movement of labor, and more. The excision of Algeria from the EEC did not occur suddenly with the former's independence. Only from the Empty Chair Crisis until the 1976 agreement did Europe finally, slowly, turn inward.[3]

French ministers and functionaries, European foreign affairs representatives, and the leaders of Houari Boumediene's government, particularly Minister of Foreign Affairs Abdelaziz Boutef-lika, all took part in the conversations and decisions that led to Algeria's exit from the EEC and to the abandonment of the expansive version of Europe that appeared possible in prior decades. Those decisions held real-life consequences beyond high-level ministerial talks. As the cases that reached the ECJ reveal, these shifts impacted the lives of workers whose careers traversed once-European borders that were no longer recognized as such. When French officials argued in the mid-1950s that including empire in the EEC would be a boon for European states overtaxed with an underemployed population (Italy) or in need of more workers (Belgium, West Germany), they built a vision of a European labor force that could move easily between continent and colony. In practice, when these movements occurred, national social security administrations challenged whether such labor could be counted as a career in Europe, leading to lasting debates about whether Algeria ever had been a part of France.

As in previous years, domestic regime changes appeared to do little to impact these talks. Indeed, although this period witnessed Boumediene forcing out Ben Bella (1965), the European Coal and Steel Community, EEC, and Euratom merging into the European Community (EC, 1967), and Charles de Gaulle leaving office (1969), the conversations between Algeria and France, and Algeria and Europe appeared little impacted by changes in leadership. Major events in the EC's history, notably de Gaulle's second veto of British membership in 1967 and the eventual accession of the United Kingdom, along with Denmark and Ireland, during the first enlargement in 1973, also barely registered in EEC-Algerian negotiations, although France's reduced might within the EC may help to explain the terms eventually settled with Algeria. Algeria's lingering economic ties with France and its increase in trade with some of the Six make clear why these upheavals did not bring a swift end to its ambiguous status vis-à-vis Europe. Little by little, however, French, EEC, and Algerian officials abandoned long-held claims about Algeria's unique status in Europe. For the EEC, this shift coincided with French disenchantment with Algeria, particularly as the Algerian government continued to nationalize formerly French industries.

In 1973, Algerian president Boumediene spoke on Radiotelevisione Italiana. "Europe," he declared, "is geographically and historically the closest continent to us, by which I mean the relations we have maintained . . . through the ages and across history."[4] Boumediene's statement echoed decades of French colonial and Eurafrican discourse about the firm connection between France and Algeria. For Boumediene, the links looked different. They afforded the Algerian government a strong position to challenge French and European policies that undercut its economy and autonomy. That the Algerian president continued to insist on Algeria's unique relationship with Europe speaks to the peculiar imbrication of Algeria and the EEC itself. Algeria's relationship with the EEC remained in flux because of inconclusive negotiations and the exigencies of external and domestic affairs in both Europe and Algeria. The relationship was rendered even more complex by the biographies of ordinary laborers like Fiege, who had taken advantage of the relatively open borders of the EEC to move across the metropolitan territories of the Six and even to Algeria. Boumediene was not wrong in claiming that Algeria's relations with Europe had not ceased. But the nature of those relations was far from fixed and their evolution represented the slow unraveling of the long-held French claim that Algeria was, indeed, a part of Europe. That it took fourteen years after Algeria's independence to conclude a new agreement should lead us to understand that Algeria's prior inclusion in Europe had been a reality. With the stroke of a pen in 1976, not only was that reality altered, but its very existence was all but erased.

"Particularly Anarchic"

The twilight years of Algeria's time in the EEC witnessed a flurry of changes to Algeria's economy and to the political calculus of the Six, both as a body and as individual states. Although Algeria's relationship to the EEC was still largely defined by its ambiguity, the consequences of Article 227 emerged in the period before formal negotiations for the 1976 accord. The exact relationship between Algeria and the EEC remained vague, affording leaders of the former some political and economic bargaining power, yet ultimately opening the door for the Six to brush aside the European rights they previously struggled to deny Algeria. The National Liberation Front's (FLN's) mouthpiece, *Révolution africaine,* described this ambiguity as a set of "particularly anarchic relations" in which European states simultaneously disavowed Algeria's rights within the EEC and extended a variety of forms of aid to the young state.[5] Increasingly, such ambiguity lost the utility it had held for Algeria and the EEC alike in the first years of independence.

Although the Evian Accords included stipulations guarding French oil interests in Algeria, by 1965, the Ben Bella administration began to scale back French benefits and push for more revenue to remain in Algeria. When the two states signed an accord on hydrocarbon later that year, French journalist Alain Murcier wrote that it "brutally tilts the balance beam in the opposite direction, giving Algeria the advantages of nationalization" with France footing the bill.[6] Jean Majorelle, an expert on France's overseas petroleum industry, reportedly despaired, "We have nothing more to do in Algeria . . . , us private capitalists. . . . Things are not at all what they were in 1958."[7] The concern of private industry may have worried the French government, but it did little to halt ongoing attempts to clarify and solidify future Franco-Algerian relations. Although the hydrocarbon accord was signed soon after Boumediene unseated Ben Bella in the June coup d'état, European administrators appeared relatively unfazed by the regime change and continued to seek agreements with Algeria and its neighbors. Two weeks after the coup, de Gaulle orchestrated the Empty Chair Crisis, effectively boycotting the EEC by refusing to seat its president in Brussels. The Empty Chair Crisis sidelined any EEC-Algerian negotiations that had been in the works. After France's return to Brussels in early 1966, EEC member state attitudes toward Algeria were characterized by uncertainty and diplomatic posturing, much as they had been previously.

Alongside Algeria's peculiar relationship to the EEC, the Six maintained a variety of relations with all three Maghrebi states, including sending experts and teachers. This European presence in the Maghreb fulfilled one of the visions the French pursued when they demanded Eurafrican policies in the 1950s: a shared responsibility toward (now-former) colonies. The French maintained a higher number of nationals in all three Maghreb states, particularly in Algeria. In 1967, for example, over 400 French *coopérants* worked in Algeria's health sector alone. Yet the number of French experts and laborers in Algeria had fallen precipitously since independence. In the first half of 1962, French workers of the railway company Société nationale des chemins de fer algériens numbered 7,581. By the first half of 1965, that number dropped to below 400.[8] Regardless of their own citizens' departure, French bureaucrats remained suspicious of the EEC-wide effort they themselves had brought about. The French consul in Tlemcen sounded pleased to report that of the two Belgian teachers in the region, one had moved to Algeria in 1962 with "very liberal ideas" and had become "disappointed with the Algerian people and authorities." The other was a young woman "purported to have not irreproachable morals," who was thus "viewed poorly by the mothers of country families."[9] Belgium, Italy, the Netherlands, and West Germany all sent experts to Algeria, but they began to analyze statistics of technical assistance by assessing figures related to all three Maghreb states rather than highlight any particular relationship between the EEC and Algeria.[10]

As the Six extended aid to Algeria, roadblocks arose in the form of individual state concerns. Italian representatives raised now-familiar complaints about the menace to their state were a Maghrebi accord to go forward, given that Italy's agricultural production closely mirrored that of the southern shores of the Mediterranean. Italy's representatives bristled at their state losing out to Algeria, a concern exacerbated by older fears about being cast as less than European. They complained that "the sacrifices to be agreed upon will be made practically by a single region—already underprivileged in relation to the rest of the Community—of a single member state." This would be compounded by labor migration rights, which would endanger nationals from "the only country in the Community that still has an excess of laborers," while proving advantageous to the other member states.[11] In other words, Italian officials believed their economy and citizens had the most to lose were the EC to embrace the Maghreb too wholeheartedly.

The Dutch, too, remained characteristically skeptical of Algeria's relationship to Europe. Emboldened to challenge France's imperial demands after Algeria's independence, Dutch representatives now took even greater steps. When the Dutch ambassador to Algeria arrived at his post in 1968, he announced that his government would not allow for "different countries that hope to establish contractual relations with the Common Market to be treated differently" and that the Maghrebi states should not expect special treatment above others, "notably Israel."[12] Such hostility toward Algeria likely had not been helped by the Algerian nationalization of Dutch oil interests one year prior. The Dutch, whom Bouteflika believed blocked Algeria's 1965 negotiations with the EEC because of their own oil interests, were scandalized when on the afternoon of Saturday, June 10, the final day of the 1967 Arab-Israeli War, Algerian authorities searched the homes of the directors of three firms with majority Dutch interests— Compagnie des pétroles d'Algérie, Shell d'Algérie, and Unilever Algérie—and alerted them that they were no longer in charge of these businesses.[13] This nationalization coincided with Algeria's seizure of other foreign-owned oil-producing enterprises. If the Dutch were willing to demonstrate that they felt little obligation to bend to Algerian desires, the Algerians, too, had signaled that they viewed the Six as something other than partners in economic affairs.

Tension over Israel impacted Algerian-European relations but did not undermine them in all cases. In particular, West German officials remained open to working with Algeria despite strong diplomatic statements such as the Algerian government's severing of ties with West Germany in May 1965 after the latter recognized Israel. Willy Brandt viewed rapprochement with Algeria as key to securing North Africa against the influence of the Soviet Union.[14] The question of Israel also increased tension about Algeria's unresolved relationship to Europe. When Israel and the EEC signed an accord in 1971, *El Moudjahid* protested that "for certain Arab countries the negotiations with the Common Market have dragged on for years."[15] Algeria's evolving relationship to France and the EEC, notably in economic terms, made these protracted negotiations even more fraught.

Independent Economies

Sheer financial sense represented only one factor in both French and Algerian decision making. Here I build on Owen White's assertion that "balance-sheet approaches to the colonial past rarely reveal . . . the multiplicity of stakeholders in particular forms of economic activity."[16] The economic links between Algeria and the EEC took on political meanings that cannot be reduced to a simple calculation. France's drive to maintain sovereignty over far-flung and nearby territories remained a priority even when many French officials began to believe that such control might be a financial drain. This was in part because of hard-to-abandon beliefs about

France's natural place within Algerian affairs, but in reality, French industry still had much to gain by being connected to Algeria, including the location of factories, the recruitment of workers, and access to natural resources. The balance-sheet approach also ignores Algerian officials' motivations and agency in determining the future of their state's relations with France and the EEC.

In 1968, the Algerian legal scholar and politician Khalfa Mameri offered possible reasons why six years after Algeria's independence, its relations with the EEC remained undefined. First, Algeria's choice to opt for a Non-Aligned position might make its leaders "prefer to postpone all decisions regarding the EEC," given its "incompatible politics." Second, and opposite, the EEC itself demonstrated "hesitations" about "the definition of new relations with this state." Finally, Mameri suggested that Algerian leaders understood the benefits afforded by the Article 227 regime and wanted to prolong the status quo as a result.[17] The answer, in fact, was all three. Yet the benefits of maintaining an undefined status became less appealing, both as the Algerian government sought closer ties outside of the EEC and as the soon-to-be-expanded EEC ceased to find use in maintaining Algeria's special place. As the Boumediene government assessed the economic needs of the nascent state, the weight of Algeria's past ties with France, and the drive to secure other bonds instead, grew to be of paramount concern.

With the 1960s coming to a close, Algeria's undefined relationship to the EEC became harder to defend as a policy in its own right, as the range of European attitudes discussed above suggests. Finger-pointing over the ambiguous state of affairs targeted different actors. Luxembourg's minister of foreign affairs and foreign trade opined that Algeria "preferred to maintain the current, more advantageous status quo and thus to preserve its privileged position vis-à-vis the Community."[18] In contrast, French ambassador to Algeria Pierre de Leusse "insisted we respond favorably to Algerian requests to restart commercial talks. It has been 15 months now that we have pushed them off."[19] De Leusse had a record of standing for Algerian interests at the heart of the French administration, requesting to be recalled from his Tunisian ambassadorial post in 1956 in protest of France's interception of an airplane carrying FLN leaders, including Ben Bella.

When the Algerian administration did attempt to open talks with the EEC, negotiations were stymied, among other things, by what EEC officials thought were overly ambitious demands from the Algerians regarding tariff rates and other trade guarantees and because of European protectionist measures that the Algerian government viewed as punitive and dangerous. In 1972, Bouteflika cited negotiation attempts in 1963, 1964, 1968, and 1970 and complained that instead, the EEC pursued "unilateral measures" that would decimate "the preferential relations that Algeria had enjoyed with the EEC." Writing to the head of the Council of Ministers, he invoked Article 227, which inserted Algeria in a "framework it certainly did not choose." At particular risk was the Algerian wine industry, "whose production was imposed upon it in the past."[20]

Wine, which *El Moudjahid* scathingly called "a clear legacy of foreign colonization, an excrescence of the French economy on our soil," would prove to be one of the most complex elements of future accords between the EEC and Algeria.[21] The choice of *excroissance* as a metaphor painted a powerful image of an unhealthy and abnormal growth jutting out of the Algerian economy. Since the second half of the nineteenth century, when French wine-makers settled in Algeria during the phylloxera outbreak, the Algerian wine industry flourished within the French economy. Although Algeria's crops allowed for the sale of affordable French table wine, this financial success was met with opposition by both southern French purveyors of cheap wine, especially in the Languedoc, and by vintners who hoped in the post–World War II era to recast wine as a luxury commodity rather than an everyday "food."[22] After Algeria's independence, these vintners were able to mount further pressure on French officials, who themselves were no longer obligated to defend the commercial interests of wine growers in Algeria. The bulk of the settler vintners had left Algeria by mid-1962, with some of the wealthiest buying up land in the Bordeaux region and others turning to Corsican soil.[23] Three years later, almost 90 percent of Algeria's vineyards operated under the self-management system.[24]

Wine, in the mid-1960s, was still Algeria's second most important export after Saharan oil, accounting for at least a quarter of its foreign currency.[25] Although a 1964 treaty secured—at a diminishing rate—the continued export of Algerian wine to France, in February 1967 the French government imposed what turned out to be a temporary suspension on it.[26] This threatened the Algerian economy in terms of foreign currency intake and agricultural employment. By then, the government had ordered over 20,000 hectares of vineyard to be uprooted, a number that would rise precipitously in the coming years. Algeria found other markets, but they were small in comparison to France. The USSR imported 280,000 hectoliters the year of France's ban, and officials there suggested distilling Algerian wine "as a palliative." West Germany appeared to be a promising partner, taking in 400,000 hectoliters.[27] Its eagerness to import Algerian wine even appeared threatening to Italy, which attempted to prevent further imports. A French official suggested that this would backfire on the Italians, likely harming Fiat's chances of receiving tractor orders from the Algerian National Agrarian Reform Office.[28]

Although it expanded partnerships outside of France, the Algerian government struggled to contend with the growing problem of the wine industry, understood as "a poisoned chalice from colonialism." This coincided with some French restrictions on Algerian citizens' entry into the metropole.[29] In early 1968, de Leusse warned Direction of External Economic Relations (DREE) director Jean-Pierre Brunet that the Algerians were invoking de Gaulle's promise to Bouteflika about financial compensation in the case that France did not respect their agreement on wine. "At the moment," he cautioned, "we are performing acrobatics."[30] In July, he wrote to François de Laboulaye, director of North Africa at the Ministry of Foreign Affairs and a close enough friend to *tutoyer* in an official communication, warning that wine had become "a real nightmare for the Algerians": "I do not know if it prevents President Boumediene from sleeping, like the Minister of Foreign Affairs [Bouteflika] told me, but it is a great subject of worry: reserves of 14 million hectoliters, a harvest said to be at least 10 million hectoliters, storage difficulties, a weight on the budget. The Algerians foist the responsibility of this situation onto us." Facing a challenging economic situation, he concluded that it was "easy [for the regime] to look for a scapegoat, namely France."[31] The EEC Council attempted to "put an end to the anarchy" by establishing a single commercial policy between all members of the Six and Algeria, in particular regarding tariff rates.[32]

Algeria's independence and the harmonization of EEC wine regulations both hardened France's stance against the lucrative

Algerian wine industry. The Algerian government, for its part, spoke of eliminating its economic dependence on the unwanted but still-necessary industry, which it planned to do by amplifying industry, including oil production. The French government faced increased pressure from the Languedoc, which now feared competition with Italy over cheap *coupage* wine. In addition, the EEC's regulations more broadly would prevent the French government from making unilateral national policies for its own industry.[33] The Algerians were aware of the issue of Midi wine interests, with de Leusse noting that his contacts in Bouteflika's office reminded him that the "opposition of vintners in the southwest does not date to today, but was already this virulent in the era of colonization. The electoral problem in the departments of the Midi has always existed."[34]

Algerian officials pressed this point as they accused the French of beginning to treat Algeria "like an ordinary Third World [*tiers monde*] state," a recrimination that accented Algeria's distinct prior status. The folding of the Algerian development fund (Caisse d'équipement pour le développement de l'Algérie) into the central fund (Caisse centrale de coopération économique) was further proof of just that and undercut previous French demands that Algerian projects be supported by funds earmarked for Europe itself. De Leusse urged his colleagues to speak about the issue of wine in particular, arguing that the appearance of unilateral decision making on the part of the French gave a worse impression than disengagement: "disinterest."[35] Although French representatives in Brussels saw themselves as upholding Algerian interests, calling for it to be treated as an associated country, the French themselves pursued policies that undermined *coupage* and limited Algeria's ability to sell wine to Europe.[36]

The question of Algerian wine remained unresolved into the early 1970s. Although wine was an agricultural question (and in part related to the Common Agricultural Policy), the political nature of the conversation instead added it to Europe's ministers of foreign affairs' portfolios.[37] The Algerians, in the eyes of the French, appeared to verge on irrational, so "haunted by the necessity of selling their wine" that they failed to see the benefits they would glean from minimum pricing regulation.[38] *El Moudjahid* criticized those "at the heart of the EEC who never lose hope of altering our country's policy of independence through economic pressures."[39] Even the French embassy in Algiers, now headed by Jean Soutou, admitted that a transitional regime approved by the Council of Ministers in 1971 was "not very favorable to the Algerians," given that it prevented Algerian wine from entering the market at lower prices than the reference price and did not secure the right for Algerian wine to be used as *coupage*. The result would be that only "quality wine," an official designation and little of which was produced in Algeria, could easily enter the market at an equal or higher price than the reference price. Soutou's office noted that "the Algerian authorities naturally considered this regime to be draconian."[40] France's pursuit of a unified EEC wine regime beneficial to its own industry undercut its pursuit of continued ties with Algeria.

Although the French reported Algerian distress following the EEC wine decisions, the Boumediene regime pursued an aggressive policy of eliminating Algerian reliance on France, in particular by literally uprooting the wine industry. One contemporary observer called Algeria's liquidation of its wine industry a key step in the full decolonization of its economy, ranked after the nationalization of the hydrocarbon industry.[41] The government gradually ramped up efforts to pull up vineyards. From 1965 to 1975, vineyards' expanse dropped from 340,000 to 210,000 hectares and wine production fell precipitously.[42] Boumediene's government committed to significant investment in other arenas. The Three-Year Plan of 1967–1969 devoted much of its budget to heavy and light industry, such as steel and textiles.[43] He launched an agrarian revolution in 1971, meant to make Algeria food self-sufficient and reduce foreign dependency, but he also ordered the nationaliza-tion of the country's natural gas deposits, signaling a new economic direction. From 1970 to 1973, 14.92 percent of Algerian invest-ment went to agriculture, while 44.7 percent went to industry.[44]

This reorientation was not without issue. The lack of agricul-tural development led to unemployment on farms, which in turn inspired an exodus to cities that exacerbated a labor problem there.[45] Facing acute domestic issues, Boumediene put on a cou-rageous face before France and the EEC. If the Six felt confident that they were stronger when they acted in concert, Boumediene showed that they could also be played off of one other. At an agri-cultural conference, he declared, "If [our] French partner refuses to buy our wine, we will refuse to buy its milk and meat. We will turn towards other international markets and thus we will remedy all inequality in the trade balance between Algeria and France."[46] He leveled a similar threat about industry. "We must be clear," he proclaimed. "If Renault does not come, it will be Volkswagen or Fiat. Or others."[47] Boumediene carried out his warning by enter-taining competition for the installation of non-French automobile factories. His decision is indicative of just how different the global economy looked after decolonization. It also demonstrates a growing frustration with France, given that past benefits had "shrunk," the balance of payments remained favorable to France, and Algerian nationals in France had experienced an uptick in xe-nophobic encounters.[48] By 1976, French observers were confident that an Oran auto manufacturing contract would go to Fiat or Volkswagen, "but certainly not a French business," and that Algeria would use the PAL color television broadcasting system, already adopted by West Germany, and not the SECAM system that had been developed in France.[49] Algerian officials proactively extracted France from its economy.

Even though Boumediene risked angering France, Algeria relied heavily on the Six, and especially West Germany. In 1973, the EEC accounted for 70 percent of Algeria's foreign purchases and 62 percent of its sales. West Germany alone bought one-fifth of its oil output, making it Algeria's top consumer of the product.[50] The following year and for the first time ever, France was not Algeria's number one client; West Germany had surpassed it.[51] Decolonization offered new possibilities for economic sovereignty, but challenging-to-break structures of trade and aid persisted in curtailing that freedom. Algeria continued to receive food aid and European Development Fund (FED) support for projects.[52] France remained the top destination for Algerian labor migration.[53]

Boumediene's invitation for European competition proved menacing to the French. Quai d'Orsay officials asserted that were Volkswagen to receive the contract for a new factory in Oran, it would go "against the spirit of cooperation instituted by the Franco-German accord of 1963" because the German firm would "have the effect of purely and simply eliminating a French firm [Renault] already in place, in a country where we hold fundamental interests."[54] In a desperate attempt to reason with the Algerians, Renault's head, Pierre Dreyfus, met with Algerian minister of industry and energy Bélaïd Abdesselam and stressed that the devaluation of the franc and revaluation of the deutsche mark distorted figures in Germany's favor.[55] Dreyfus appeared convinced that Algeria's leaders failed to grasp the math he presented, rather than acknowledge that they might hold a range of motivations. In another instance, Soutou reported that the director general of the Société nationale de constructions méchaniques (SONACOME) attempted to play European car manufactures against one another regarding a possible contract for a factory in Oran.[56] Algerian maneuvering disconcerted French officials, making clear that the latter no longer held the sway they once took for granted.

Despite falling trade figures and the attack on their wine industry, the Algerian government still held clout in its negotiations with Europe, particularly thanks to its oil, which invited new openings. Its significance was so great that French economist Maurice Byé described Algeria's economic policy as "sowing oil."[57] Even Italy, in contrast to its attitude toward Algerian wine, was a growing client for Algerian oil, along with iron and olive oil.[58] With the nationalization of the hydrocarbon industry in 1971, the Algerian press proclaimed "victory" in the "battle" of oil, celebrating the "historic decisions of revolutionary power." A French scholar at the time noted that in Europe the reaction was concern over depending on "politically unstable" energy sources.[59] Yet Algeria continued to draw strength from its oil. In 1973, the Arab-Israeli War precipitated the oil shock, further demonstrating to French officials that Algeria operated autonomously from French control.[60] This served as a backdrop for contentious discussions and underscored for Algerians that the EEC refused to serve the interests of Third World or Arab states.

The Negotiating Table

In early 1974, an Algerian communiqué took aim at the EC, declaring that it was "regrettable" that the EC did not move to secure accords with the Maghreb states. The EC maintained "its old-fashioned attitude of selfish concerns" in the face of the "pressure of the current energy crisis." It cited Boumediene's interview with a Belgian newspaper in which he declared, "We are not going to beg. We want justice."[61] The reference to the energy crisis advertised the leverage Algerian representatives brought to the negotiating table. As historian Aurélie Élisa Gfeller argues, the oil shock marked "the end of European dominance over the Third World."[62] It bolstered Algeria's confidence about Europe's willingness to cooperate, although it also raised questions of whether the EC would now turn its attention to collaboration with the Gulf states.[63] The justice that Boumediene demanded alluded to older economic and social issues, notably related to development and education, that could be traced to decades of French colonial rule. It also implied justice in the present, such as fair treatment of migrant workers' families and competitive commercial tariff rates. The Algeria that approached renewed negotiations with the EC in December of that year was at once emboldened by the power on display since the oil shock and concerned about securing for its population the strongest support possible from integrated Europe.

By the launch of these talks, the EEC counted three new members: Denmark, Ireland, and the United Kingdom. Of the three, the Algerian press appeared most interested in Britain because of now-established oil industry ties and longer-term critiques of British imperialism. On the industrial side, for example, Algeria's state-owned oil company, Sonatrach, had requested that the John Brown firm, which built the Haoud el Hamra–Arzew pipeline, recruit 300 British technicians to replace French specialists who had left Algeria. By mid-1971, the British embassy estimated that at least 120 technicians were already there.[64] From the imperial angle, Algerian authorities criticized British policies toward Rhodesia and South Africa and tensions rose when Algeria detained British pilots during the 1967 Moïse Tshombe affair in which the former prime minister of the Democratic Republic of the Congo was kidnapped in a hijacking by unknown assailants—rumored to be the French secret service—and held in Algeria.[65] Ahead of the EEC enlargement, *El Moudjahid* hoped that the expansion would "overturn American hegemony." Yet it also argued that "a large weakling will be sacrificed: the Commonwealth. . . . London did not hesitate to deliver a coup de grâce to its protectees in order to take its place in the concert of *grands ensembles*." This type of threat could extend to the whole of the Third World, which might suffer from the additional pressures from the West. For the Algerians, this was an especially salient fear, given that *El Moudjahid* viewed the Six's policy toward Algeria in the past few years as so restrictive that it bordered on a "boycott."[66] The threat to the Commonwealth fell along racialized lines: months earlier, *El Moudjahid* warned that "for London, the Commonwealth boils down to New Zealand's butter and Australia's fruit, forgetting a large section of Africa and the Asian continent."[67]

Algerian officials seemed to carry few illusions about what Europe might cede. Messaoud Aït Chaalal represented Algeria when the negotiations relaunched in 1974. The Algeria-born Jean Durieux of the EC's Direction of Commercial Exchange and Development represented the EEC. Algerian officials leveled a detailed series of demands. They sought a comprehensive agreement (*accord global*) that would secure economic and financial cooperation (including oil production), commercial preferences (including the wine trade), and security for Algerian workers.[68] They demanded a higher cap on oil purchases to a figure above what they could actually produce, challenged European propositions for the wine section of the treaty, and pushed for better standing with regard to the proposed quotas. Aït Chaalal demanded the transfer to Algeria of family allowances. He also asked the EEC to participate in worker development comprising literacy and training.[69] The Algerians rejected commercial nondiscrimination clauses on the grounds that they might eventually need to exercise discrimination in order to boycott organizations working with Israel. Further still, they suggested that the EEC's emphasis on Algerian security appeared to menace its sovereignty, which might invite "political 'interpretations.'"[70] By April 1975, the EEC delegation made clear that their offer on wine was final and could not be improved. This offer did not include the guarantee of minimum sale (*écoulement minimum*) the Algerian delegation sought.[71] One month later, the Danish representative, Niels Ersbøll, suggested that the question of petrol be removed from the negotiation's mandate. This idea was met by the general acclamation of the EEC representatives, except for France's DREE chief, Émile Cazimajou, who warned that if this happened, Algeria would likely cease negotiations altogether.[72]

When the EEC renewed negotiations with Algeria, it concurrently pursued accords with other Mediterranean states, such as Malta, Spain, and Israel. France's European Commissioner, Claude Cheysson, who was responsible for relations with developing countries, hoped that Maghreb leaders would feel pressure after witnessing the relative ease of upcoming trade and aid negotiations between the EEC and Egypt, Jordan, and Turkey.[73] The existing accords between the EEC and Morocco and Tunisia were set to expire in August 1975, adding urgency to a new agreement, while overall, the range of accords complicated negotiations with Algeria because of overlapping interests and the variety of domestic demands that impacted negotiations. Algerian officials, for instance, informed an EEC representative that their government would attempt to keep EEC-Arab state talks suspended until the EEC agreed not to apply its Israeli regulations to products from the territories Israel occupied in 1967—oranges from Gaza, for example.[74] Cazimajou warned that ignoring Algeria's tactic, coupled with the risk of the Moroccan and Tunisian accords lapsing at the end of August, could lead to a dangerous outcome for future EEC relations with the "Arab countries of the Mediterranean."[75]

Algeria's Exit

On April 26, 1976, Luxembourger prime minister Gaston Thorn and Algerian minister of foreign affairs Bouteflika signed the Co-operation Agreement between the European Economic Community and the People's Democratic Republic of Algeria, which each individual state's government would ratify in the coming months. Although it maintained some labor and commercial relations, it treated Algeria as a third party like any other. The European delegation arrived in Algiers a day after signing a similar accord with Tunisia. They left the very evening of the signature, off to Rabat to sign the EEC-Morocco accord.[76] This left little time for events marking the accord beyond the signing ceremony itself.

The agreement opened with a preamble noting that the contracting parties "wish[ed] to demonstrate their common desire to maintain and strengthen their friendly relations in accordance with the principles of the United Nations Charter."[77] It made no reference to French Algeria or Article 227. The articles that followed left open the possibility for cooperation in the oil industry, set tariffs for a range of agricultural products, and introduced heavy limitations on Algeria's wine exports. Only four articles addressed labor, in comparison to thirty on trade. These four articles provided for commercial nondiscrimination, the transfer of family allowances and pensions, and the legality of future bilateral agreements that could secure more favorable conditions between Algeria and a given member state.[78] Article 56 limited the accord's geographic boundaries "to the territories to which the Treaty establishing the European Economic Community applies under the conditions laid out in that Treaty" and to Algeria.[79] Unspoken was the reality that Algeria itself had once figured into that territorial equation.

The day after the accord's signing, *Le Monde* ran a 428-word article on the Maghreb treaties that quoted Tunisian minister of foreign affairs Habib Chatti talking about the rights of Palestinians; Algerian and Moroccan officials were not referenced because the article went to press before their treaties' signing. The following day, *Le Monde* ran a two-line announcement of the Algerian accord.[80] The Algerian press commented favorably on the accord, with *Révolution africaine* noting its balanced nature and the possibility of expanding some of the provisions, especially related to labor. At the signing ceremony, Bouteflika declared that now Europe could move beyond the Cold War poles and embrace Mediterranean security and Europe's "particular mission." Like Chatti, he took the opportunity to evoke the "dispossession of the Palestinian people's national rights" and to accuse the EEC of abdicating its role. The situation could improve, he argued, if the Mediterranean states came together "in friendship and cooperation."[81] A French official in the Algiers embassy, however, argued that European-Algerian relations experienced more failures than successes in the first half of the 1970s, which would lead Algerian officials to look toward Arab states for development assistance and stronger ties.[82]

Indeed, with the accord, the era of Algeria as a seventh member state came to a close. The treaty represented the end of the reign of Article 227. The Treaty of Rome's legacy in Algeria—or rather, the legacy of Algeria in the Treaty of Rome—had defined the independent state's relationship with integrated Europe for over a decade, even as that exact relationship remained difficult to define. In the barely remarked-upon April signing, a new relationship emerged: One that was neither peculiar nor unique.

Algeria at the European Court of Justice

On a more human scale, the slow excision of Algeria from the EEC, starting in 1962 and ending in 1976, jeopardized the livelihoods of non-French Europeans who now had to prove that they had ever worked outside of their own home borders, but within Europe, and thus were eligible for the protections the EEC guaranteed to migrant laborers. The opening made by Algeria in the Treaty of Rome and the thorny question of how integrated Europe related to the remaining dependent overseas holdings and, in the case of France, French Overseas Departments, lingered. The same issues the EEC debated about Algeria would come to the fore in a newer set of debates in the years, even decades, to come.

Cases argued before the ECJ forced European officials to face difficult questions about what position Algeria had ever held in relationship to the EEC. In their careful attempts to answer that question, the reality of Algeria's special status, and in particular what that meant for non-French Europeans after independence, became impossible to deny. The ECJ was, by the 1970s, a long-established institution within Europe's integration scheme, having been founded alongside the ECSC by the Treaty of Paris. The ECJ's purpose was to ensure that member states followed and applied laws uniformly. As such, the judges' decisions, typically informed by the opinion of an impartial advocate-general, led to recommendations to be handed back to a national court in order for the latter to apply EEC law. When they weighed in on the subject of Algeria, this typically involved reminding the member states that until recently, they had all agreed that Algeria was a part of France.

Gerd Fiege's, Ulrich Horst's, and Auguste Hirardin's careers reflected the labor mobility of the postwar era. Fiege lived in Algeria from 1951 to 1963. Horst, a German scientist employed by S. N. Repal (National Society for Petroleum Research and Exploitation in Algeria), lived there from July 1960 until the end of June 1962, when he took part in the settler migration to metropolitan France.[83] He worked for the company for another month. Hirardin, a Belgian citizen, worked in continental France on and off from 1930 until his retirement in 1972, and from January 1957 to March 1961 in Algeria. The ECJ records leave Fiege's and Hirardin's professions unspecified. Although Fiege, Horst, and Hirardin almost certainly never met, their collective experience in Algeria and, more significantly, what came after, forced European lawmakers to reckon with the long-term implications of Algeria's former legal status and relationship to the EEC. Each man pursued a labor complaint up to the ECJ in the 1970s. Together, the three trials—the "Algerian cases," as they came to be known—set a precedent for how European law must be interpreted vis-à-vis an Algeria now in its second decade of independence and how that would impact people who moved between Algeria and continental Europe decades earlier. In the realms of labor and law, Article 227 of the Treaty of Rome had a very long life.

After Algeria's independence, the ECJ saw cases arise because of questions of Algeria's relationship with the EEC. In 1963, the Hamburg-based firm C. Mackprang ran afoul of European law when it failed to acquire a certificate showing the EEC origin of wheat bran it imported from Algeria. Algerian authorities refused to provide the certificate, countering with the seemingly unimpeachable—but as we have seen, malleable—assertion that since independence, Algeria was not part of the EEC. Mackprang demanded that the commission "take a special decision enabling and compelling the Member States to grant the benefit of the Community system to goods imported from Algeria during 1963 when sufficient evidence is put forward to show that the product is in fact of Algerian origin." The court heard the case in 1971 and did not view this argument favorably.[84] In contrast, when it encountered questions of the rights of European nationals who had worked in Algeria prior to independence, the court took pains to emphasize Europe's obligation to recognize that EEC rights in Algeria were a legal reality. These decisions demonstrate the aftereffects of Algeria having once being counted as a region of the EEC.

The first of the Algerian cases, Fiege's suit against the Caisse régionale d'assurance maladie of Strasbourg, reached the ECJ in 1973. The French insurance office denied Fiege payments for his years working in Algeria, arguing that he had no right to claim a member state pension for that time. Advocate-General Warner argued that France had to recognize Fiege's claim.[85] Two years later, the court heard Horst's case against the Bundesknappschaft (Federal Mineworkers Association). German courts had similarly rebuffed Horst when he attempted to collect a pension inclusive of his time in Algeria.[86] In both cases, the ECJ recommended that the state courts find in favor of the German men and recognize their work in Algeria as legitimate parts of their European careers.

With *Horst,* the ECJ laid out a timeline of applicability that rewrote the periodization of Algeria's inclusion in the EEC. The first and most obvious period was prior to June 30, 1962; all member states would be required to recognize any labor done during those insurance periods (this pertained to social security payouts) as being under French legislation. The second period, July 1, 1962 to January 18, 1965, demanded the same treatment because Algeria still figured on the list for Regulation 3 of the Council of the EEC, regarding social security for migrant workers. Although then eliminated from this list, under transitional rules those rights remained in place from January 19 to July 31, 1965. Under these regulations, European workers employed in Algeria until the middle of 1965, three full years after Algeria's independence, still stood to benefit from a member state social security regime.[87]

In 1976, one year after the *Horst* ruling, Nancy's regional director of social security brought Hirardin before the ECJ. The French social security office argued that Hirardin did not merit an old-age pension inclusive of his Algerian working years because the contribution periods completed in Algeria before July 1, 1962 were applicable only to French nationals unless Hirardin could prove, in accordance with a September 4, 1962 decree, that he had "shown devotion to France or . . . rendered exceptional service to that country."[88] Italian advocate-general Alberto Trabucchi argued that this was unlawful because it privileged one member state's nationals (French) over another (Belgian). Trabucchi added the caveat that such rights should not apply to someone who began working in Algeria after independence, which would "have consequences which, to put it mildly, would be surprising."[89] Trabucchi tempered Warner's findings in *Horst* by insisting that Algeria's independence terminated member state workers' right to count their North African salaries toward an EEC pension. His recommendation also castigated the French for attempting to apply retroactively a punitive "alien" labor regime for work done prior to Algeria's independence. The court found in Hirardin's favor on "the principle of the equal treatment of laborers," noting that there was "no doubt" that the French social security administration was obligated to compensate labor in Algeria completed before January 19, 1965.[90]

The Algerian cases attest to one of the ways that Algeria's former juridical status within both France and the EEC carried long-term implications for the structuring of European rights regimes. Although French social security offices guaranteed support for former settler colonists, they felt no such obligation to other Europeans; those workers' home states in turn took the opportunity to emphasize that Algeria had never been a part of Europe. The result was a small cohort of people who had to prove that they had, in fact, crossed within the borders of Europe during their careers. In these three cases, European state social security offices attempted to abdicate their financial obligations to Europeans who had labored in French Algeria on the grounds that independent Algeria was not a part of the EEC. Although the ECJ rejected this argument, it is clear that for the administrations of EEC member states, willfully forgetting the very recent past could be a useful and financially appealing tool. The long, twisted road to an EEC-Algeria accord demonstrates continuity from the mid-1950s until the mid-1970s in which Algeria's relationship to Europe was not automatically altered by its newfound independence. In contrast, the ECJ cases are examples of attempts to claim that those relations had already been broken.

The court insisted that the EEC accept that Algeria had been within the EEC until July 1962 and that some rights lingered for a further three years. It also enforced a type of break, as in Trabucchi's insistence that European rights should not extend to new European arrivals after Algeria's independence. The Algerian cases reinforce the reality that Europe's borders were not fixed at the founding of the EEC. The fact that these laborers' rights were debated years after highlights the degree to which states, firms, and individuals could make use of that ambiguity after 1962. The cases became key precedent for future rulings related to the limits of European territory or rights precisely because they raised thorny issues of the sharing of responsibility toward citizens from other member states and demanded acknowledgment of transnational labor migration.

That the human impact of Algeria's years in the EEC proved the hardest puzzle to unravel speaks to the unintended legacy of Article 227 and France's attempts to sustain its empire through European integration. It also demonstrates the complexity of the emergence of a new category of laborer: the trans-European migrant. What kinds of rights did European law afford a German national who had worked in metropolitan France and French Algeria? How much protection was any European laborer owed by integrated Europe's institutions or its member states' governments? These were new questions and Algeria's EEC status pushed them to the fore. They have remained there ever since. As recently as

2013, the European Union's European Economic and Social Committee cited *Fiege* and *Hirardin* as precedent mandating the equal treatment of member state workers "beyond the EU's borders."[91]

Formerly European Migrants

There is at least one example of an Algerian worker bringing his case to the ECJ. Tayeb Belbouab, born in 1924, worked in continental French coal mines for nearly thirteen years before moving to West Germany in 1960 "to avoid possible political difficulties." While living in the Federal Republic, Belbouab became an Algerian national as a result of independence, working in German mines until he became eligible for an old-age pension in 1974. The German administration rejected his pension application on the grounds that he was not a European national. This would mean he could not claim his years in France to be paid by the German administration through EEC provisions for member state reciprocity. Italian advocate-general Francesco Capotorti cited *Horst* and argued in favor of Belbouab in 1978, contending that it would be "illogical and in substance discriminatory" were a worker "who has lost French nationality and become Algerian to be placed, with regard to the application of Community social security provisions, in a less favorable position than those whose ties with the French state were looser as was the case for nationals of the French Union."[92] The ECJ ruled that because Belbouab was a French national when he worked in France, he was entitled to the full pension he demanded in West Germany.[93] Belbouab's success coincided with France and West Germany's attempts to curtail Algerian immigration, which culminated in labor recruitment freezes in 1974 and

1973, respectively.[94] Thus, although Belbouab found satisfaction, many of his fellow citizens did not.

At the diplomatic level, Algeria's full extraction from the EEC proved long and uneven. At a human level, exclusion from Europe began well before 1976, 1965, or even 1962. When the Algerian government negotiated with the EEC member states, the latter saw a means of maintaining economic hierarchies. But the former maintained that their state had legal recourse to claim European benefits, forcing the Six to grapple with the elasticity of the European borders they now hoped would keep Algerians out. The 1976 accord stripped Algeria of any semblance of privilege in Europe. For citizens of Algeria, the denial of European rights was nothing new. The very same imperial assumptions that allowed the French to convince their European partners to include French Algeria in the EEC also prevented EEC officials from ever accepting Algerian people as a part of Europe. On the face of it, Algeria's years in the EEC may appear to have existed only on paper, a set of promises for economic and social relations that never came to fruition. But the human impact of Article 227, as these cases demonstrate, could be profound. After years of claiming that Algeria was French and was in the EEC, the erasure of that contention forced people who had traversed these now-hardened borders to prove that they had never left Europe. At the same time, the ECJ's support of their claims shows that the erasure would never be complete. Algeria's years in the EEC created a lasting impact on Europe itself.

Why did French officials attempt to hold on for so long? It is clear that there were commonsense business motivations for maintaining close ties. The remnants of the wine industry and the fear that another state's businesses would enjoy the benefits of establishing factories there led the French to grip tightly to a bond that was crumbling in their hands. Beyond sheer economic determinism, it took time to unlearn the belief that Algeria was French. Pride for—or a desperate grasping at—the vestiges of French prestige suggest that bureaucrats struggled to understand a France that was not defined by its presence overseas. At the same time, French and EEC disgust (or feigned disgust) at the long life of Portuguese colonialism offered an outlet for reframing themselves as forward-moving and suggesting that colonialism was a relic of a bygone era.[95] This smugness belies the plodding, even excruciating, nature of Algeria's extraction from Europe.

The EEC became a Europe of nation-states slowly and haltingly. That this transition proved incomplete until at least 1976—sixteen years after the Year of Africa and fourteen years after Algeria's independence—demonstrates how long-lasting and deeply ingrained assumptions about Europe's, and especially France's, role in former colonial holdings would be. When Bouteflika returned to Algeria in May 1974 following a trip to Cairo, he addressed the EEC via a press conference. Bouteflika foregrounded the importance for the EEC to collaborate with the Arab world, as he termed it, in part because this would lead to a more equitable future. He harkened back to the early days of the EEC, declaring, "Because I speak in the name of Algeria, it should be recalled that France signed the Treaty of Rome considering Algeria to be an integrated part of France and, by consequence, legally and historically we Algerians would have had the same rights as any other member of the European Community."[96] Bouteflika's use of the past conditional tense (*nous aurions eu*) underscores the futures never realized during the nearly two decades between the signing of the Treaty of Rome and the signing of the EEC-Algeria accord. For the EEC, those rights proved easy to curtail, despite the occasional setback in the courts. After over a century of declaring Algeria French and years of claiming it as European, the French had finally abandoned the notion of Algeria as an integrated part of their metropole and turned away from Algérie européenne.

Conclusion

"We're from Europe—Let Us In!"

In mid-June 2016, the conservative *Daily Mail* published a front-page photo of a group of Iraqi and Kuwaiti people—including small children—among boxes in the back of a truck. The headline blared, "As politicians squabble over border controls, yet another lorry load of migrants arrives in UK declaring . . . We're from Europe—let us in!"[1] This inflammatory front page, appearing just one week before Britons went to the polls to decide whether the United Kingdom (UK) should remain in the European Union (EU), stoked one of Brexit supporters' greatest fears: the arrival of people who, thanks to their movement within the EU, could claim the right to live in the UK. This book has detailed an earlier and lesser known history of Europe's contraction: Algeria's slow departure from the European Economic Community (EEC). As in the case of Algeria, in Brexit debates the fear of who might be able to claim European rights arose, now compounded by a deep Euroscepticism.

Headlines in Britain's right-wing press maintained their momentum throughout the referendum process. On June 23, the day

Fig. C.1   *Daily Mail*, June 16, 2016. dmg media licensing

of the vote, the *Sun* ran a front-page headline screaming "Independence Day" and promising readers, "You can free UK from clutches [*sic*] of the EU today." The next day, in an early print edition, the *Daily Mail*'s jubilant front page declared "We're Out!"[2] Brexit had won. To Brexit supporters, the stakes of the Leave campaign were clear: the restoration of sovereignty, as the *Sun*'s headline trumpeted, and the liberation of Britain from the dangers of its continental obligations. This historic vote did not lead to a swift exit, however, but rather to years of negotiations revealing the challenges of leaving a supranational organization, given the intertwined nature of trade, labor circulation, and more. As for the Iraqi and Kuwaiti individuals whose photo appeared a week prior, footage soon proved that they had never claimed to be from Europe, forcing the *Daily Mail* to print a correction.[3]

The EU's recent history features important flashpoints of immigration anxiety, reflecting the ongoing ramifications of European notions of outsiderness. Such anxiety underlines the long history of European leaders attempting to draw borders and the equally long history of local stakeholders exercising their own agency in border-making processes.[4] Beginning in the 2010s, the rise in asylum seekers and other migrants from Syria, Afghanistan, and elsewhere coming to the EU, known in the press as the "migrant crisis," brought into stark relief the complexities of the EU's borders. As European studies scholar Jan Ifversen wrote, "People escaping across the Mediterranean are questioning the borders of Europe and dramatically exposing past entanglements again."[5] Like the German, Belgian, and Algerian workers who traveled within European borders before July 1962 and demanded commensurate rights after, these new arrivals forced European politicians to grapple with the meaning of the EU's borders.

Wrestling with such questions invited new waves of political extremism in Europe, with fringe and mainstream political parties in France, Britain, and elsewhere flourishing by sowing panic about an onslaught of unassimilable, needy foreigners pounding at the gates and posing a grave danger to citizens' material and cultural well-being.[6] Headlines suggesting that a toddler in jaunty red socks was menacing emblematized this historical moment in which the arrival of people characterized as "other" could be cast as an existential threat. That the child's ancestors were born in Iraq or Kuwait, places where British imperial administrators had long attempted to exert particular versions of borders, reminds us of the range of ways in which European administrators have attempted to exercise power through delineations of space.

Conversely, overseas Europe also forms an important part of the EU's efforts to keep out unwanted populations. Mayotte, a French overseas department in the Comoros Archipelago in the Indian Ocean, although less mediatized than the Italian island of Lampedusa, is similarly surveilled as a hub of clandestine migration and its attendant danger and tragedy.[7] Mayotte, French Guiana, Guadeloupe, and Réunion all house at least one migrant detention facility, operating as the outer barrier, and in some cases the first line of defense, against the migration maligned by European politicians and their constituents.[8] That greater France—and the peripheries of the EU—are pivotal in the alleged protection of Europe highlights the ambivalence of a Europe dependent on and fearful of the lands and peoples beyond the continent.[9] Since 1995, the French have implemented a visa in Mayotte drawing legal differentiation between those Comorians who have the right to live in Mayotte and those who do not. The Moroni (Grande Comore)-born writer Soeuf Elbadawi satirized the visa, which transformed Comorians into "'illegal migrants' on the 'Land of the Ancestors,'" inspiring him to rewrite France's national anthem, "La Marseillaise":

> Come on! Drowned children of brotherhood
> The day of mourning has arrived
> On us blows a wind of tyranny
> Bloody sharks stand ready[10]

Disentangling the Seventh Member State

Although it took Brexit to bring EU affairs to the attention of many people living both in and outside of the EU's limits, in reality the reports of Brexit's unprecedented nature were overstated. Algeria's history with and within integrated Europe shows that leaving Europe has a precedent. Accounting for the years after the Six agreed to name Algeria as a constitutive part of integrated Europe undermines contemporary understandings of Europe's "natural" geopolitical limits. The EU's history cannot and must not be told without a discussion of the place of empire in its forerunners' foundational treaties and institutions. For thirty years following the end of World War II, integrating Europe stood as a paramount concern to French officials. So too did maintaining the empire. Algeria, ultimately named in the Treaty of Rome and therefore juridically integrated into the EEC, held the greatest stakes for these officials. French administrators went so far as to antagonize, even alienate, their European partners in order to secure development funds and a European-wide agreement naming Algeria as a part of France. Both the funds and the agreement, in their own ways, would stave off the growing might of anti-imperial nationalists fighting for Algeria's independence. This French diplomatic tactic resulted in a European geography markedly different from what would come to be understood as the natural expanse for integrated European institutions by the time the twelve members of the European Communities signed the Maastricht Treaty in 1992.

At first glance, then, this appears to be a history of opening and possibility, with Algerian people poised to enjoy the benefits not just of French but also European citizenship. From the outset, this idea received little support from Paris, to say nothing of the opposition from Brussels. EEC officials certainly could envision Algerian land as a part of Europe; Algerian people complicated this picture. As much as Algeria's links to the EEC suggest a history of what could have been, ultimately this is a chronicle of why that did not come to pass. French and European assumptions about race and religion drove EEC officials to ignore Algeria's status as a potential seventh member state. These assumptions closed off the possibilities of an expansive, egalitarian Europe, even as they inadvertently invited the independent Algerian government to make demands on the EEC for funding, social security rights, and labor circulation for over a decade to come.

The inclusion of Algeria in the Treaty of Rome through Article 227 made this newly sovereign state's disentanglement from Europe a challenging and lengthy affair. For five years while still holding French departmental status and for fourteen years following its independence, Algeria was a part of the EEC, or at least, it was not *not* part of the EEC. This remarkable reality signals that decolonization cannot be reduced to one celebratory day or a single document. Similarly, the intricate dealings between the Six also suggest that Algeria's exclusion from European status was an ongoing act.[11] Algeria only departed from Europe—and with it, transformed its relationship to France—slowly and unevenly over the course of more than a decade. Algerians may have celebrated their independence in July 1962, but their representatives fought to keep up close ties with the EEC. These officials understood the potential uses of a European connection to secure economic benefits and support migrant workers. Of course, this was not the first time that bureaucrats had leveraged Algeria's place in Europe to forward a national agenda. French civil servants had done precisely the same thing beginning in the mid-1950s as they grasped at a diplomatic weapon to stave off Algerian nationalism.

After Algeria's independence, the composition of Algeria's population now made its inclusion in Europe appear to be an "absurdity," as one official dubbed it, yet officials in Europe and Algeria on the whole saw little reason for pursuing a swift break.[12] Despite the ongoing economic and labor ties between the Six and Algeria, the mythology of Algeria's decolonization, invented in the aftermath of independence, allowed French officials to reframe Algerians as purely foreign and definitively non-French.[13] The coding of Algerians as racially "other" was a process that began before European integration and continued afterward. Algeria's naming in the Treaty of Rome did not inspire a rewriting of racial assumptions in the eyes of the Six's leaders. However, it did introduce the legal reality that Algerian Muslims were owed the same rights as Europeans, suggesting that integrated Europe's citizenship regime could be opened to people from formerly colonized spaces who, under national law, had long been denied equality. Algeria's 1976 treaty with the EEC erased this possibility, yet the human impact of its inclusion resonated for decades to come.

The border of integrated Europe once crossed Algeria, but it no longer does. These new borders cannot be used to keep all North Africans out, given their multigenerational presence in continental France. But when French politicians across the political spectrum grouse about the presence of North African migrants and their children and grandchildren diluting supposedly real French values, they erase the long history of French borders that encompassed the Maghreb, large swaths of the African continent, and territories across the globe. By gatekeeping identity, they attempt to draw fresh lines distinguishing between who counts as French and who is deemed unassimilable.

As I was working on this book in late summer 2020, news from France made the erasure of Algeria's European years more salient. When the trial of the surviving alleged perpetrators of the January 2015 murders of Charlie Hebdo cartoonists and journalists, Hyper Cacher shoppers, and a Montrouge police officer began in September, the same language that dominated the aftermath of those events and the November 2015 attacks reemerged. Politicians and reporters launched polemics about the supremacy of *laïcité,* or secularism, above all other republican values and warned of the dangers of communitarianism, roughly meaning ethnoreligious groups living in and identifying with their enclave.[14] The othering of people of color and Muslims in France, through the perpetual demand that they integrate to a circumscribed model of French republican citizenship, serves as a constant effort to reinforce "real" Frenchness in appearance, background, and daily lived experience and behavior. Algeria's years in the EEC add another layer to this complex history, as an acknowledgment of this reality would force European officials to accept a version of history inclusive of people beyond the borders of what they now consider Europe.

The term *Fortress Europe*—once used by Nazi Germany to denote its defense tactics—is now employed to signify an EU girding itself against the arrival of populations deemed impossible to acculturate or provide for.[15] This book has asked where "Europe" was or may be located. Thanks to French machinations, the EEC stretched into the African continent, comprising land and possibly peoples who had long been denied rights as French citizens, let alone as Europeans. Was Algeria ever actually the seventh member state of the European Economic Community? Its bygone status as a constitutive part of integrated Europe suggests a past future for Europe that could have been more expansive than what we know today. An account of French officials' political imaginaries signals why those possibilities were foreclosed. Nevertheless, Algeria's European years invite us to imagine a world where communities of color and Muslim people living across Europe are not treated as racialized outsiders in need of education to "become" European. By birthright, they may have been European all along.

Notes

Introduction

1. Assemblée Nationale, *Journal officiel, Débats parlementaires* 98, August 19, 1947 session, 4408–4409.
2. Jean-Pierre Peyroulou, *Guelma, 1945: Une subversion française dans l'Algérie coloniale* (Paris: La Découverte, 2009), 197–202; Joshua Cole, "Massacres and Their Historians: Recent Histories of State Violence in France and Algeria in the Twentieth Century," *French Politics, Culture & Society* 28, no. 1 (2010): 111–113.
3. Manfred Halpern, "The Algerian Uprising of 1945," *Middle East Journal* 2, no. 2 (April 1948): 191–202.
4. Alan S. Milward with the assistance of George Brennan and Federico Romero, *The European Rescue of the Nation-State,* 2nd ed. (London: Routledge, 2000). Gary Wilder calls the "French imperial nation-state" an "internally contradictory artifact of colonial modernity that was simultaneously . . . Franco-African and Afro-French, national and transnational." Gary Wilder, *The French Imperial Nation-State: Negritude and Colonial Humanism between the Two World Wars* (Chicago: University of Chicago Press, 2005), 21–22.
5. Choosing terminology for Algeria's populations is challenging. All terms I use are at best imperfect. I use "settler" to demarcate the

population of European origin in Algeria, at points subsuming Algeria's Jewish population under this term because of their French citizenship status. I use "Algerian" and "Muslim" to mean individuals the French once categorized as *indigène* (a term for Indigenous people that can be understood as a pejorative) or *musulman* (Muslim), while in reality this population represented a diverse mix of Berber ethnic groups and Arab peoples.

6. Laure Blévis, "La citoyenneté française au miroir de la colonisation: Étude des demandes de naturalisation des 'sujets français' en Algérie coloniale," *Genèses* 53, no. 4 (2003): 25–47; Naomi Davidson, *Only Muslim: Embodying Islam in Twentieth-Century France* (Ithaca, NY: Cornell University Press, 2012).

7. Jean-Jacques Jordi, *1962: L'arrivée des Pieds-Noirs* (Paris: Éditions Autrement, 1995); Joëlle Hureau, *La mémoire des pieds-noirs de 1830 à nos jours* (Paris: Olivier Orban, 1987); Eric Savarese, *L'invention des pieds-noirs* (Paris: Séguier, 2002); Samuel Kalman, *French Colonial Fascism: The Extreme Right in Algeria, 1919–1939* (London: Palgrave Macmillan, 2013).

8. Mark Mazower, "An International Civilization? Empire, Internationalism and the Crisis of the Mid-Twentieth Century," *International Affairs* 82, no. 3 (2006): 561.

9. Herrick Chapman, *France's Long Reconstruction: In Search of the Modern Republic* (Cambridge, MA: Harvard University Press, 2018), 262–263. On migration history, see Alexis Spire, *Étrangers à la carte: L'administration de l'immigration en France, 1945–1975* (Paris: Grasset, 2005); Vincent Viet, *La France immigrée: Construction d'une politique, 1914–1997* (Paris: Fayard, 1998); Patrick Weil, *How to Be French: Nationality in the Making since 1789,* trans. Catherine Porter (Durham, NC: Duke University Press, 2008); Amelia H. Lyons, *The Civilizing Mission in the Metropole: Algerian Families and the French Welfare State during Decolonization* (Stanford, CA: Stanford University Press, 2013); Neil MacMaster, *Colonial Migrants and Racism: Algerians in France, 1900–1962* (New York: St. Martin's, 1997); Clifford Rosenberg, *Policing Paris: The Origins of Modern Immigration Control between the Wars* (Ithaca, NY: Cornell University Press, 2006).

10. Frederick Cooper, *Citizenship between Empire and Nation: Remaking France and French Africa, 1945–1960* (Princeton, NJ: Princeton University Press, 2014); Séverine Awenengo Dalberto, "La première carte d'identité d'Afrique occidentale française (1946–1960): Identifier et s'identifier au Sénégal au temps de la citoyenneté impériale," *Annales: Histoire, sciences sociales* 75, no. 1 (2020): 113–151.

11. On borders, see Hélène Blais, *Mirages de la carte: L'invention de l'Algérie coloniale, XIXe–XXe siècle* (Paris: Fayard, 2014); Adrian Little, "The Complex Temporality of Borders: Contingency and Normativity," *European Journal of Political Theory* 14, no. 4 (2015): 429–447; Stuart Elden, *The Birth of Territory* (Chicago: University of Chicago Press, 2013), 322–330; Jordan Branch, *The Cartographic State: Maps, Territory and the Origins of Sovereignty* (Cambridge: Cambridge University Press, 2014); Peter Sahlins, *Boundaries: The Making of France and Spain in the Pyrenees* (Berkeley: University of California Press, 1989).

12. Mathilde von Bülow, "The Telefunken Affair and the Internationalisation of the Algerian War, 1957–59," *Journal of Strategic Studies* 28, no. 4 (2005): 703–729; Mathilde von Bülow, "Franco-German Intelligence Cooperation and the Internationalization of Algeria's War of Independence (1954–62)," *Intelligence and National Security* 28, no. 3 (2013): 397–419.

13. Matthew Connelly, *A Diplomatic Revolution: Algeria's Fight for Independence and the Origins of the Post–Cold War Era* (New York: Oxford University Press, 2002).

14. Phillip C. Naylor, *France and Algeria: A History of Decolonization and Transformation* (Gainesville: University Press of Florida, 2000).

15. On race and religion in the construction of Europe, see Emily Marker, *Black France, White Europe: Youth, Race, and Belonging in the Postwar Era* (Ithaca, NY: Cornell University Press, forthcoming).

16. Yves Montarsolo, *L'Eurafrique: Contrepoint de l'idée d'Europe: Le cas français de la fin de la deuxième guerre mondiale aux négociations des Traités de Rome* (Aix-en-Provence: Publications de l'Université de Provence, 2010), 261.

17. Florence Renucci, "Le rôle des anonymes? L'inspectrice générale du travail Lucrèce Guelfi et 'ses hommes' face à la réforme du droit du

travail en Afrique," presented at La réception du droit du travail par les milieux professionnels et intellectuels (XIXe–XXe siècles) colloquium, November 2015, Université de Bourgogne, Dijon, https://lir3s.u-bourgogne.fr/phonotheque/c-1049.

18. Ann Laura Stoler, *Along the Archival Grain: Epistemic Anxieties and Colonial Common Sense* (Princeton, NJ: Princeton University Press, 2010).

19. Véronique Dimier, *The Invention of a Development Aid Bureaucracy: Recycling Empire* (London: Palgrave Macmillan, 2014).

20. René Girault, "La France entre l'Europe et l'Afrique," in *The Relaunching of Europe and the Treaties of Rome: Actes du colloque de Rome 25–28 Mars 1987,* ed. Enrico Serra (Brussels: Bruylant, 1989), 352.

21. Cited in Dimier, *Invention,* 47–48.

22. Mark Mazower, *No Enchanted Palace: The End of Empire and the Ideological Origins of the United Nations* (Princeton, NJ: Princeton University Press, 2009).

23. René Girault, *Être historien des relations internationales* (Paris: Publications de la Sorbonne, 1998), 357.

24. Stanley Hoffmann, "Obstinate or Obsolete? The Fate of the Nation-State and the Case of Western Europe," in *Debates on European Integration: A Reader,* ed. Mette Eilstrup-Sangiovanni (London: Palgrave Macmillan, 2006), 143.

25. Kiran Klaus Patel, "Provincialising European Union: Co-operation and Integration in Europe in a Historical Perspective," *Contemporary European History* 22, no. 4 (2013): 649–673.

26. CAOM 81 F 2256: Délégation générale du Gouvernement en Algérie, commerce intérieur et extérieur, "Association de la Turquie à la Communauté économique européenne," April 9, 1960; CAEF B 0062126 (formerly B 25343): Ministère de l'économie et des finances, Direction des finances extérieures, Comptes-rendus de réunions des conseillers financiers français à Paris, May 18, 1960; Megan Brown, "Drawing Algeria into Europe: Shifting French Policy and the Treaty of Rome (1951–1964)," *Modern & Contemporary France* 25, no. 2 (2017): 202.

27. Lauren Stokes, *Fear of the Family: Guest Workers and Family Migration in the Federal Republic of Germany* (Oxford: Oxford University Press, forthcoming).

28. Guia Migani, "La CEE ou la France, l'impossible choix de Sylvanus Olympio, président du Togo," *Matériaux pour l'histoire de notre temps* 77 (2005): 27.

29. Todd Shepard, "À l'heure des 'grands ensembles' et de la guerre d'Algérie: L''état-nation' en question," trans. Jennifer Dybmann, *Monde(s): Histoire, espaces, relations* 1 (2012): 113–134; Jeffrey James Byrne, *Mecca of Revolution: Algeria, Decolonization and the Third World Order* (New York: Oxford University Press, 2016).

30. Byrne, *Mecca of Revolution;* Matthew Connelly, "Taking Off the Cold War Lens: Visions of North-South Conflict during the Algerian War for Independence," *American Historical Review* 105, no. 3 (2000): 739–769.

31. Patrick Pasture, "The EC / EU between the Art of Forgetting and the Palimpsest of Empire," *European Review* 26, no. 3 (2018): 1–37; Benjamin Stora, *La gangrène et l'oubli: La mémoire de la guerre d'Algérie* (Paris: La Découverte, 2005).

32. Greenland's exit in the 1980s falls outside the scope of this book. Unlike Algeria, Greenland's citizens were given the option to choose whether to leave or not. Greenland was then afforded what is now called Overseas Countries and Territories status. Kiran Klaus Patel, *Project Europe: A History* (Cambridge: Cambridge University Press, 2020), 3, 209–220.

33. Julia Nordblad, "The Un-European Idea: Vichy and Eurafrica in the Historiography of Europeanism," *European Legacy: Toward New Paradigms* 19, no. 6 (2014): 711–729.

34. One of the most thorough recent studies of Eurafrica, by Peo Hansen and Stefan Jonsson, offers a brief overview, focused on negotiations for the Treaty of Rome. Peo Hansen and Stefan Jonsson, *Eurafrica: The Untold History of European Integration and Colonialism* (London: Bloomsbury, 2014), 226–234. On Eurafrica and former colonies' (though rarely Algeria's) relationship to integrated

Europe, see Dimier, *Invention;* Karis Muller, "Reconfigurer
l'Eurafrique," *Matériaux pour l'histoire de notre temps, Europe et Afrique
au tournant des indépendances* 77 (2005): 52–60; Giuliano Garavini,
*After Empires: European Integration, Decolonization, and the Challenge
from the Global South, 1957–1986* (Oxford: Oxford University Press,
2012); Montarsolo, *L'Eurafrique;* Marie-Thérèse Bitsch and Gérard
Bossuat, eds., *L'Europe unie et l'Afrique: De l'idée d'Eurafrique à la
Convention de Lomé I: Actes du colloque international de Paris, 1er et 2
avril 2004* (Brussels: Bruylant, 2005); Adekeye Adebajo and Kaye
Whiteman, eds., *The EU and Africa: From Eurafrique to Afro-Europa*
(New York: Columbia University Press, 2012); Papa Dramé and
Samir Saul, "Le projet d'Eurafrique en France (1946–1960): Quête
de puissance ou atavisme colonial?" *Guerres mondiales et conflits
contemporains* 216, no. 4 (2004): 95–114; Louis Sicking, "A Colonial
Echo: France and the Colonial Dimension of the European
Economic Community," *French Colonial History* 5 (2005): 207–228;
Martin Rempe, "Decolonization by Europeanization? The Early
EEC and the Transformation of French-African Relations," *KFG
Working Paper Series* 27 (May 2011): 3–20. Brian Shaev, although
demonstrating the Section française de l'Internationale ouvrière's
simultaneous interest in European internationalism and the Algerian
crisis, still does not give full weight to the EEC treaty, arguing that
it "avoided a direct entanglement in the Algerian War." Brian Shaev,
"The Algerian War, European Integration, and the Decolonization
of French Socialism," *French Historical Studies* 41, no. 1 (2018): 82.

35. Hélène B. Ducros, "Beyond Eurafrica: Encounters in a Globalized
World," *EuropeNow,* published online March 1, 2018, https://www
.europenowjournal.org/2018/02/28/introduction-2/.

36. Shepard, "A l'heure des 'grands ensembles,'" 116.

37. Muriam Haleh Davis, *Markets of Civilization: Islam and Racial Capitalism
in Algeria* (Durham, NC: Duke University Press, forthcoming); Joseph
Bohling, *The Sober Revolution: Appellation Wine and the Transformation of
France* (Ithaca, NY: Cornell University Press, 2018). On trans-Saharan
scholarship, see Ralph A. Austen, *Trans-Saharan Africa in World History*
(Oxford: Oxford University Press, 2010).

38. Cited in Peo Hansen and Stefan Jonsson, "A Statue to Nasser? Eurafrica, the Colonial Roots of European Integration, and the 2012 Nobel Peace Prize," *Mediterranean Quarterly* 24, no. 4 (2013): 6.

39. Hugues Tertrais, "Le patronat français et la guerre d'Indochine," in *L'esprit économique impérial (1830–1970): Groupes de pression et réseaux du patronat colonial en France et dans l'empire,* ed. Hubert Bonin, Catherine Hodeir, and Jean-François Klein (Paris: Publications de la Société française d'histoire d'outre-mer, 2008), 192.

40. Dimier, *Invention;* Garavini, *After Empires;* Guia Migani, *La France et l'Afrique sub-saharienne, 1957–1963: Histoire d'une décolonisation entre idéaux eurafricains et politique de puissance* (Brussels: Peter Lang, 2008); Karis Muller, "Iconographie de l'Eurafrique," in *L'Europe unie et l'Afrique,* 9–33; Karis Muller, "Shadows of Empire in the European Union," *The European Legacy* 6, no. 4 (2001): 439–451; Karis Muller, "'Concentric Circles' at the Periphery of the European Union," *Australian Journal of Politics and History* 46, no. 3 (2000): 322–335.

41. Cooper, *Citizenship between Empire and Nation.*

42. Gary Wilder, *Freedom Time: Negritude, Decolonization, and the Future of the World* (Durham, NC: Duke University Press, 2015).

43. Wilder, *Freedom Time;* Thomas Yarrow, "Remains of the Future: Rethinking the Space and Time of Ruination through the Volta Resettlement Project, Ghana," *Cultural Anthropology* 32, no. 4 (2017): 566–591.

44. Connelly, *Diplomatic Revolution,* 133–135.

45. Jessica Lynne Pearson, *The Colonial Politics of Global Health: France and the United Nations in Postwar Africa* (Cambridge, MA: Harvard University Press, 2018). See also Jennifer Johnson, *The Battle of Algeria: Sovereignty, Health Care, and Humanitarianism* (Philadelphia: University of Pennsylvania Press, 2016).

46. Muriam Haleh Davis, "'The Transformation of Man' in French Algeria: Economic Planning and the Postwar Social Sciences, 1958–62," *Journal of Contemporary History* 52, no. 1 (2017): 74.

47. Jacques Marseille, *Empire colonial et capitalisme français: Histoire d'un divorce* (Paris: Albin Michel, 1984); Daniel Lefeuvre, *Chère Algérie: La France et sa colonie, 1930–1962* (Paris: Flammarion, 2005).

48. Samir Saul, *Intérêts économiques français et décolonisation de l'Afrique du Nord (1945–1962)* (Geneva: Librairie Droz, 2016), 713–721.

49. Elise Huillery, "The Black Man's Burden: The Cost of Colonization of French West Africa," *Journal of Economic History* 74, no. 1 (2014): 1–38; Denis Cogneau, Yannick Dupraz, and Sandrine Mesplé-Somps, "Fiscal Capacity and Dualism in Colonial States: The French Empire 1830–1962," Paris School of Economics Working Paper no. 2018–27 (2019), halshs-01818700v3; Marlous van Waijenburg, "Financing the African Colonial State: The Revenue Imperative and Forced Labor," *Journal of Economic History* 78, no. 1 (2018): 40–80.

50. Irwin M. Wall, *France, the United States, and the Algerian War* (Chicago: University of Chicago Press, 2001), 6.

51. Bitsch and Bossuat, *L'Europe unie et l'Afrique;* Adebajo and Whiteman, *The EU and Africa;* Garavini, *After Empires;* Lilith Mahmud, "#Eurostop: Toward a Feminist Decolonial Critical Theory of Europe," in *North Africa and the Making of Europe: Governance, Institutions and Culture,* ed. Muriam Haleh Davis and Thomas Serres (London: Bloomsbury Academic, 2018), 266.

52. Bitsch, "Introduction," in *L'Europe unie et l'Afrique,* 5.

53. For a reevaluation of the *trente glorieuses,* see Rémy Pawin, "Retour sur les 'Trente Glorieuses' et la périodisation du second XXe siècle," *Revue d'histoire moderne et contemporaine* 60–61, no. 1 (2013): 155–175; Céline Pessis, Sezin Topçu, and Christophe Bonneuil, eds., *Une autre histoire des 'Trente Glorieuses': Modernisation, contestations et pollutions dans la France d'après-guerre* (Paris: La Découverte, 2013); Chapman, *France's Long Reconstruction,* 16.

54. Although in this hypothetical the laborer is a man, in reality women represented an important population of migrant laborers in Europe. Stokes, *Fear of the Family.*

1. Eurafrican Dreams, Imperial Realities

1. Conseil de la République, *Journal officiel, Débats parlementaires* 107, August 29, 1947 session, 1922.

2. Peo Hansen and Stefan Jonsson's work on Eurafrica showcases the intertwined relationship of federalism and imperialism. Peo Hansen and Stefan Jonsson, *Eurafrica: The Untold History of European Integration and Colonialism* (London: Bloomsbury, 2014).

3. Edward Ousselin, "Victor Hugo's European Utopia," *Nineteenth-Century French Studies* 34, nos. 1 and 2 (2005–2006): 40–41; Edward Ousselin, *The Invention of Europe in French Literature and Film* (London: Palgrave Macmillan, 2009), 64–68; Maurice Agulhon, "Victor Hugo et l'Europe: Les États-Unis d'Europe," in *Penser les frontières de l'Europe du XIXe au XXIe siècle,* ed. Gilles Pécout (Paris: Presses Universitaires de France, 2004), 41–51.

4. Europeans had a history of using ruins from classical antiquity to justify colonization. Gavin Murray-Miller, *The Cult of the Modern: Trans-Mediterranean France and the Construction of French Modernity* (Lincoln: University of Nebraska Press, 2017), 43–44; Bonnie Effros, "Museum-building in Nineteenth-Century Algeria: Colonial Narratives in French Collections of Classical Antiquities," *Journal of the History of Collections* 28, no. 2 (2016): 243–259; Patricia Lorcin, "Rome and France in Africa: Recovering Colonial Algeria's Latin Past," *French Historical Studies* 25, no. 2 (Spring 2002): 295–329.

5. Charles-Robert Ageron, "L'idée d'Eurafrique et le débat colonial franco-allemand de l'entre-deux-guerres," *Revue d'histoire moderne et contemporaine* 22, no. 3 (1975): 446–475; Benjamin Thorpe, "Eurafrica: A Pan-European Vehicle for Central European Colonialism (1923–1939)," *European Review* 26, no. 3 (2018): 503–513.

6. Sven Beckert, "American Danger: United States Empire, Eurafrica, and the Territorialization of Industrial Capitalism, 1870–1950," *American Historical Review* 122, no. 4 (2017): 1137–1170.

7. The dream of "perpetual peace" had long roots by then, particularly in Immanuel Kant's treatise of that name. In it, Kant declared, "The law of nations shall be founded on a federation of free states." Immanuel Kant, "Perpetual Peace: A Philosophical Sketch," https://www .mtholyoke.edu/acad/intrel/kant/kant1.htm#fn8. See Dina Gusejnova,

European Elites and Ideas of Empire, 1917–1957 (Cambridge: Cambridge University Press, 2016), 69–97, especially 74–81.

8. Carole Fink, "Minority Rights as an International Question," *Contemporary European History* 9, no. 3 (2000): 385–400; Susan Pedersen, *The Guardians: The League of Nations and the Crisis of Empire* (Oxford: Oxford University Press, 2015); Naoko Shimazu, *Japan, Race and Equality: The Racial Equality Clause of 1919* (London: Routledge, 1998).

9. "World War I casualties," compiled by Nadège Mougel, *Repères,* Centre européen Robert Schuman, http://www.centre-robert -schuman.org/userfiles/files/REPERES%20%E2%80%93%20 module%201-1%20-%20explanatory%20notes%20%E2%80 %93%20World%20War%20I%20casualties%20%E2%80 %93%20EN.pdf.

10. "The 200 Largest Cities in the United States by Population 2021," *World Population Review,* https://worldpopulationreview.com/us -cities; "Europe Cities by Population 2021," *World Population Review,* https://worldpopulationreview.com/continents/cities/europe.

11. AEI, "Aristide Briand, Gustav Stresemann and the Unity of Europe," *European Studies Teachers' Series* 9 (1970): 2, http://aei.pitt.edu /41263/1/A5303.pdf.

12. Gusejnova describes Coudenhove-Kalergi's father as an "Orientalist scholar and diplomat." Gusejnova, *European Elites,* 74–75.

13. Richard Coudenhove-Kalergi, "Afrika," *Paneuropa* 5, no. 2 (1929): 3, cited in Hansen and Jonsson, *Eurafrica,* 28.

14. Richard Coudenhove-Kalergi, "The Pan-European Outlook," *International Affairs* 10, no. 5 (1931): 639.

15. Hansen and Jonsson, *Eurafrica,* 17–69; Ruth Ben-Ghiat, "Modernity Is Just Over There: Colonialism and Italian National Identity," *Interventions* 8, no. 3 (2006): 380–393.

16. Richard Coudenhove-Kalergi, "Europe To-Morrow," *International Affairs* 18, no. 5 (1939): 625.

17. Nedjib Sidi Moussa, "Les Messalistes et la gauche française: Alliances, ruptures et transactions dans l'entre-deux-guerres," *Vingtième siècle: Revue d'histoire* 131 (2016): 72.

18. Manu Goswami, "Imaginary Futures and Colonial Internationalisms," *American Historical Review* 117, no. 5 (2012): 1463–1464.

19. J. Ayo Langley, "Pan-Africanism in Paris, 1924–1936," *Journal of Modern African Studies* 7, no. 1 (April 1969): 69–94; Michael Goebel, "'The Capital of Men without a Country': Migrants and Anticolonialism in Interwar Paris," *American Historical Review* 121, no. 5 (2016): 1444–1467.

20. CVCE: Richard Coudenhove-Kalergi, *Europe Must Unite* (Glarus, Switzerland: Paneuropa Editions, 1939). Published in German in 1938 as *Kommen die Vereinigten Staaten von Europa?* https://www.cvce .eu/en/obj/richard_coudenhove_kalergi_europe_must_unite_1938 -en-87035567-586c-4a12-99e7-6857ee13f146.html. In fact, communist thinkers, including Vladimir Lenin and Karl Kautsky, had plenty to say about a United States of Europe, but in their own terms. Erik van Ree, "Lenin's Conception of Socialism in One Country, 1915–17," *Revolutionary Russia* 23, no. 2 (2010): 159–181; Leon Trotsky, "Disarmament and the United States of Europe," 1945 English-language reprint of piece published in 1929, http://phl .bibliotecaleontrotsky.org/arquivo/themi-eua/II-1929/themi1929 /disarmament_%20unitedstatesofeurope.pdf; Leon Trotsky, "Is the Time Ripe for the Slogan: 'The United States of Europe'?" *Pravda*, June 30, 1923, https://www.marxists.org/archive/trotsky/1923/06 /europe.htm.

21. Stephen G. Gross, "Gold, Debt and the Quest for Monetary Order: The Nazi Campaign to Integrate Europe in 1940," *Contemporary European History* 26, no. 2 (2017): 287–309.

22. Marco Antonsich, "*Geopolitica:* The 'Geographical and Imperial Consciousness' of Fascist Italy," *Geopolitics* 14, no. 2 (2009): 267.

23. Ambracia (present-day Arta, Greece) fell to Rome in 189 BCE. My thanks to Kyle Mahoney for discussing this poem with me. Hans Lamers and Bettina Reitz-Joosse, "Lingua Lictoria: The Latin Literature of Italian Fascism," *Classical Receptions Journal* 8, no. 2 (2016): 237–240.

24. Julia Nordblad, "The Un-European Idea: Vichy and Eurafrica in the Historiography of Europeanism," *European Legacy: Toward New*

Paradigms 19, no. 6 (2014): 711–729. On Mohammed El Maadi's Eurafricanism and his links to the French right-wing Cagoule network, see Joshua Cole, *Lethal Provocation: The Constantine Murders and the Politics of French Algeria* (Ithaca, NY: Cornell University Press, 2019), 202–228, especially 227–228.

25. CAOM 1AFFPOL/2318: Georges Le Brun Kéris, "L'Union européenne," lecture at the Collège libre des sciences sociales et économiques, section d'outre-mer, Paris, 1951–1952 school year.

26. CAOM 1AFFPOL/2314: Léopold Sédar Senghor, "L'intégration des pays d'outre-mer dans la Communauté européenne," *Le Monde,* October 6, 1953.

27. Cited in Todd Shepard, "The Birth of the Hexagon: 1962 and the Erasure of France's Supranational History," in *Vertriebene and Pieds-Noirs in Postwar Germany and France: Comparative Perspectives,* ed. Manuel Borutta and Jan C. Jansen (London: Palgrave Macmillan, 2016), 59.

28. This coincided with the emergence of "integration" policy in France, itself a direct response to the crisis in Algeria. Todd Shepard, "Algeria, France, Mexico, UNESCO: A Transnational History of Anti-Racism and Decolonization, 1932–1962," *Journal of Global History* 6 (2011): 273–297.

29. Emphasis original. William Cohen, ed., *Robert Delavignette on the French Empire: Selected Writings,* trans. Camille Garnier (Chicago: University of Chicago Press, 1977), 88.

30. Eugène Guernier, "La Communauté européenne à la recherche de son âme," *Hommes et mondes* 83 (1953): 349.

31. Official cited in Jessica Lynne Pearson, "Defending Empire at the United Nations: The Politics of International Colonial Oversight in the Era of Decolonisation," *Journal of Imperial and Commonwealth History* 45, no. 3 (2017): 526. See also Jessica Lynne Pearson, *The Colonial Politics of Global Health: France and the United Nations in Postwar Africa* (Cambridge, MA: Harvard University Press, 2018). MAEF-N 378PO 6 581: "Anglo-French Ministerial Discussions on Colonial Policy in Africa," March 31, 1952.

32. Gaston Riou, "L'Eurafrique," *Hommes et mondes* 13, no. 53 (1950): 586. On the French Union and the formation of the United Nations, see Jessica Lynne Pearson, "The French Empire Goes to San Francisco: The Founding of the United Nations and the Limits of Colonial Reform," *French Politics, Culture & Society* 38, no. 2 (2020): 35–55. On Riou's interwar enthusiasm for European integration, see Joseph Bohling, "Colonial or Continental Power? The Debate over Economic Expansion in Interwar France, 1925–1932," *Contemporary European History* 26, no. 2 (2017): 229.

33. Gaston Riou, "Nation, internations," *Hommes et mondes* 14, no. 55 (1951): 278.

34. Laurent Dubois contends that French universalism in fact emerged out of the emancipatory agitation of enslaved peoples in Guadeloupe and elsewhere. Laurent Dubois, *A Colony of Citizens: Revolution and Slave Emancipation in the French Caribbean, 1787–1804* (Chapel Hill: University of North Carolina Press, 2004).

35. European self-confidence in their civilizational standard-bearing was nothing new. Kalypso Nicolaïdis, "Southern Barbarians? A Post-colonial Critique of EUniversalism," in *Echoes of Empire: Memory, Identity and Colonial Legacies,* ed. Kalypso Nicolaïdis, Berny Sèbe, and Gabrielle Maas (London: Tauris, 2015), 293–296.

36. Pierre Fistié, "L'Afrique du Nord et la destinée occidentale," *Le Monde,* February 8, 1951; "Réponse à Monsieur P. Fistié: L'Europe doit faire son mea-culpa," *L'Algérie libre,* February 24, 1951, 1–2.

37. A prolific novelist, Nord's works included *Un bastion de l'empire* (1940), *Le guet-apens d'Alger* (1955), and *Vols de vautours sur le Congo* (1961), although many more of his works took place outside of the French Empire. Pierre Nord, *L'Eurafrique: Notre dernière chance* (Paris: Librairie Arthème Fayard, 1955), 114, 11.

38. Once the independent Algerian government rejected further testing, the French turned their attention to test sites and mineral extraction in the Pacific. See Natacha Gagné and Marie Salaün, "Les chemins de la décolonisation aujourd'hui: Perspectives du Pacifique insulaire," *Critique internationale* 60, no. 3 (2013): 111–132; Christine

Demmer, "Une nouvelle stratégie kanake," *Vacarme* 39, no. 2 (2007): 43–48.

39. "Réponse à Monsieur P. Fistié."

40. Cited in Jean Fremigacci, "Les parlementaires africains face à la construction européenne, 1953–1957," *Matériaux pour l'histoire de notre temps* 7, no. 1 (2005): 16.

41. Fistié, "L'Afrique du Nord et la destinée occidentale."

42. Fistié, "L'Afrique du Nord et la destinée occidentale."

43. The classic account of French assimilationist and associationist ideologies is found in Raymond Betts, *Assimilation and Association in French Colonial Theory, 1890–1914* (New York: Columbia University Press, 1961).

44. Nord, *L'Eurafrique,* 103–104.

45. Given this explicit reference to race and creed, this group presumably comprised at least in part Muslim Algerians. HAEU AMG-254: Albert Gordiani, "Campagne de solidarité métropole-Algérie," speech to Bougie youth, July 19, 1956.

46. Andrew M. Daily, "Race, Citizenship, and Antillean Student Activism in Postwar France, 1946–1968," *French Historical Studies* 37, no. 2 (2014): 340–341.

47. The best-known example may be the association of British women's suffrage with the end of World War I. Birgitta Bader-Zaar, "Women's Suffrage and War: World War I and Political Reform in a Comparative Perspective," in *Suffrage, Gender and Citizenship: International Perspectives on Parliamentary Reforms,* ed. Irma Sulkunen, Seija-Leena Nevala-Nurmi, and Pirjo Markkola (Newcastle upon Tyne, UK: Cambridge Scholars Publishing, 2009), 193–218.

48. On prisoners of war's treatment in Vichy camps, see Sarah Ann Frank, *Hostages of Empire: Colonial Prisoners of War in Vichy France* (Lincoln: University of Nebraska Press, 2021).

49. Kristen Stromberg Childers, *Seeking Imperialism's Embrace: National Identity, Decolonization, and Assimilation in the French Caribbean* (Oxford: Oxford University Press, 2016), 70, 124.

50. James E. Genova, "Constructing Identity in Post-war France: Citizenship, Nationality, and the Lamine Guèye Law, 1946–1953," *International History Review* 26, no. 1 (2004): 60.

51. Gary Wilder, *The French Imperial Nation-State: Negritude and Colonial Humanism between the Two World Wars* (Chicago: University of Chicago Press, 2005), 134.

52. Frederick Cooper, *Citizenship between Empire and Nation* (Princeton, NJ: Princeton University Press, 2014), 67–123; Senghor cited on 80–81.

53. Tyler Stovall, *White Freedom: The Racial History of an Idea* (Princeton, NJ: Princeton University Press, 2021), 157.

54. Cooper, *Citizenship between Empire and Nation*, 5–6; Genova, "Constructing Identity," 71–72.

55. On the racialization of Islam in relation to North Africans, see Naomi Davidson, *Only Muslim: Embodying Islam in Twentieth-Century France* (Ithaca, NY: Cornell University Press, 2012); Muriam Haleh Davis, *Markets of Civilization: Islam and Racial Capitalism in Algeria* (Durham, NC: Duke University Press, forthcoming); Judith Surkis, *Sex, Law, and Sovereignty in French Algeria, 1830–1930* (Ithaca, NY: Cornell University Press, 2019), 181–216.

56. Patrick Weil, *How to Be French: Nationality in the Making since 1789*, trans. Catherine Porter (Durham, NC: Duke University Press, 2008), 219; Mamadou Diouf, "The French Colonial Policy of Assimilation and the Civility of the *Originaires* of the Four Communes (Senegal): A Nineteenth Century Globalization Project," *Development and Change* 29 (1998): 671–696; Cooper, *Citizenship between Empire and Nation*.

57. James McDougall, *A History of Algeria* (Cambridge: Cambridge University Press, 2017), 134–136, 166–178.

58. Dónal Hassett, *Mobilizing Memory: The Great War and the Language of Politics in Colonial Algeria, 1918–39* (Oxford: Oxford University Press, 2019).

59. Martin Thomas, *The French Empire at War, 1940–1945* (Manchester, UK: Manchester University Press, 1998), 159–190.

60. Martin Evans, *Algeria: France's Undeclared War* (Oxford: Oxford University Press, 2012), 94–95.

61. McDougall, *History of Algeria*, 179–180.

62. Martin Thomas, "From Sétif to Moramanga: Identifying Insurgents and Ascribing Guilt in the French Colonial Post-war," *War in History* 25, no. 2 (2018): 227–253.

63. Jean-Pierre Peyroulou, *Guelma, 1945: Une subversion française dans l'Algérie coloniale* (Paris: La Découverte, 2009), 135–153.

64. Alexis Spire, "D'une colonie à l'autre: La continuation des structures coloniales dans le traitement de l'immigration algérienne en France," in *L'esclavage, la colonisation, et après . . . France, États-Unis, Grande-Bretagne,* ed. Patrick Weil and Stéphane Dufoix (Paris: Presses Universitaires de France, 2005), 390.

65. Weil, *How to Be French,* 224.

66. James McDougall, "The Impossible Republic: The Reconquest of Algeria and the Decolonization of France, 1945–1962," *Journal of Modern History* 89 (2017): 788.

67. McDougall, *History of Algeria,* 183–185.

68. Under the Fourth Republic, the Parliament was split into the National Assembly, which held the power to make laws, and the Council of the Republic, a consultative body whose power was comparatively small. Representatives in the latter were called councillors of the Republic until 1948, then known as senators—a moniker that mirrored the senate that the Council of the Republic replaced and foreshadowed the senate that would supersede the council once the Fifth Republic came to be.

69. Assemblée Nationale, *Journal officiel, Débats parlementaires* 94, August 10, 1947 session, 4220.

70. Assemblée Nationale, August 10, 1947 session, 4221.

71. Punctuation original. Johanny (Joanny) Berlioz, "L'Afrique du Nord, foyer d'activité pro-hitlérienne et antifrançaise," *Cahiers du communisme* 4 (1945): 49; Assemblée Nationale Constituante, *Journal officiel, Débats* 47, April 13, 1946 session, 1789; Assemblée Nationale Constituante, *Journal officiel, Débats* 81, August 22, 1946 session, 3261.

72. Allison Drew, *We Are No Longer in France: Communists in Colonial Algeria* (Manchester, UK: Manchester University Press, 2014), 39–40.

73. Conseil de la République, *Journal officiel, Débats parlementaires* 107, August 29, 1947 session, 1918. On mobilizations of French revolutionary symbols and language during the Algerian War, see Timothy Scott Johnson, "Histories We Repeat," *Journal of the History of Ideas* blog, October 19, 2016, https://jhiblog.org/2016/10/19/histories-we-repeat/; Guy Pervillé, "Les principes de 1789 et le mouvement national algérien," *Revue française d'histoire d'outre-mer* 76, no. 282–283 (1989): 231–237.

74. Conseil de la République, *Journal officiel, Débats parlementaires* 107, August 29, 1947 session, 1920.

75. Assemblée Nationale, *Journal officiel, Débats parlementaires* 109, September 1, 1947 session, 4815.

76. *Journal officiel de la République Française,* Loi n° 47-1853 du 20 septembre 1947 portant statut organique de l'Algérie, September 21, 1947, 9470–9474.

77. Emphasis original. Written in 1943, Viard published this piece three years later. CAOM BIB AOM B283: Paul-Émile Viard, "Essai d'une organisation constitutionnelle de la 'Communauté française," in *La Communauté française* (Paris: Éditions Renaissances, 1946), 19, 21. On Viard, see Florence Renucci, "La 'décolonisation doctrinale' ou la naissance du droit d'outre-mer (1946–début des années 1960)," *Revue d'histoire de sciences humaines* 24, no. 1 (2011): 70–71.

78. Jacques Lambert, *Manuel de législation algérienne* (Algiers: Librairie des Facultés, 1952), 51.

79. Florence Renucci, "Le démontage de l'empire colonial français dans les nouveaux manuels de droit de l'après-guerre (1949–1952)," in *Démontage d'empires,* ed. Jean Fremigacci, Daniel Lefeuvre, and Marc Michel (Paris: Riveneuve éditions, 2012), 161.

80. Lambert, *Manuel de législation algérienne,* 61–63.

81. Samir Saul, *Intérêts économiques français et décolonisation de l'Afrique du Nord (1945–1962)* (Geneva: Librairie Droz, 2016), 43.

82. Assemblée Nationale, *Journal officiel, Débats parlementaires* 28, March 4, 1948 session, 1340.

83. Assemblée Nationale, March 4, 1948 session, 1340–1342.

84. All of the Comoros islands gained their independence in 1975, except Mayotte, which is now a French department.

85. Assemblée Nationale, March 4, 1948 session, 1334, 1341.

86. *Journal officiel, Lois et décrets* 223, Loi nº 47-1853 du 20 septembre 1947 portant statut organique de l'Algérie, September 21, 1947, 9471.

87. Walter Lipgens, *A History of European Integration 1945–1947: The Formation of the European Unity Movement,* trans. P. S. Falla and A. J. Ryder (Oxford: Oxford University Press, 1982), 296–316.

88. Nicholas J. White, "Reconstructing Europe through Rejuvenating Empire: The British, French, and Dutch Experiences Compared," *Past & Present* S6, no. 210 (2011): 219–220.

89. Rik Schreurs, "A Marshall Plan for Africa? The Overseas Territories Committee and the Origins of European Co-operation in Africa," in *Explorations in OEEC History,* ed. Richard T. Griffiths (Paris: OECD, 1997), 88.

90. Hansen and Jonsson, *Eurafrica,* 112–117.

91. Raphaël Saller, "Special Report of OEEC on the Strasbourg Plan," Council of Europe Parliamentary Assembly, May 27, 1954, http:// semantic-pace.net/tools/pdf.aspx?doc=aHR0cDovL2Fzc2VtYmx5 LmNvZS5pbnQvbncveG1sL1hSZWYvWDJILURXLWV4dHIu YXNwP2ZpbGVpZD01ODEmbGFuZz1FTg==&xsl=aHR0cDovL3 NlbWFudGljcGFjZS5uZXQvWHNsdC9QZGGvWFJlZi1XRC1BV C1YTUwyUERGLnhzbA==&xsltparams=ZmlsZWlkPTU4MQ==.

92. On Britain's influence on European integration, see Laura Kottos, "A 'European Commonwealth': Britain, the European League for Economic Co-operation, and European Debates on Empire, 1947–1957," *Journal of Contemporary European Studies* 20, no. 4 (2012): 497–515.

93. MAEF-N 378PO 6 581: Diplomatie, Direction d'Afrique-Levant, "Note sur la coopération franco-britannique en Afrique Noire," January 10, 1949.

94. "L'Afrique est aujourd'hui (une des) frontières de l'Occident." MAEF-N 378PO 6 581: DELFRA Washington to Diplomatie, transmitted to DELFRA London (Diplo / 3382–86), July 3, 1949.
95. MAEF-N 378PO 6 581: Massigli, DELFRA London to Diplomatie, Afrique-Levant, Direction économique, Diplo / 2564 à 66, September 24, 1949.
96. MAEF-N 378PO 6 581: Massigli to Diplomatie, Afrique-Levant, Diplo / 2423, September 7, 1949.
97. MAEF-N 378PO 6 788: Direction générale des Affaires politiques, Direction d'Afrique-Levant, "Note sur la position des territoires français d'outre-mer dans la question de l'intégration européenne," October 14, 1952, 5.

2. Reforming Empire, Forming Europe

1. Conseil de la République, *Journal officiel, Débats parlementaires* 31, April 1, 1952 session, 793–816.
2. The standard narrative of European integration historians emphasizes the institutions' stabilizing outcome. See Mark Gilbert, *European Integration: A Concise History* (Lanham, MD: Rowman & Littlefield, 2012), 16.
3. Malika Rahal, "La place des réformistes dans le mouvement national algérien," *Vingtième siècle: Revue d'histoire* 83 (2004): 163–164.
4. For a challenge to the *immobiliste* trope, see Richard Vinen, *Bourgeois Politics in France, 1945–1951* (Cambridge: Cambridge University Press, 1995), 173–215.
5. Conseil de la République, *Journal officiel, Débats parlementaires* 31, April 1, 1952 session, 799.
6. Robert Schuman, Declaration of May 9, 1950, *European Issue* 204 (2011), robert-schuman.eu/en/doc/questions-d-europe/qe-204-en. pdf; Etienne Deschamps, "Robert Schuman, un apôtre oublié de l'Eurafrique?" in *Quelles architectures pour quelle Europe? Des projets d'une Europe unie à l'Union européenne (1945–1992): Actes des deuxièmes journées d'étude de la Maison de Robert Schuman, Metz, 9, 10 et 11 mai 2010,* ed. Sylvain Schirmann (Brussels: Peter Lang, 2011), 75–92.

7. Ed Naylor, ed., *France's Modernising Mission: Citizenship, Welfare and the Ends of Empire* (London: Palgrave Macmillan, 2018).

8. "'Entre la France et l'Allemagne une rivalité ruineuse doit faire place à l'intérêt commun,' déclare à Nantes M. Schuman," *Le Monde,* May 23, 1950.

9. In Guernier's breathless words, "to labor towards the expansion of Europe into Africa is to labor for peace." Eugène Guernier, *Le destin des continents, trois continents—trois civilisations—trois destins* (Paris: Librairie Félix Alcan, 1936), 257.

10. Conseil de la République, *Journal officiel, Débats parlementaires* 31, April 1, 1952 session, 799. International relations scholars have long theorized the importance of marriage and other gendered metaphors in diplomatic contexts. Frank Costigliola recalled an American foreign service officer telling him that "NATO is a marriage" involving the "exchange of bodily fluids, in terms of sharing blood together." He posits that such language forces historians to reevaluate the purportedly rational comportment of diplomats and consider the emotional element of their work. Frank Costigliola, "The Nuclear Family: Tropes of Gender and Pathology in the Western Alliance," *Diplomatic History* 21, no. 2 (1997): 163. Links between sex and diplomacy also extended beyond metaphor. See Katharine H. S. Moon, *Sex among Allies: Military Prostitution in US-Korea Relations* (New York: Columbia University Press, 1997). Anti-imperial activists challenged marriage and family metaphors with more visceral biological imagery, equating colonialism to gangrene. Elizabeth Buettner, "Extended Families or Bodily Decomposition? Biological Metaphors in the Age of European Decolonization," in *Rhetorics of Empire: Languages of Colonial Conflict after 1900,* ed. Martin Thomas and Richard Toye (Manchester, UK: Manchester University Press, 2017), 208–227.

11. CAOM 1AFFECO / 695: Léon Feix, Henri Lozeray, Georges Thévenin, and Henri Barbé, PCF, "Proposition, tendant à inviter le Gouvernement à dénoncer les clauses des récents accords de Londres ayant trait aux territoires d'Afrique et arrêter tous les négociations en

cours sur le pool franco-allemand en raison de ses conséquences
africaines," Assemblée de l'Union Française, annex, July 25, 1950.

12. Danièle Joly, *The French Communist Party and the Algerian War*
(London: Macmillan, 1991).

13. CAOM 1AFFECO / 695: "Intervention faite à Strasbourg par M.
Diop Ousmane Socé, Sénateur du Sénégal, Délégué de la France au
Conseil de l'Europe, le Plan Schuman et l'Afrique," August 14, 1950.

14. Siba N'Zatioula Grovogui, *Beyond Eurocentrism and Anarchy: Memories
of International Order and Institutions* (London: Palgrave Macmillan,
2006), 96–98.

15. CAOM 1AFFECO / 695: Raphaël Saller, "L'avenir économique de
l'Afrique et le pool franco-allemand de l'acier et du charbon,"
Marchés coloniaux (June 3, 1950): 1247–1248.

16. Cited in Gérard Bossuat, *L'Europe des Français, 1943–1959: La IVe
République aux sources de l'Europe communautaire* (Paris: Publications de
la Sorbonne, 1996), 105.

17. CAOM 1AFFECO / 752: Ministère de l'outre-mer, "Inclusion des
pays d'outre-mer français dans la Communauté européenne,"
November 5, 1950, 2.

18. An important exception is Muriam Haleh Davis. Muriam Haleh
Davis, "The Sahara as the 'Cornerstone' of Eurafrica: European
Integration and Technical Sovereignty Seen from the Desert,"
Journal of European Integration History 23, no. 1 (2017): 97–112;
Muriam Haleh Davis, "'The Transformation of Man' in French
Algeria: Economic Planning and the Postwar Social Sciences,
1958–62," *Journal of Contemporary History* 52, no. 1 (2017): 86–87.

19. On Algeria's coal deposits, see Samir Saul, *Intérêts économiques français
et décolonisation de l'Afrique du Nord (1945–1962)* (Geneva: Librairie
Droz, 2016), 528.

20. Stéphane Mourlane, "Actions culturelles et coopération
méditerranéenne: Le projet italien d'Eurafrica au début des années
1950," in *La construction d'un espace euro-méditerranéen: Genèses, mythes
et perspectives,* ed. Houda Ben Hamouda and Mathieu Bouchard
(Brussels: P.I.E. Peter Lang, 2012), 23–31.

278 Notes to Pages 78-82

21. CAOM 1AFFECO / 752: Ministère de l'outre-mer, "Inclusion des pays d'outre-mer français dans la Communauté européenne," November 5, 1950, 2.

22. AN 363AP / 17: G. L. S. Mercier, Chambre syndicale des mines d'Algérie, to René Mayer, December 8, 1950.

23. CAOM 81 F 2136: Jacques Hasse, "L'Algérie ne saurait faire les frais du pool charbon-acier (Plan Schuman)," *Dépêche quotidienne d'Algérie,* February 7, 1951.

24. CAOM 81 F 2136: "M. Robert Schuman commente son plan," *L'Écho d'Oran,* April 21, 1951.

25. See Eric T. Jennings, *Vichy in the Tropics: Pétain's National Revolution in Madagascar, Guadeloupe, and Indochina, 1940–1944* (Stanford, CA: Stanford University Press, 2001), especially 79–104.

26. Guy Pervillé, "La politique algérienne de la France (1830–1962)," *Le genre humain* 32, no. 1 (1997): 27.

27. Further wording accounted for the Saar. CVCE: Treaty of Paris, Article 79, http://www.cvce.eu/en/obj/treaty_establishing_the _european_coal_and_steel_community_paris_18_april_1951-en -11a21305-941e-49d7-a171-ed5be548cd58.html.

28. Dominque Custos, "Implications of the European Integration for the Overseas," in *EU Law of the Overseas: Outermost Regions, Associated Overseas Countries and Territories, Territories Sui Generis,* ed. Dimitry Kochenov (Alphen aan den Rijn: Kluwer Law International, 2011), 94–96.

29. Assemblée Nationale, *Journal officiel, Débats parlementaires* 104, October 24, 1950 session, 7119.

30. The North Atlantic Treaty, Article 6, https://www.nato.int/cps/en /natolive/official_texts_17120.htm; Timothy Andrews Sayle, "'A Great List of Potential Mistakes': NATO, Africa, and British Efforts to Limit the Global Cold War," *Cold War History* 16, no. 1 (2016): 19–36.

31. MAEF-N 122PO / D / 67: Hauteclocque, DELFRA Brussels, to Diplomatie, 261–270, October 8, 1951.

32. MAEF-N 122PO / D / 67: DELFRA Brussels to Diplomatie, ca. April 1952.

33. AEI: "Treaty Constituting the European Defense Community," 167, https://aei.pitt.edu/5201/1/5201.pdf.
34. AN C//16282: "Proposition [no. 353] à inviter le Gouvernement à prendre en considération les nécessités de la défense nationale et la sauvegarde de l'Union Française dans l'élaboration du Traité instituant la Communauté européenne de défense proposé à la ratification des Chambres," Assemblée de l'Union française, annex, October 23, 1952; AN C//16282: "Projet de rapport fait au nom de la Commission des relations extérieures sur la proposition n° 353," n.d.
35. The journal *La Fédération* and its affiliated group originated with corporatist Vichy sympathizers in late 1944 and only partially gained respectability (while maintaining hardline anti-communism) in the ensuing years. See Antonin Cohen, "De la révolution nationale à l'Europe fédérale: Les métamorphoses de la troisième voie aux origines du mouvement fédéraliste français, La Fédération (1943–1948)," *Le Mouvement social* 217, no. 4 (2006): 56–58.
36. CVCE: "Pour ou contre l'armée européenne," *Fédération: Revue de l'ordre vivant* 101 (June 1953): 494–503, 508–510, https://www.cvce.eu/en/obj/for_or_against_a_european_army_from_federation_june_1953-en-e698c20f-a575-4dd0-8bb9-7177e88c364b.html.
37. CAOM 1AFFPOL/3255: Institut des hautes études de défense nationale, Direction des études, "Travail en comités: Problèmes soulevés par l'intégration de l'Union française dans une Communauté européenne," December 24, 1952.
38. State Department official in 1956, cited in Sayle, "'A Great List of Potential Mistakes,'" 23.
39. CAOM 1AFFPOL/3255: "Le projet de Communauté européenne de défense et l'Union française—Bordereau analytique," sent by J. Iehlé, Inspecteur de la France d'outre-mer, Chef de la section de documentation du Ministre de la France d'outre-mer to Chef de l'État-Major Particulier du Ministre and Chef du Service de la Défense Nationale (00553CAM/DOC), "Communauté européenne de défense," May 20, 1953.

40. CAOM 1AFFPOL/3255: Iehlé, "Note de Synthèse: La Communauté européenne de défense et l'Union française," April 25, 1953.

41. BDIC Q pièce 10408 (1)-(2): CELPUF, Conférence plénière des 13 et 14 janvier 1953.

42. Todd Shepard, "The Birth of the Hexagon: 1962 and the Erasure of France's Supranational History," in *Vertriebene and Pieds-Noirs in Postwar Germany and France: Comparative Perspectives,* ed. Manuel Borutta and Jan C. Jansen (London: Palgrave Macmillan, 2016), 64.

43. CAOM 1AFFPOL/219: "'Les territoires d'outre-mer ne doivent pas être associés à l'Europe sans garanties durables' déclare M. Louis Jacquinot," *Le Figaro,* October 31, 1953.

44. "Le plan allemand pour la conquête de l'Europe," *L'Express,* November 14, 1953, 6–7.

45. CVCE: Union française des fédéralistes, "Communauté européenne de défense?" pamphlet, 1954, https://www.cvce.eu/en/obj/european _defence_community_1954-en-4ff354e2-5b9f-411b-b59d -bc6a49d3ee95.html.

46. MAEF-N 378PO/6/788: Saffroy, DELFRA Luxembourg, to Diplomatie, 159, December 13, 1952.

47. Assemblée Nationale, *Journal officiel, Débats parlementaires* 84, August 29, 1954 session, 4439.

48. Assemblée Nationale, *Journal officiel, Débats parlementaires* 85, August 30, 1954 session, 4469.

49. Assemblée Nationale, *Journal officiel, Débats parlementaires* 85, August 30, 1954 session, 4471.

50. Joseph Bohling, *The Sober Revolution: Appellation Wine and the Transformation of France* (Ithaca, NY: Cornell University Press, 2018); Owen White, *The Blood of the Colony: Wine and the Rise and Fall of French Algeria* (Cambridge, MA: Harvard University Press, 2021).

51. BDIC Q pièce 10408 (1)-(2): CELPUF, Conférence plénière des 13 et 14 janvier 1953.

52. Frantz Fanon, *The Wretched of the Earth,* trans. Constance Farrington (New York: Grove, 1963), 51.

53. Gary Wilder, "Framing Greater France between the Wars," *Journal of Historical Sociology* 14, no. 2 (2001): 198–225.

54. CAOM 1AFFPOL / 3255: "Assemblée ad hoc chargée d'élaborer un projet de Traité instituant une Communauté politique européenne, session de janvier 1953, amendement n° 30 au rapport de la Commission constitutionnelle"; CAOM 1AFFPOL / 3255: "Interventions de M. Senghor, député du Sénégal à l'Assemblé ad hoc, chargée d'élaborer un projet de Traité instituant une Communauté politique européenne," January 8, 1953.

55. CAOM 1AFFPOL / 3255: Yvon Gouet to Direction des affaires politiques, "L'Union européenne," February 9, 1953.

56. Ann Laura Stoler, *Carnal Knowledge and Imperial Power: Race and the Intimate in Colonial Rule* (Berkeley: University of California Press, 2010).

57. CAOM 1AFFPOL / 3255: "Interventions de M. Senghor, député du Sénégal à l'Assemblé ad hoc, chargée d'élaborer un projet de Traité instituant une Communauté politique européenne," January 9, 1953.

58. CAOM 1AFFPOL / 2318: Georges Le Brun Kéris, "L'Union européenne," lecture at the Collège libre des sciences sociales et économiques, section d'outre-mer, Paris, 1951–1952 school year.

59. AN C / / 15639: Assemblée Nationale, Commission des Territoires d'outre-mer, November 12, 1953.

60. CAOM 1AFFPOL / 2314: Michel Debré, "Construit-on l'Europe," *L'information économique & financière,* November 26, 1952.

61. Giuliano Garavini, *After Empires: European Integration, Decolonization, and the Challenge from the Global South, 1957–1986* (Oxford: Oxford University Press, 2012), 12.

62. "Final Communiqué of the Asian-African Conference," April 24, 1955, published in Kweku Ampiah, *The Political and Moral Imperatives of the Bandung Conference of 1955: The Reactions of the US, UK and Japan* (Folkestone, UK: Global Oriental, 2007), 222–228.

63. Anne-Isabelle Richard, "The Limits of Solidarity: Europeanism, Anti-Colonialism and Socialism at the Congress of the Peoples of

Europe, Asia and Africa in Puteaux, 1948," *European Review of History / Revue européenne d'histoire* 21, no. 4 (2014): 532.

64. Sukarno opening speech, Bandung Conference, published in Ampiah, *The Political and Moral Imperatives of the Bandung Conference,* 233–240.

65. CVCE: Paul Ély to Antoine Pinay, April 28, 1955, https://www.cvce .eu/en/obj/lettre_du_general_ely_a_antoine_pinay_sur_la _conference_de_bandung_saigon_28_avril_1955-fr-f71582f5-0631 -4b0d-a1a9-4d7a75eeffdb.html.

66. CAOM 23 APC 18: Octave Meynier to Louis Robin, Secrétaire général du syndicat de la presse nord-africaine, April 30, 1955.

67. Megan Brown, "Le Rallye Méditerranée-le-Cap: Racing towards Eurafrica?" *French Politics, Culture & Society* 38, no. 2 (2020): 80–104.

68. Jeffrey James Byrne, *Mecca of Revolution: Algeria, Decolonization and the Third World Order* (New York: Oxford University Press, 2016), 41.

69. Martin Thomas, "France Accused: French North Africa before the United Nations, 1952–1962," *Contemporary European History* 10, no. 1 (2001): 91–121; Maryliz Racine, "Le passage à l'ère post-westphalienne: Les politiques européennes et impériales de la France pendant la IVe République (1944–1958)" (PhD diss., Université Laval and Aix-Marseille Université, 2020), 297–306.

70. INA: "La loi-cadre Defferre de 1956," Radiodiffusion-Télévision Française, December 4, 1956, https://fresques.ina.fr/independances /fiche-media/Indepe00120/la-loi-cadre-defferre-de-1956.html; Thomas Jackson, "The *loi-cadre* and the Colonial Mind: Reform between Discourse, Myth and History" (PhD diss., University of Sheffield, 2018); Tony Chafer, *The End of Empire in French West Africa: France's Successful Decolonization?* (Oxford: Berg, 2002), 163–192.

71. Emphasis original. Martin Shipway, "Gaston Defferre's *Loi-Cadre* and Its Application 1956 / 57: The Last Chance for a French African 'Empire-State' or Blueprint for Decolonisation?" in *Francophone Africa at Fifty,* ed. Tony Chafer and Alexander Keese (Manchester, UK: Manchester University Press, 2013), 16.

72. Frederick Cooper, "Modernizing Colonialism and the Limits of Empire," *SSRC Items & Issues* 4, no. 4 (2003): 3.

73. Todd Shepard, *The Invention of Decolonization: The Algerian War and the Remaking of France* (Ithaca, NY: Cornell University Press, 2006). Compare to Jacques Marseille, *Empire colonial et capitalisme français: Histoire d'un divorce* (Paris: Albin Michel, 1984); Daniel Lefeuvre, *Chère Algérie: La France et sa colonie, 1930–1962* (Paris: Flammarion, 2005).

74. MAEF-N 378PO / 6 / 1213: "L'Union française et la Communauté européenne, rapport du Centre d'études de politique étrangère," July 1953.

75. CAOM 81 F 1134: "Convention du Conseil de l'Europe sur le traitement réciproque des nationaux, compte-rendu de la réunion interministérielle tenue au Ministère des affaires étrangères le 16 novembre 1954."

76. Council of Europe, "European Convention on Establishment and Protocol thereto," signed December 13, 1955, Paris, https://www.coe.int/en/web/conventions/full-list/-/conventions/rms/090000168006457f.

77. CAOM 81 F 1133: Ferrandi, Ministère de l'Intérieur, Direction des affaires algériennes, "Projet de convention européenne concernant la sécurité sociale des travailleurs migrants," summary of March 26, 1955 meeting, SGCI.

78. Constantine councilor El-Hadi Mostefaï hurled the accusation of the French Union being treated like a "poor relation" during the *statut organique* debate. Conseil de la République, *Journal officiel, Débats parlementaires* 107, August 29, 1947 session, 1920.

79. CAOM 81 F 2136: "Tamzali," *Dépêche quotidienne d'Algérie*, April 3, 1952; Conseil de la République, *Journal officiel, Débats parlementaires* 31, April 1, 1952, 799.

80. MAEF-C 20QO / 792: Defferre to Secrétaire d'État aux Affaires Étrangères, "Problèmes posés pour la France d'outre-mer par le projet de Marché commun européen," May 17, 1956. For an extended analysis of Defferre, European integration, and

decolonization, see Anne-Laure Ollivier, "Entre Europe et Afrique: Gaston Defferre et les débuts de la construction européenne," *Terrains et Travaux* 8, no. 1 (2005): 14–33.

3. The Ultimatum for the Treaty of Rome

1. This represented an iteration of the "last chance" myth to which Fourth Republic politicians ascribed. Charles-Robert Ageron, "L'Algérie, dernière chance de la puissance française," *Relations internationales* 57 (Spring 1989): 113–139.

2. Gérard Bossuat, *L'Europe des Français, 1943–1959: La IVe République aux sources de l'Europe communautaire* (Paris: Publications de la Sorbonne, 1996); Papa Dramé and Samir Saul, "Le projet d'Eurafrique en France (1946–1960): Quête de puissance ou atavisme colonial?" *Guerres mondiales et conflits contemporains* 216, no. 4 (2004): 95–114.

3. Kiran Klaus Patel, *Project Europe: A History* (Cambridge: Cambridge University Press, 2020), 26.

4. Sally Engle Merry, "Colonial Law and Its Uncertainties," *Law and History Review* 28, no. 4 (November 2010): 1071.

5. Matthew Connelly, *A Diplomatic Revolution: Algeria's Fight for Independence and the Origins of the Post–Cold War Era* (New York: Oxford University Press, 2002), 82.

6. Zohra Drif, *Inside the Battle of Algiers: Memoir of a Woman Freedom Fighter,* trans. Andrew Farrand (Charlottesville, VA: Just World Books, 2017), 198–200.

7. Connelly, *Diplomatic Revolution*.

8. Martin Thomas, "France Accused: French North Africa before the United Nations, 1952–1962," *Contemporary European History* 10, no. 1 (2001): 91–121; Jessica Lynne Pearson, *The Colonial Politics of Global Health: France and the United Nations in Postwar Africa* (Cambridge, MA: Harvard University Press, 2018); Brian Digre, "The United Nations, France, and African Independence: A Case Study of Togo," *French Colonial History* 5 (2004): 193–206.

9. The cartoon, drawn by David Low, shows History (an old, bearded man) shaking Stalin's unwilling hand, saying, "Congratulations, Joe! It could never have been begun without your inspiration!" A sign behind them reads, "European Union—Under Construction at Last." CVCE: Low, February 1, 1949, https://www.cvce.eu/en/obj/cartoon_by_low _on_the_impact_of_thecold_war_on_the_plan_for_a_united_europe _1_february_1949-en-248a65df-e4d9-4857-85cd-aea943d575b2.html.

10. Cited in Peo Hansen and Stefan Jonsson, "A Statue to Nasser? Eurafrica, the Colonial Roots of European Integration, and the 2012 Nobel Peace Prize," *Mediterranean Quarterly* 24, no. 4 (2013): 18.

11. Cited in Hansen and Jonsson, "A Statue to Nasser?" 6.

12. CVCE: Étienne Hirsch, "A Guide to Euratom," *The New Scientist,* March 26, 1959, https://www.cvce.eu/obj/a_guide_to_euratom _from_the_new_scientist_26_march_1959-en-b3528159-ad01-40cf -a4b0-7f6a51daf9b8.html.

13. SP MEC 24: Chérif Mécheri, "Note à l'attention de Monsieur le Président [René Coty]," June 28, 1957.

14. CVCE: Centre européen de la culture, Mouvement européen, *Questions et réponses, Marché commun, Euratom* (Geneva: Centre européen de la culture, 1957), https://www.cvce.eu/obj/questions_et _reponses_marche_commun_euratom-fr-a2183675-d849-4a2f-9b7a -05d2f80c6f8a.html; CVCE: Étienne Deschamps, "L'échec d'Euratom," https://www.cvce.eu/obj/l_echec_d_euratom-fr -ed07967d-d4b8-4224-acd9-fb9cb15b9947.html; Bossuat, *L'Europe des Français,* 294.

15. Henri Rieben, "L'Euratom: Une nécessité vitale et urgente pour la France et pour l'Europe," *Revue économique et sociale: Bulletin de la Société d'études économiques et sociales* 15, no. 1 (1957): 40.

16. CAEF 5A-0000116 / 2: "L'Eurafrique troisième force mondiale, Conférence faite par M. Eugène Guernier au 349ème déjeuner-conférence du CMEF," speech delivered January 16, 1957.

17. Michel Dumoulin, "La crise européenne de la Belgique à la veille de la signature des Traités de Rome," *Journal of European Integration History* 23, no. 1 (2017): 31–40.

18. MAEF-N 122PO/D/74: Raymond Bousquet, DELFRA Brussels, to Christian Pineau, Diplomatie, Direction générale politique— Europe, 1909/EU, "Débat au Sénat sur le projet de loi portant approbation des Traités de Rome," December 2, 1957, 12–13.

19. Raymond Bertrand, "The European Common Market Proposal," *International Organization* 10, no. 4 (1956): 570. Bertrand, an economist, had served as chief of the Western European Division of the International Monetary Fund.

20. MAEF-C 20QO/792: Gaston Defferre to Secrétaire d'état aux affaires étrangères, "Problèmes posés pour la France d'outre-mer par le projet de Marché commun européen," May 17, 1956. Within a few days, Defferre had also written to Prime Minister Guy Mollet. Guia Migani details this in her excellent study of the negotiations for associating the TOM with the Common Market. Guia Migani, "L'association des TOM au Marché commun: Histoire d'un accord européen entre cultures économiques différentes et idéaux politiques communs, 1955–1957," in *L'Europe Unie et l'Afrique: De l'idée d'Eurafrique à la Convention de Lomé I: Actes du colloque international de Paris, 1er et 2 avril 2004,* ed. Marie-Thérèse Bitsch and Gérard Bossuat (Brussels: Bruylant, 2005), 233–251, especially 234–235.

21. Catherine Hodeir, "Le grand patronat colonial français face à la décolonisation, 1945–1962: Problématiques, sources, conclusions," *Outre-mer* 88, no. 330–331 (2001): 141.

22. MAEF-C 20QO/719: "Note d'information sur les Territoires d'outre-mer et le Marché commun," n.d. but likely August 1956.

23. Cited in Giuliano Garavini, *After Empires: European Integration, Decolonization, and the Challenge from the Global South, 1957–1986* (Oxford: Oxford University Press, 2012), 54–55. Mollet had a record of expressing skepticism about assimilation. Brian Shaev, "The Algerian War, European Integration, and the Decolonization of French Socialism," *French Historical Studies* 41, no. 1 (2018): 73.

24. Ann Laura Stoler, *Along the Archival Grain: Epistemic Anxieties and Colonial Common Sense* (Princeton, NJ: Princeton University Press, 2010).

25. MAEF-C 20QO / 792: Defferre to Secrétaire d'état aux affaires étrangères, "Problèmes posés pour la France d'outre-mer par le projet de Marché commun européen," May 17, 1956.

26. MAEF-N 122PO / D / 73: Bousquet to Pineau, 1324 / CM, "Le Marché commun et les Territoires d'outre-mer," September 30, 1956.

27. MAEF-C 20QO / 719: DE-CE, "Participation de la France au Marché commun compte tenu de ses responsabilités d'outre-mer," May 24, 1956.

28. MAEF-C 20QO / 792: Defferre to Secrétaire d'état aux affaires étrangères, "Problèmes posés pour la France d'outre-mer par le projet de Marché commun européen," May 17, 1956.

29. CVCE: "Projet de procès-verbal de la conférence des ministres des affaires étrangères des états membres de la CECA," May 29–30, 1956, https://www.cvce.eu/obj/projet_de_proces_verbal_de_la _conference_de_venise_29_30_mai_1956-fr-af6e5adf-01a5-4f22 -88cd-8354a265e5db.html.

30. Preparatory documents make no allusion to the subject. See, for example, CVCE: Secrétariat du comité intergouvernemental, "Note confidentielle sur la préparation de la conférence de Venise (Luxembourg, 16 mai 1956)," https://www.cvce.eu/obj/note _confidentielle_sur_la_preparation_de_la_conference_de_venise _luxembourg_16_mai_1956-fr-f47791ad-32df-4218-a20e -0eed89ee1bd0.html.

31. I am indebted here to scholarship found in Bitsch and Bossuat, *L'Europe Unie et l'Afrique*. In particular, see Vincent Dujardin, "Le monde politique belge face au traité d'association des PTOM au Marché commun," 301–318; Guido Thiemeyer, "West German Perceptions of Africa and the Association of the Overseas Territories with the Common Market, 1956–1957," 269–286; Lorenzo Pacifici, "L'Italie et la question de l'association des PTOM au cours des négociations pour la création de la CEE," 253–268; and Anjo G. Harryvan and Jan van der Harst, "A Bumpy Road to Lomé: The Netherlands, Association, and the Yaoundé Treaties, 1956–1969," 319–344.

32. Harryvan and van der Harst, "A Bumpy Road to Lomé," 322.

33. Thiemeyer, "West German," 274–275. My translation from the German.

34. MAEF-C 20QO/726: DE-CE, Marché commun, "Note sur les observations et conditions principales à prendre en considération pour l'entrée de l'Algérie dans la Communauté du marché européen," August 21, 1956.

35. MAEF-N 122PO/D/73: Bousquet to Pineau, 1324/CM, "Le Marché commun et les Territoires d'outre-mer," September 30, 1956.

36. MAEF-N 122PO/D/73: Bousquet to Pineau, 1324/CM.

37. On Cartier, see Todd Shepard, *The Invention of Decolonization: The Algerian War and the Remaking of France* (Ithaca, NY: Cornell University Press, 2006), 68; Martin Evans, *Algeria: France's Undeclared War* (Oxford: Oxford University Press, 2012), 200–201.

38. MAEF-N 122PO/D/71: "Projet de rapport franco-belge sur la participation éventuelle des Pays et Territoires d'outre-mer au Marché commun européen," October 2, 1956. Sent by Bousquet to Pineau, October 8, 1956. On the European Payments Union, see S. F. Goodman, *The European Union,* 3rd ed. (London: Macmillan, 1996), 187–188.

39. MAEF-N 122PO/D/71: Bousquet to Pineau—Direction Politique, "Le Marché commun et les Territoires d'outre-mer," October 8, 1956.

40. Nicholas Pas, "La guerre d'Algérie vue des Pays-Bas (1954–1962)," *Vingtième siècle: Revue d'histoire* 86, no. 2 (2005): 43–58.

41. This was Bousquet's appraisal of Marjolin's speech. Emphasis original. MAEF-N 122PO/D/71: Bousquet to Pineau, 1742/DE, Direction générale politique—Europe, "Séance des chefs de délégation du 29 novembre," December 5, 1956, 24.

42. HAEU AD-52: François Georges-Picot, "Le Marché commun par l'Eurafrique," *L'action fédéraliste européenne* 2, no. 9 (1957): 4.

43. Samir Saul, *Intérêts économiques français et décolonisation de l'Afrique du Nord (1945–1962)* (Geneva: Librairie Droz, 2016), 601.

44. MAEF-C 20QO/726: DE-CE, Marché commun, "Les échanges commerciaux de l'Algérie," August 22, 1956.

45. MAEF-N 122PO/D/72: "Résumé de la conférence des chefs de délégation du 29 novembre 1956," November 30, 1956, 21. Sent by Bousquet to Pineau, 1742/DE, December 5, 1956.

46. MAEF-N 122PO/D/72: "Résumé de la conférence des chefs de délégation du 29 novembre 1956."

47. Bousquet's paraphrase of a January 27 article. MAEF-N 122PO/D/74: Bousquet to Pineau, Direction générale politique—Europe, 318/EU, "L'opinion flamande et le Marché commun," February 9, 1957.

48. MAEF-C 20QO/719: Ad Hoc Group for the Overseas Territories, "Rapport au comité des chefs de délégation," December 20, 1956, 5.

49. MAEF-N 122PO/D/74: Bousquet to Pineau, Direction générale des affaires économiques, 184/EU, "Territoires d'outre-mer," January 25, 1957.

50. Raphaëlle Branche and Sylvie Thénault, "Le secret sur la torture pendant la guerre d'Algérie," *Matériaux pour l'histoire de notre temps* 58, no. 1 (2000): 57–63; Paola Paissa, "Le silence sur la torture pendant la guerre d'Algérie: Analyse d'un corpus de presse française (1957 et 2000)," *Mots: Les langages du politique* 103 (2013): 39–54.

51. Denis Barbet and Jean-Paul Honoré, "Ce que taire veut dire: Expressions et usages politiques du silence," *Mots: Les langages du politique* 103 (2013): 8.

52. Emphasis original. SP 2 BA 32: R. Frank, "Problèmes posés par la mise en œuvre d'un marché commun européen," January 2, 1957.

53. Todd Shepard, "Thinking between Metropole and Colony: The French Republic, 'Exceptional Promotion,' and the 'Integration' of Algerians, 1955–1962," in *The French Colonial Mind Volume I: Mental Maps of Empire and Colonial Encounters,* ed. Martin Thomas (Lincoln: University of Nebraska Press, 2011), 313–316.

54. SP MEC 24: Mécheri to René Coty, "Le Marché commun européen et les Territoires d'outre-mer français," January 24, 1957.

55. MAEF-N 122PO / D / 74: Bousquet to Pineau, Direction générale des affaires économiques, 184 / EU, "Territoires d'outre-mer," January 25, 1957.

56. MAEF-C 20QO / 627: Assemblée de l'Union Française, "Compte rendu analytique de l'Assemblée de l'Union Française," January 24, 1957 session, 8–10.

57. Eric T. Jennings, *Free French Africa in World War II: The African Resistance* (Cambridge: Cambridge University Press, 2015), 2.

58. Irwin M. Wall, "The French Communists and the Algerian War," *Journal of Contemporary History* 12, no. 3 (1977): 521–543.

59. MAEF-C 20QO / 627: Assemblée de l'Union Française, January 24, 1957 session, 17–22.

60. MAEF-C 20QO / 719: Laloy, Diplomatie to Direction générale politique—Europe, "Direction des organisations européennes," November 24, 1956.

61. Xavier de Glowczewski, "La guerre d'Algérie au miroir de la presse allemande (1958–1962)," *Revue d'Allemagne* 31, no. 3 / 4 (1999): 541–553.

62. MAEF-C 20QO / 720: Maurice Couve de Murville to Pineau, "Inclusion de l'Afrique dans le Marché commun européen," January 7, 1957.

63. MAEF-N 122PO / D / 71: Bousquet to Pineau, 1914 / EU, "Comité des Chefs de délégation des 19 et 20 décembre—Fonds d'investissement," December 22, 1956.

64. MAEF-N 122PO / D / 71: Bousquet to Pineau, 82 / EU, "Réunion du Comité des chefs de délégation—Association des Territoires d'outre-mer au Marché commun," January 7, 1957.

65. Vincent Genin, "Les Rolin, le sacrifice d'une famille d'intellectuels," RTBF, https://www.rtbf.be/14-18/thematiques /detail_les-rolin-le-sacrifice-d-une-famille-d-intellectuels?id =8286145.

66. MAEF-N 122PO / D / 55: Direction des organisations européennes, "Proposition de la résolution de l'Assemblée Consultative du Conseil de l'Europe sur les 'atrocités' françaises en Algérie," March 21, 1957.

67. Hodeir, "Le grand patronat colonial français face à la décolonisation," 141.
68. MAEF-N 122PO / D / 73: Bousquet to Pineau, Direction générale politique—Europe, 1840 / EU, "Relance européenne (Marché commun et Euratom sous l'angle politique). L'action de M. Spaak 1956–1957," November 22, 1957.
69. Connelly, *Diplomatic Revolution*, 6.
70. MAEF-C 20QO / 720: DE-CE, "Accord des chefs de gouvernement sur l'Algérie et les Départements d'Outre-Mer au regard du Marché commun," February 22, 1957.
71. Emphasis original. MAEF-N 122PO / D / 73: Bousquet to Pineau, 1840 / EU, "Relance européenne."
72. Peo Hansen and Stefan Jonsson, *Eurafrica: The Untold History of European Integration and Colonialism* (London: Bloomsbury, 2014), 230.
73. MAEF-N 122PO / D / 73: Bousquet to Pineau, 1840 / EU, "Relance européenne."
74. MAEF-N 122PO / D / 72: Bousquet to Pineau, Direction générale des affaires économiques, 403 / EU, "Conférence des Premiers ministres, association des Territoires d'outre-mer au Marché commun," February 21, 1957, 3.
75. MAEF-N 122PO / D / 73: Bousquet to Pineau, 1840 / EU, "Relance européenne."
76. MAEF-N 122PO / D / 72: Bousquet to Pineau, 403 / EU, "Conférence des Premiers ministres," 1.
77. MAEF-N 122PO / D / 72: Bousquet to Pineau, Direction générale des affaires économiques, 409 / EU, "Comité des chefs de délégation du 20 février. Proposition de la délégation italienne relative aux conséquences de l'inclusion de l'Algérie dans le Marché commun européen en ce qui concerne le minerai et le fer algériens," February 21, 1957.
78. Garavini, *After Empires*, 50.
79. MAEF-N 122PO / D / 71: Bousquet to Pineau, Direction des affaires économiques, 78 / EU, "Éditorial de 'La Libre Belgique' sur M. SPAAK," January 7, 1957.

80. MAEF-N 122PO / D / 73: Bousquet to Pineau, Direction des affaires économiques, "Le parti catholique et le Fonds d'investissements dans les TOM," March 13, 1957.

81. MAEF-N 122PO / D / 74: Bousquet to Pineau, Direction générale politique—Europe, 462 / EU, "L'opinion belge et Val Duchesse," March 5, 1957.

82. 122PO / D / 73: Bousquet to Pineau, Direction générale politique— Europe, 1865 / EU, "Relance européenne (Marché commun et Euratom sous l'angle politique). L'action de M. Spaak 1956–1957," November 30, 1957.

83. MAEF-N 122PO / D / 72: Bousquet to Pineau, Direction des affaires économiques, 457 / EU, "Comité des chefs de délégation des 28 février–3 mars 1957. Application à l'Algérie et aux Départements français d'outre-mer du Traité instituant le Marché commun— Décisions des chefs de délégation," March 6, 1957, 1–2.

84. MAEF-N 122PO / D / 72: Bousquet to Pineau, Direction des affaires économiques, 456 / EU, "Comité des chefs de délégation des 28 février–3 mars 1957. Application à l'Algérie et aux Départements français d'outre-mer du Traité instituant le Marché commun—Débat au groupe du Marché commun," March 4, 1957, 3.

85. MAEF-N 122PO / D / 72: Bousquet to Pineau, 457 / EU, "Comité des chefs de délégation," 2–3.

86. Fiona Murray, *The European Union and Member State Territories: A New Legal Framework under the EU Treaties* (The Hague: Asser Press, 2012), 15–18. See also Vincent Coussirat-Coustère, "Article 227," in *Traité instituant la CEE: Commentaire article par article,* ed. Vlad Constantinesco, Jean-Paul Jacqué, Robert Kovar, and Denys Simon (Paris: Economica, 1992), 1419–1430. AN 20000293 / 4 (dérogation): "Note sur les dispositions du Traité de Rome relatives à l'Algérie," February 10, 1959.

87. MAEF-N 122PO / D / 73: Diplomatie to DELFRA Brussels, 94, November 2, 1957.

88. Thomas W. Zeiler, "The Expanding Mandate of the GATT: The First Seven Rounds," in *The Oxford Handbook on the World Trade Organization,* ed. Amrita Narlikar, Martin Daunton, and Robert M.

Stern (Oxford: Oxford University Press, 2012), 105; Todd Shepard, "Algeria, France, Mexico, UNESCO: A Transnational History of Anti-Racism and Decolonization, 1932–1962," *Journal of Global History* 6 (2011): 286–287.

89. MAEF-N 122PO / D / 74: "Conférence des Ministres des affaires étrangères du 16 octobre. Résumé des débats," annexed document, Bousquet to Pineau, Direction générale politique, 1701 / DE, "Conférence des Ministres des affaires étrangères du 16 octobre," October 19, 1957.

90. MAEF-N 122PO / D / 74: Bousquet to Pineau, Direction générale politique, "Comité intérimaire de Bruxelles, Sessions des 23 et 24 octobre—État de la discussion du Traité instituant la CEE devant le GATT," annex, October 28, 1957, 6.

91. Garavini, *After Empires*, 35–44, 68–69.

4. Algérie Européenne

1. CDHA: Marzocchi, Directeur du commerce intérieur et extérieur, secrétaire général adjoint des affaires économiques algériennes, "Le Marché algérien et l'Europe," *France Outremer* 36, no. 354 (May 1959): 60–61.

2. SP CM 7: Michel Debré to Maurice Couve de Murville, Diplomatie, July 23, 1960.

3. Guia Migani, "L'association des TOM au Marché commun: Histoire d'un accord européen entre cultures économiques différentes et idéaux politiques communs, 1955–1957," in *L'Europe unie et l'Afrique: De l'idée d'Eurafrique à la Convention de Lomé I: Actes du colloque international de Paris, 1er et 2 avril 2004,* ed. Marie-Thérèse Bitsch and Gérard Bossuat (Brussels: Bruylant, 2005), 237.

4. On the SGCI, see Ben Soetendorp, *Foreign Policy in the European Union: Theory, History and Practice* (London: Routledge, 2014), 52; Anne Dulphy and Christine Manigand, "Le Secrétariat général du Comité interministériel pour les questions de coopération économique européenne," *Histoire@Politique* 8, no. 2 (2009): 1–14.

5. On continuities between the Fourth and Fifth Republics, see Herrick Chapman, *France's Long Reconstruction: In Search of the Modern Republic* (Cambridge, MA: Harvard University Press, 2018).

6. CAOM 81 F 2255: Jacques Pélissier, Directeur de l'agriculture et des forêts du ministère de l'Algérie to Ministre de l'agriculture, "Production agricole de l'Algérie—Intégration dans le cadre du Marché commun européen," May 30, 1958.

7. CAOM 81 F 2128: Conseil de la République, "Avis présenté," Léon Motais de Narbonne, Sénateur, Commission de la France d'outre-mer, July 12, 1957.

8. MAEF-C 20QO / 792: Jean Jourdain, Président de l'Union syndicale des producteurs de sucre et de rhum de l'Ile de la Réunion, Conseiller économique, to Maurice Faure, Secrétaire d'état aux affaires étrangères, January 9, 1958.

9. ANMT 98 AS N 603: Confédération générale du patronat de l'Algérie, *Rapport de synthèse: Édition provisoire,* December 16, 1958.

10. MAEF-C 20QO / 712: Mille to Jacques Donnedieu de Vabres, Secrétaire d'état et direction économique, April 12, 1958.

11. "Algerier flüchten in die Bundesrepublik," *Frankfurter Allgemeine,* February 25, 1958.

12. AN 20000293 / 4: Draft memo, likely SGCI, "L'Algérie et le Marché commun," March 16, 1959.

13. AN 20000293 / 4: SGCI, CE / 2862, "Compte-Rendu de la réunion relative aux conditions d'application du Traité de Rome à l'Algérie et aux Départements d'outre-mer (article 227 du Traité) tenue au SGCI le 24 septembre 1959," October 21, 1959.

14. Amelia H. Lyons, "French or Foreign? The Algerian Migrants' Status at the End of Empire (1962–1968)," *Journal of Modern European History* 12, no. 1 (2014): 127–129.

15. Muriam Haleh Davis, "'The Transformation of Man' in French Algeria: Economic Planning and the Postwar Social Sciences, 1958–62," *Journal of Contemporary History* 52, no. 1 (2017): 75. See also James McDougall, "The Impossible Republic: The Reconquest of Algeria and the Decolonization of France, 1945–1962," *Journal of Modern History* 89 (2017): 795–798.

16. Muriam Haleh Davis, "Restaging Mise en Valeur: 'Postwar Imperialism' and the Plan de Constantine," *Review of Middle East Studies* 44, no. 2 (2010): 176–178.

17. He was referencing the 1934 case *Castanié v Vve Hutarto*. Emphasis original. Pierre-François Gonidec, "L'association des pays d'outre-mer au Marché commun," *Annuaire français de droit international* 4 (1958): 598–599.

18. CAOM 81 F 2255: Salah Bouakouir, Délégué général du gouvernement en Algérie to Premier Ministre, Secrétariat général pour les affaires algériennes, "Place de l'agriculture algérienne dans la politique agricole commune de la Communauté économique européenne," February 18, 1960.

19. CAOM 81 F 188: De Wailly to Donnedieu de Vabres, February 12, 1959.

20. MAEF-C 20QO/721: De Carbonnel to Diplomatie, August 5, 1958.

21. Denis Barbet and Jean-Paul Honoré, "Ce que taire veut dire. Expressions et usages politiques du silence," *Mots: Les langages du politique* 103 (2013): 13–14. There are multiple modes of preterition. Francisca Snoeck Henkemans, "La prétérition comme outil de stratégie rhétorique," trans. Sivan Cohen-Wiesenfeld, *Argumentation et analyse du discours* 2 (2009), doi: 10.4000/aad.217.

22. CAOM 81 F 1134: Ministère de l'intérieur [?], "La libre circulation des travailleurs," December 8, 1959.

23. Malick W. Ghachem, "The 'Trap' of Representation: Sovereignty, Slavery and the Road to the Haitian Revolution," *Historical Reflections / Réflexions historiques* 29, no. 1 (2003): 123–124.

24. CAOM 81 F 1134: SGCI, "Avant-projet de règlement de la Communauté économique européenne sur la libre circulation des travailleurs," July 9, 1959.

25. CAOM 81 F 1134: SGCI, "Études générales: Marché commun (Application de l'article 227)," n.d. [likely October–December 1960].

26. MAEF-N 105PO/1/156: Bousquet to Pineau, "Propagande MNA en Belgique," 1515/MLA, September 11, 1959. The editorial was published in June.

27. MAEF-N 105PO / 1 / 158: DELFRA Bonn to Couve de Murville, Direction d'Europe, "a / s Interview Abd-El-Krim," June 5, 1959.

28. MAEF-N 105PO / 1 / 156: François Seydoux, Bonn, to Delahaye, Diplomatie, 1272–75, March 15, 1961.

29. MAEF-C 20QO / 792: Groupe de Travail Algérie, SGCI, "Participation éventuelle de l'Algérie à une Zone de libre échange," April 17, 1957.

30. CAOM BIB AOM 20773 / 1959: Jean Pouderoux, "La Communauté économique européenne et l'Algérie," *Communautés et continents* 51, no. 3 (1959): 12.

31. Muriam Haleh Davis, *Markets of Civilization: Islam and Racial Capitalism in Algeria* (Durham, NC: Duke University Press, forthcoming), chap. 4.

32. John Agnew, "The Myth of Backward Italy in Modern Europe," in *Revisioning Italy: National Identity and Global Culture,* ed. Beverly Allen and Mary Russo (Minneapolis: University of Minnesota Press, 1997), 23–42; Antonio Gramsci, "Some Aspects of the Southern Question," in *The Gramsci Reader: Selected Writings 1916–1935,* ed. David Forgacs (New York: New York University Press, 2000), 171–185.

33. Robert Aldrich, "Homosexuality in the French Colonies," *Journal of Homosexuality* 41, no. 3 (2002): 201–218; Chiara Beccalossi, "The 'Italian Vice': Male Homosexuality and British Tourism in Southern Italy," in *Italian Sexualities Uncovered, 1789–1914,* ed. Valeria P. Babini, Chiara Beccalossi, and Lucy Riall (London: Palgrave Macmillan, 2015), 185–206.

34. Maura O'Connor, "Civilizing Southern Italy: British and Italian Women and the Cultural Politics of European Nation Building," *Women's Writing* 10, no. 2 (2003): 256–257.

35. Carmine Conelli, "Challenging the Domestic Colonial Archive: Notes on the Racialization of the Italian Mezzogiorno," in *Postcolonial Europe: Comparative Reflections after the Empires,* ed. Lars Jensen, Julia Suárez-Krabbe, Christian Groes, and Zoran Lee Pecic (Lanham, MD: Rowman & Littlefield, 2017), 35–36.

36. CAOM BIB AOM 20773 / 1959: Pouderoux, "La Communauté économique européenne et l'Algérie," 12.
37. CAOM 81 F 2363: Commission d'étude de l'agriculture dans le cadre du Marché commun, "Note relative aux départements d'Algérie," June 9, 1958.
38. Lauren Stokes, *Fear of the Family: Guest Workers and Family Migration in the Federal Republic of Germany* (Oxford: Oxford University Press, forthcoming).
39. Rita Chin, *The Guest Worker Question in Postwar Germany* (Cambridge: Cambridge University Press, 2007), 7.
40. MAEF-C 20QO / 726: Gorse, Brussels, to Diplomatie, June 16, 1960.
41. AN 20000293 / 4: Gorse to DAEF, "Extension à l'Algérie et aux DOM des clauses du Traité de Rome (art. 227)," January 25, 1961.
42. CAOM 81 F 1133: Yves Roland-Billecart, March 22, 1961.
43. CAOM 81 F 1133: Christian Delaballe, Ministre d'état chargé des affaires algériennes to Morin, SGCI, "Application à l'Algérie des dispositions du Traité de Rome," June 26, 1961.
44. "'Hort auf, den Massenmord zu unterstützen': Ein Spiegel-Gespräch mit dem Ministerpräsidenten der algerischen Exilregierung, Ferhat Abbas," *Der Spiegel,* August 19, 1958, 36–37.
45. MAEF-C 20QO / 726: Leduc, Bonn, to Delahaye, Diplomatie, August 18, 1959.
46. Köhler, "Gemeinsamer Markt," *Frankfurter Allgemeine Zeitung,* October 19, 1957.
47. MAEF-N 105PO / 1 / 158: Leduc to Diplomatie, 603–605, March 10, 1958.
48. MAEF-C 20QO / 726: DE-CE, "Extension à l'Algérie des opérations du Fonds européen de développement," November 28, 1959.
49. MAEF-C 20QO / 726: DE-CE, "Algérie et Marché commun," December 30, 1959.
50. AN 2 DE 69: "Note sur la politique européenne," June 30, 1960.
51. MAEF-N 105PO / 1 / 159: Seydoux to Diplomatie, 2555–57, October 31, 1958.

52. Emphasis original. MAEF-C 260QO / 26: "Premier comité européen de salut public," n.d.

53. HAEU AD-4: "Les fédéralistes européens en face du drame algérien," October 1956.

54. Leila J. Rupp, "Constructing Internationalism: The Case of Transnational Women's Organizations, 1888–1945," *American Historical Review* 99, no. 5 (1994): 1592–1593.

55. Gary Wilder, *Freedom Time: Negritude, Decolonization, and the Future of the World* (Durham, NC: Duke University Press, 2015).

56. HAEU AD-16: Mouvement fédéraliste européen, Turin section, pamphlet, n.d.

57. HAEU AD-16: MFE, "Communiqué du comité central," Paris, April 3, 1962.

58. MAEF-C 260QO / 26: "Mouvement fédéraliste européen se déclare 'persuadés que l'Algérie doit obtenir son indépendance,'" February 25, 1961.

59. Cited in Samir Saul, *Intérêts économiques français et décolonisation de l'Afrique du Nord (1945–1962)* (Geneva: Librairie Droz, 2016), 9.

60. MAEF-N 105PO / 1 / 159: J. Fernand-Laurent, DELFRA Hamburg, to Seydoux, "Voyage de journalistes au Sahara," January 14, 1960. Giuliano Garavini calls OPEC's launch "a vital element of the Third World's new activism and of the increasingly global reach of some of its ideas." Giuliano Garavini, *After Empires: European Integration, Decolonization, and the Challenge from the Global South, 1957–1986* (Oxford: Oxford University Press, 2012), 34–35. On OPEC, see Giuliano Garavini, *The Rise and Fall of OPEC in the Twentieth Century* (Oxford: Oxford University Press, 2019). Organized tours were a well-worn mode of propaganda for the French state. Véronique Dimier, *The Invention of a Development Aid Bureaucracy: Recycling Empire* (London: Palgrave Macmillan, 2014), 48–53.

61. MAEF-N 105PO / 1 / 158: Gaston Palewski to Diplomatie, Service d'information et de presse, 637-IP, "Émission à télévision italienne," April 17, 1958.

62. MAEF-N 105PO / 1 / 156: Seydoux to Diplomatie, Service d'information et de presse," January 23, 1959.

63. CAEF B 0062126 (formerly B 25343): Ministère de l'économie et affaires financières, direction des finances extérieures, Compte-rendu de la réunion des conseillers financiers, October 9, 1959.

64. AN 19771468 / 228: Hendus to Gorse, "Présentation au Fonds européen de développement de projets concernant l'Algérie," September 21, 1960, VIII / C / 21.962; AN 19771468 / 228: Burgard, Caisse d'équipement pour la développement de l'Algérie to Mayoux, SGCI, "Présentation au Fonds européen de développement d'un projet d'équipement public pour l'Algérie," August 1, 1961; AN 19771468 / 228: Putod, Caisse d'équipement pour la développement de l'Algérie, département de l'équipement public, to Direction financière et technique du FED, February 1, 1962.

65. "Aide des Six à la Réunion," Le Monde, March 4, 1961.

66. MAEF-C 20QO / 726: Seydoux to Diplomatie, July 3, 1959. Mathilde von Bülow, West Germany, Cold War Europe and the Algerian War (Cambridge: Cambridge University Press, 2016).

67. MAEF-C 20QO / 726: DAEF, note for Olivier Wormser and Valery, June 4, 1959.

68. MAEF-C 20QO / 726: DE-CE, "Extension à l'Algérie des opérations du Fonds de développement de la CEE," October 3, 1959.

69. MAEF-C 20QO / 726: Seydoux to Couve de Murville, "Visite de M. Coup de Fréjac le 18 décembre 1959, entretien avec MM. Leduc, Rivain, Biclet, Schricke, Féquant et Morizet," December 24, 1959.

70. Véronique Dimier, "Recycling Empire: French Colonial Administrators at the Heart of European Development Policy," in The French Colonial Mind Vol. 1: Mental Maps of Empire and Colonial Encounters, ed. Martin Thomas (Lincoln: University of Nebraska Press, 2011), 251–274.

71. CAOM BIB AOM 20285 / 1960: "La politique européenne en Afrique doit rester solidaire," Marchés tropicaux et méditerranéens 16, no. 762 (1960): 1383.

72. HAEU: Jean-Marie Palayret and Anaïs Legendre, "Histoire interne de la Commission européenne 1958–1973," interview with Jacques Ferrandi, Ajaccio, May 28–29, 2004, archives.eui.eu/en/files/transcript/15190.pdf.

73. Dimier, *Invention,* 23–25, 2.

74. AN AG / 5(F) / 2558: Bonn to Hallstein, translation of dépêche de l'Agence DPA en provenance de Bruxelles, "Motifs de la démission d'Allardt de la Commission de la CEE," June 8, 1960.

75. AN AG / 5(F) / 2558: Translated excerpt of "Brouille à la Commission de la CEE au sujet d'anciens territoires coloniaux," *Westfaelische Rundschau,* June 9, 1960.

76. AN AG / 5(F) / 2558: Translated excerpt of Hilde Purwin, "À la CEE à Bruxelles, on reste entre soi," *Neue Rhein Zeitung,* June 26, 1960.

77. MAEF-N 105PO / 1 / 150: Commandement en chef des forces françaises en Allemagne, Groupement des services de sécurité, 510 / CCFFA / GSS, "Renseignements sur Heinrich Hendus, nommé Consul général de la République fédérale à Alger," March 9, 1956.

78. MAEF-C 20QO / 722: Tofkin [?], Diplomatie, to Direction générale des affaires politiques, Mission de liaison pour les affaires algériennes, June 10, 1960.

79. HAEU: Ferrandi interview.

80. MAEF-C 20QO / 726: DE–CE, "Algérie et Fonds européen de développement," August 3, 1960.

81. MAEF-C 20QO / 726: DE–CE, annexed to "Algérie et Fonds européen de développement," "Projet de lettre de présentation au Président de la Commission économique européenne," August 3, 1960.

82. MAEF-N 378PO / 6 / 1773: Jean-Pierre Brunet, "Négociations sur le renouvellement de l'association des pays d'Afrique," March 1962.

83. AN 20000293 / 4: SGCI, CE / 2797, "Fonds de développement de la Communauté économique européenne—Intervention en Algérie," May 10, 1962.

84. CAOM BIB AOM 20773 / 1959: Pouderoux, "La Communauté économique européenne et l'Algérie," 6. Perhaps Pouderoux borrowed the term from an economist who employed it a year earlier. Cited in Muriam Haleh Davis, "The Sahara as the 'Cornerstone' of Eurafrica: European Integration and Technical Sovereignty Seen from the Desert," *Journal of European Integration*

History 23, no. 1 (2017): 97. Dimier employs the term herself in describing the regime of African states in relation to European development aid entities. Dimier, *Invention, 73.*

85. "L'Algérie et le Marché commun," *Le Monde*, December 25, 1958.

5. French Supremacy in Europe after Algerian Independence

1. HAEU CM2 / 1963–885: Herbst, EEC Commission, to Calmes, Council of EEC, January 3, 1963.

2. Frederick Cooper and Randall M. Packard, eds., *International Development and the Social Sciences: Essays on the History and Politics of Knowledge* (Berkeley: University of California Press, 1998); Urban Vahsen, "Africa Policy in a European Framework? The Federal Republic of Germany and Sub-Saharan Africa in the 1960s," *Outre-Mers: Revue d'histoire* 98, no. 372–373 (2011): 95–106.

3. Tony Chafer, "Chirac and 'la Françafrique': No Longer a Family Affair," *Modern & Contemporary France* 13, no. 1 (2006): 7–23.

4. Benjamin Stora, "Les algériens à Paris pendant la guerre d'Algérie: Installation, travail et conditions de vie," in *Le Paris des étrangers depuis 1945,* ed. Antoine Marès and Pierre Milza (Paris: Éditions de la Sorbonne, 1995), n.p.; Pierrette Meynier and Gilbert Meynier, "L'immigration algérienne en France: Histoire et actualité," *Confluences Méditerranée* 77, no. 2 (2011): 219–234; Maud Anne Bracke, "May 1968 and Algerian Immigrants in France: Trajectories of Mobilization and Encounter," in *1968 in Retrospect: History, Theory, Alterity,* ed. Gurminder K. Bhambra and Ipek Demir (London: Palgrave Macmillan, 2009), 115–130.

5. On the 1963 and 1969 Yaoundé Conventions and their successor, Lomé, see Marie-Thérèse Bitsch and Gérard Bossuat, eds., *L'Europe unie et l'Afrique: De l'idée d'Eurafrique à la Convention de Lomé I: Actes du colloque international de Paris, 1er et 2 avril 2004* (Brussels: Bruylant, 2005); Adekeye Adebajo and Kaye Whiteman, eds., *The EU and Africa: From Eurafrique to Afro-Europa* (New York: Columbia University Press, 2012).

6. Cited in Jeffrey James Byrne, *Mecca of Revolution: Algeria, Decolonization and the Third World Order* (New York: Oxford University Press, 2016), 273.

7. Reza Zia-Ebrahimi, "Courting the Former Colony: Algeria's Special Position in French Third World Policy, 1963," *Journal of North African Studies* 17, no. 1 (2012): 23–44.

8. On the remarkable range of the Algerian government's international connections, see Byrne, *Mecca of Revolution*.

9. MAEF-C 21QO / 1462: DE-CE, "Note a / s le Maghreb et la Communauté économique européenne," October 11, 1962. This echoed decades-old questions of French nationality, citizenship, and (perhaps murkiest of all) identity. Catherine Coquéry-Vidrovitch, "Nationalité et citoyenneté en Afrique occidentale française: Originaires et citoyens dans le Sénégal colonial," *Journal of African History* 42 (2001): 285–305; Emmanuelle Saada, *Empire's Children: Race, Filiation, and Citizenship in the French Colonies*, trans. Arthur Goldhammer (Chicago: University of Chicago Press, 2012); Lorelle D. Semley, "'Evolution Revolution' and the Journey from African Colonial Subject to French Citizen," *Law and History Review* 32, no. 2 (2014): 267–307; Frederick Cooper, *Citizenship between Empire and Nation: Remaking France and French Africa, 1945–1960* (Princeton, NJ: Princeton University Press, 2014); Christina Elizabeth Firpo, *The Uprooted: Race, Children, and Imperialism in French Indochina, 1890–1980* (Honolulu: University of Hawai'i Press, 2016).

10. Cited in Jacques Marseille, *Empire colonial et capitalisme français: Histoire d'un divorce* (Paris: Albin Michel, 1984), 373.

11. On the genesis of the French hexagon concept, see Eugen Weber, "L'hexagone," in *Les lieux de mémoire: La nation, Vol. II: Le territoire, l'état, le patrimoine,* ed. Pierre Nora (Paris: Gallimard, 1986), 97–116; Todd Shepard, "The Birth of the Hexagon: 1962 and the Erasure of France's Supranational History," in *Vertriebene and Pieds-Noirs in Postwar Germany and France: Comparative Perspectives,* ed. Manuel Borutta and Jan C. Jansen (London: Palgrave Macmillan, 2016), 53–69.

12. "Algeria: France-Algeria Independence Agreements (Evian Agreements)," *International Legal Materials* 1, no. 2 (1962): 214–230.

13. Strikethrough original. MAEF-C 21QO / 1462: DE-CE, "Le Maghreb et la Communauté économique européenne," October 11, 1962.

14. MAEF-C 21QO / 1462: Jean-Marc Boegner to Diplomatie, "Politique agricole commune et Algérie," August 9, 1962.

15. MAEF-C 21QO / 1462: Valéry to Boegner, August 17, 1962.

16. MAEF-C 21QO / 1462: Boegner to Diplomatie, "L'Algérie et la CEE," August 22, 1962.

17. "Construction de 6 hôpitaux blocs," *Journal officiel de l'État Algérien* 1, no. 6 (August 14–17, 1962): 64.

18. AN 20000293 / 4: Henri Rochereau to Louis Joxe, Ministre d'état chargé des affaires algériennes, September 25, 1962.

19. HAEU CM2 / 1963–885: Calmes to Permanent Representatives, February 11, 1963.

20. Laredj Sekkiou, *L'Algérie et la Communauté économique européenne* (Nyon, Switzerland: J. Allamand, 1971), 31.

21. Mahfoud Bennoune, *The Making of Contemporary Algeria, 1830–1987: Colonial Upheavals and Post-independence Development* (Cambridge: Cambridge University Press, 1988), 104; Owen White, *The Blood of the Colony: Wine and the Rise and Fall of French Algeria* (Cambridge, MA: Harvard University Press, 2021), 211–215.

22. Todd Shepard, *The Invention of Decolonization: The Algerian War and the Remaking of France* (Ithaca, NY: Cornell University Press, 2006), 55–68.

23. Jean-Jacques Jordi, *1962: L'arrivée des pieds-noirs* (Paris: Éditions Autrement, 1995), 56–57.

24. Yann Scioldo-Zürcher, *Devenir métropolitain: Politique d'intégration et parcours de rapatriés d'Algérie en metropole (1954–2005)* (Paris: Éditions de l'École des hautes études en sciences sociales, 2010), 187–196.

25. Pertti Ahonen, *After the Expulsion: West Germany and Eastern Europe, 1945–1990* (Oxford: Oxford University Press, 2003).

26. BDIC 4° delta 998 / 6: "Mesures prises par la République fédérale allemande en faveur des expulsés, réfugiés et sinistrés," September 29, 1960.

27. Shepard, *The Invention of Decolonization*.

28. AD-BdR 137 W 457: Provisional Committee of European Youth to M. P. Havard, Union départementale des associations familiales, Amsterdam, July 24, 1962.

29. Sung-Eun Choi, *Decolonization and the French of Algeria: Bringing the Settler Colony Home* (London: Palgrave Macmillan, 2016), 8.

30. Shepard, *The Invention of Decolonization,* 230–238; Connelly, *Diplomatic Revolution,* 285.

31. Stora, "Les algériens à Paris," n.p.

32. CAOM 81 F 1506: C. Husson, SGCI, CE/5.048, "Notification de la modification apportée à l'annexe 3 du règlement n° 4 du Conseil de la CEE par l'autorité compétente néerlandaise," August 13, 1962; CAOM 81 F 1506: Christian Delaballe, Ministère d'état chargé des affaires algériennes to DELFRA Algiers, 7208–1005, "Circulaire relative à l'application du règlement n° 3 de la Communauté économique européenne applicable aux travailleurs migrants," October 25, 1962.

33. CAOM 81 F 1506: "Note relative au Centre de Sécurité sociale des travailleurs migrants," October 10, 1962.

34. MAEF-C 21QO/1462: "Relations financières franco-algériennes," October 31, 1962.

35. Emmanuelle Comtat, "La question du vote *pied-noir,*" *Pôle sud* 24, no. 1 (2006): 75–88.

36. MAEF-C 21QO/1462: DE-CE, "L'Algérie et la Communauté économique européenne," February 7, 1963.

37. MAEF-C 21QO/1462: Boegner to Diplomatie, March 11, 1964; B. Layer, Secrétaire d'état auprès du Premier ministre, chargé des affaires algériennes to DELFRA Algiers, March 14, 1964; Delahaye on behalf of the DREE, telegram to DELFRA Algiers, April 20, 1964.

38. AN 19880053/195: SGCI, JS/MP no. CE/1516, "Sur les relations commerciales franco-algériennes," February 17, 1964.

39. MAEF-C 21QO/1462: Boegner to Diplomatie, May 19, 1964.

40. Byrne, *Mecca of Revolution.*

41. HAEU CM2/1963–885: Herbst, EEC Commission, to Calmes, Council of EEC, January 3, 1963.

42. HAEU CM2 / 1963–885: Councils of the EEC and CEEA, "Addendum au projet de compte rendu sommaire de la réunion restreinte à l'occasion de la 243ème réunion du Comité des représentants permanents," January 28, 1963.

43. MAEF-C 21QO / 1462: Diplomatie, "Démarches algériennes auprès de la CEE," January 3, 1964.

44. AN 19880053 / 196: Représentant permanente de la République Française et de la Communauté auprès des Communautés européennes—Conseiller financier, 404 CF, "L'Algérie et le Marché commun," January 7, 1963.

45. Claude Zarka, "Chronique économique," *Annuaire de l'Afrique du Nord: 1962* 1 (1963): 538–539.

46. Bennoune, *The Making of Contemporary Algeria*, 90.

47. MAEF-N 378PO / 6 / 1496: DELFRA Algiers to Ministre d'état chargé des affaires algériennes, "Évolution récente de la situation en Algérie," November 29, 1962.

48. Elizabeth Schmidt, *Cold War and Decolonization in Guinea, 1946–1958* (Athens: Ohio University Press, 2007), 166–179.

49. I. William Zartman, *The Politics of Trade Negotiations between Africa and the European Economic Community: The Weak Confront the Strong* (Princeton, NJ: Princeton University Press, 1971), 19–20n9.

50. Bitsch and Bossuat, *L'Europe unie et l'Afrique;* Guia Migani, *La France et l'Afrique sub-saharienne, 1957–1963: Histoire d'une décolonisation entre idéaux eurafricains et politique de puissance* (Brussels: Peter Lang, 2008).

51. Zartman, *The Politics of Trade Negotiations*, 25–26.

52. Council of Europe (no author), "Europe and Africa," (booklet), (Strasbourg, 1960), 34–35.

53. CVCE: "La Convention de Yaoundé," July 20, 1963, https://www.cvce.eu/en/obj/the_yaounde_convention_20_july_1963-en-52d35693-845a–49ae-b6f9-ddbc48276546.html.

54. MAEF-N 378PO / 6 / 1773: Margerie, Bonn, to Diplomatie, 650 / 54, "Reserve allemande quant à l'aide financière aux pays africains associés," November 21, 1962.

55. MAEF-N 378PO / 6 / 1494: Margerie, Bonn, to Diplomatie, 6646 / 49, "Aide financière allemande à l'Algérie," October 7, 1964.

56. MAEF-N 378PO / 6 / 1496: DELFRA Algiers to Secrétaire d'état auprès du Premier ministre chargé des affaires algériennes, 1423 / AP, "À la recherche d'un second souffle?" March 6, 1963; Robert A. Mortimer, "Algerian Foreign Policy: From Revolution to National Interest," *Journal of North African Studies* 20, no. 3 (2015): 466–482.

57. Bennoune, *The Making of Contemporary Algeria,* 101.

58. Jacques Garello, Claude Bensoussan, and Claude Zarka, "Chronique économique," *Annuaire de l'Afrique du Nord: 1963* 2 (1964): 606.

59. B. Zoubir, "Chronique économique Algérie," *Annuaire de l'Afrique du Nord: 1967* 6 (1968): 439.

60. MAEF-N 378PO / 6 / 1493: Courcel, DELFRA London, 3778, October 3, 1962.

61. MAEF-N 378PO / 6 / 1493: Courcel to Secrétariat d'état aux affaires algériennes, 2512 / 14, "Visite de M. Boumaza à Londres," May 30, 1964.

62. Philippe Cabanius-Matraman, "Chronique économique Algérie," *Annuaire de l'Afrique du Nord: 1965* 4 (1966): 295.

63. "Avis aux importateurs de produits en provenance de Suède," *Journal officiel de l'État Algérien* 1, no. 2 (July 17, 1962): 24.

64. Byrne, *Mecca of Revolution,* 143.

65. "Avis aux importateurs de textiles et de café vert en provenance de l'étranger," *Journal officiel de l'État Algérien* 1, no. 4 (July 27–31, 1962): 35.

66. MAEF-C 21QO / 1462: Gorse to Diplomatie, May 19, 1964.

67. MAEF-C 21QO / 1462: Gorse to Diplomatie, May 19, 1964.

68. Jacob Abadi, "Algeria's Policy toward Israel: Pragmatism and Rhetoric," *Middle East Journal* 56, no. 4 (2002): 616–641.

69. AN 19880053 / 196: Wahl, DREE, to SGCI, 2424, "Position de l'Algérie vis-à-vis du Marché commun," November 19, 1964. This was just after the cooling of the Moroccan-Algerian conflict over territory in western Algeria. Patricia Berko Wild, "The Organization of African Unity and the Algerian-Moroccan Border Conflict: A Study of New Machinery for Peacekeeping and for the

Peaceful Settlement of Disputes among African States," *International Organization* 20, no. 1 (Winter 1966): 21–25.

70. AN 19880053 / 196: Wahl to SGCI, 2424.

71. Herrick Chapman, *France's Long Reconstruction: In Search of the Modern Republic* (Cambridge, MA: Harvard University Press, 2018), 270–271.

72. HAEU CM2 / 1964–1347: EEC Council, "Aide-mémoire du secrétariat, compte rendu de l'exposé fait par la Commission devant le Comité des Représentants permanents le 21 mai 1964 sur les résultats de la deuxième série de conversations exploratoires avec le gouvernement algérien," May 22, 1964.

73. HAEU CM2 / 1964–1347: EEC Council, "Aide-mémoire du secrétariat."

74. MAEF-C 21QO / 1462: Louis Dauge, DELFRA Algiers, to Diplomatie, Finances, May 30, 1964.

75. Todd Shepard, "À l'heure des 'grands ensembles' et de la guerre d'Algérie: L'"état-nation' en question," trans. Jennifer Dybmann, *Monde(s): Histoire, espaces, relations* 1 (2012): 113–134.

76. MAEF-C 21 QO / 1462: Secrétariat d'état auprès du Premier ministre chargé des affaires algériennes to SGCI, "Application à l'Algérie des règlements n° 3 et 4 sur la sécurité sociale des travailleurs migrants," May 28, 1964.

77. MAEF-C 21QO / 1462: Morin, SGCI, "Application à l'Algérie des règlements n° 3 et 4 sur la sécurité sociale des travailleurs migrants," June 8, 1964; Service des affaires générales, affaires sociales, secrétaire d'état auprès du Premier ministre, chargé des affaires algériennes, to SGCI, "Application à l'Algérie des règlements n° 3 et 4 sur la sécurité sociale des travailleurs migrants," May 28, 1964.

78. Irwin M. Wall, *France, the United States, and the Algerian War* (Chicago: University of Chicago Press, 2001), 203–204.

79. Anthony Teasdale, "The Fouchet Plan: De Gaulle's Intergovernmental Design for Europe," *LEQS Paper* 117 (2016): 1–3.

80. MAEF-C 21QO / 1462: DE-CE, "L'Algérie et la Communauté économique européenne," February 7, 1963.

81. Guia Migani, "Avant Lomé: La France, l'Afrique anglophone et la CEE (1961–1972)," *Modern & Contemporary France* 26, no. 1 (2018): 45–49.

82. Opland, "Franse les voor gevorderden," cartoon, 1963.

83. Ian Coller, *Arab France: Islam and the Making of Modern Europe, 1789–1831* (Berkeley: University of California Press, 2010); Black Central Europe, https://blackcentraleurope.com.

84. Pierre Moussa, *Les chances économique de la communauté franco-africaine* (Paris: Armand Colin, 1957).

85. Arend Lijphart, *The Trauma of Decolonization: The Dutch and West New Guinea* (New Haven, CT: Yale University Press, 1966).

86. MAEF-C 21QO / 1462: Boegner to Diplomatie, May 29, 1963.

87. MAEF-C 21QO / 1462: Boegner to Diplomatie, June 18, 1963.

88. MAEF-C 21QO / 1462: Crouy, DELFRA Hague to Diplomatie, June 20, 1963.

89. On Franco-German relations and the Algeria War, see Mathilde von Bülow, *West Germany, Cold War Europe and the Algerian War* (Cambridge: Cambridge University Press, 2016).

90. Cited in Jeffrey Glen Giauque, *Grand Designs and Visions of Unity: The Atlantic Powers and the Reorganization of Western Europe, 1955–1963* (Chapel Hill: University of North Carolina Press, 2002), 200.

91. On Renault's tardy installation in Algeria in 1959, see Daniel Lefeuvre, *Chère Algérie: La France et sa colonie, 1930–1962* (Paris: Flammarion, 2005), 471–473.

92. MAEF-C 21QO / 1462: Gorse to DREE, March 2, 1963.

93. Michael Sutton, *France and the Construction of Europe, 1944–2007: The Geopolitical Imperative* (New York: Berghahn, 2007), 134–136.

94. HAEU CM2 / 1963–885: Calmes to Permanent Representatives, February 11, 1963; Martin Dedman, *The Origins and Development of the European Union, 1945–2008: A History of European Integration* (London: Routledge, 2010), 101–102.

95. Byrne, *Mecca of Revolution,* 170.

96. MAEF-C 21QO / 1462: Boegner to Diplomatie, June 18, 1963.

97. MAEF-N 378PO / 6 / 1773: Diplomatie to DELFRA Brussels, 10666 / 68, "Des rapports de la CEE avec l'Algérie," June 19, 1963.

98. Byrne, *Mecca of Revolution*.

99. MAEF-C 21QO/1462: Colonel Degas, Premier ministre, Secrétariat général à la Défense, Chef du centre d'exploitation du renseignement, to DAEF, "Position de l'Algérie face au Marché commun," September 2, 1963.

100. MAEF-C 21QO/1462: Pierre de Leusse to Diplomatie, September 14, 1963.

101. MAEF-C 21QO/1462: Diplomatie, "Démarches algériennes auprès de la CEE," January 3, 1964.

102. MAEF-C 21QO/1462: DE-CE, likely to Delahaye, "Conversations exploratoires CEE/Algérie," February 29, 1964.

103. HAEU CM2/1964–1347: EEC press release, "Conversations CEE/Algérie," February 27, 1964.

104. AN 19950190/7: SGCI, "Projet de règlement relatif à l'organisation du marché européen du sucre," January 25, 1965.

105. AN 20040335/4: Préfecture de la Réunion, cabinet to M. le Ministre d'état chargé des départements et territoires d'outre-mer, "Expulsion de la Réunion de deux ressortissants allemands," August 10, 1965.

106. AN 20040335/4: Heuman, Diplomatie, direction des conventions administratives et des affaires consulaires to Ministre d'état chargé des départements et territoires d'outre-mer, "Expulsion de la Réunion de deux ressortissants allemands," July 8, 1965; AN 20040335/4: West Germany embassy to Diplomatie, Direction des conventions administratives et des affaires consulaires, June 29, 1965; AN 20040335/4: West Germany embassy to Diplomatie, June 30, 1965.

107. AN 20040335/4: Préfecture de la Réunion to Ministre d'état chargé des départements et territoires d'outre-mer, "Expulsion de la Réunion de deux ressortissants allemands," August 10, 1965.

108. AN 20040335/4: Hugues Vinel, Ministère d'état chargé des départements et territoires d'outre-mer to Ministre du travail, sous-direction de la réglementation de l'emploi et de l'immigration, 1420, "Intervention de l'ambassade de la République fédérale d'Allemagne a/s expulsion deux de ses ressortissants de la Réunion," August 31, 1965.

109. AN 20040335 / 4: Ministère du travail, sous-direction de la réglementation de l'emploi et de l'immigration to Ministère d'état départements et territoires d'outre-mer, "Situation de Messieurs Horsting et Erb, de nationalité allemande," December 3, 1965.

110. "De Gaulle à Adenauer: 'L'Union franco-allemande permet une vaste organisation de l'Europe,'" *L'Indépendant,* July 4, 1962, 12.

111. Houari Boumediene, "The Future of the Algerian Revolution," *Journal of Modern African Studies* 6, no. 3 (1968).

112. MAEF-C 0034SUP / 90: Diplomatie, Direction des Affaires politiques, Sous-direction Algérie, "Note: L'Algérie et la CEE," January 24, 1967.

113. Mark Gilbert, *European Integration: A Concise History* (Lanham, MD: Rowman & Littlefield, 2012), 79–83.

114. N. Piers Ludlow, "Challenging French Leadership in Europe: Germany, Italy, the Netherlands and the Outbreak of the Empty Chair Crisis of 1965–1966," *Contemporary European History* 8, no. 2 (1999): 231–233.

6. Algeria, France, and the Europe of Nation-States

1. G. *Fiege v Caisse régionale d'assurance maladie de Strasbourg* (Case 110 / 73), opinion of Advocate-General Warner, September 19, 1973, *European Court Reports 1973–01001,* 1014. All ECJ documents cited available on EUR-Lex, https://eur-lex.europa.eu/.

2. Jeffrey James Byrne, *Mecca of Revolution: Algeria, Decolonization and the Third World Order* (New York: Oxford University Press, 2016).

3. Fátima Fernández, "Une 'sortie' en cachette: La discrète disparition de l'Algérie du Marché commun européen (1957–1976)," *Maghreb Review* 44, no. 1 (2019): 91–111.

4. MAEF-N 21PO / 112: Soutou to Diplomatie, 933, "Interview du Président Boumediene à la Radio-Télévision Italienne (Suite)," April 15, 1973.

5. "'Révolution africaine': L'Algérie et la CEE doivent ouvrir des négociations officielles," *Le Monde,* April 1, 1970.

6. Alain Murcier, "Les accords franco-algériens sur les hydrocarbures 'décapitalisent' l'activité pétrolière au Sahara," *Le Monde diplomatique,* August 1965, 2.

7. AN 19820750 / 37: Pierre Desprairies, Société des pétroles d'Afrique équatoriale, to Jean Blancard, September 23, 1965.

8. Viviane Michel and Jean-Jacques Régnier, "Aperçu sur la coopération technique française en Afrique du Nord depuis l'indépendance," *Annuaire de l'Afrique du Nord: 1967* 6 (1968): 166–167.

9. MAEF-N 21PO / 220: A. Dargent, Consulat Tlemcen, to DELFRA Algiers, "Coopération (française et étrangère)," January 25, 1965.

10. MAEF-N 21PO / DE / 418: CEE—Le Conseil, S / 286 / 65, "Note d'information—Relevé des données techniques et financières les plus caractéristiques concernant les actions de coopération technique mises en œuvre ou envisagées par les États membres de la Communauté à l'égard de l'Algérie, du Maroc et de la Tunisie," April 6, 1965.

11. AN 19950190 / 7: EEC Council, "Relations avec les pays du Maghreb: Aide-mémoire du secrétariat," S / 38 / 65, January 14, 1965, annex II: "Déclaration générale faite par la délégation italienne à l'occasion de la réunion du 9 décembre 1964."

12. MAEF-N 21PO / DE / 418: Leusse, Algiers, to Diplomatie and DELFRA Brussels / Haye, 1471 / 72, April 4, 1968.

13. MAEF-N 21PO / DE / 418: Gorse to DREE, 5866 / 67, December 28, 1965; MAEF-N 21PO / 353: Dutch embassy in Algiers to Diplomatie, June 11, 1967.

14. Philipp Hirsch, "The Cold War, the Arab World, and West Germany's 'Mediterranean Moment,' 1967–73," *Cold War History* (2019): 161–178.

15. MAEF-N 21PO / DE / 418: Basdevant to Diplomatie, Direction d'Afrique-Levant, "Réactions de l'Algérie à la réunion des Ministres des affaires étrangères des membres de la CEE," May 18, 1971.

16. Owen White, "Roll Out the Barrel: French and Algerian Ports and the Birth of the Wine Tanker," *French Politics, Culture & Society* 35, no. 2 (2017): 126.

17. Aflakh [Khalfa] Mameri, "L'adhésion de l'Algérie à la Communauté économique européenne," *Revue algérienne des sciences juridiques, économiques et politiques* (1968): 434. Although this article's published author attribution is "Aflakh," I attribute this article to Khalfa Mameri and suggest that the misidentification is due to someone transliterating Arabic from left to right. I am grateful to Benjamin L. Smith for discussing Mameri's identity with me.

18. MAEF-N 21PO / DE / 418: "Rien n'empêche l'Algérie d'adhérer à la CEE, déclare le président du conseil de la Communauté," AFP, March 28, 1969.

19. MAEF-N 21PO / 82: Pierre de Leusse to Bernard Tricot, January 11, 1968.

20. MAEF-N 21PO / DE / 418: Bouteflika to Président du Conseil des Ministres, March 10, 1972, transmitted by Messaoud Ait-Chaalal to Calmes, March 16, 1972.

21. MAEF-N 21PO / DE / 418: "Quelques remarques," *El Moudjahid,* ca. June 25, 1973. Sent by DELFRA Algiers to Michel Jobert, Diplomatie, sous-direction d'Algérie, June 25, 1973.

22. On the early years of contestation, see Elizabeth Heath, "The Color of French Wine: Southern Wine Producers Respond to Competition from the Algerian Wine Industry in the Early Third Republic," *French Politics, Culture & Society* 35, no. 2 (2017): 89–110 and John Strachan, "The Colonial Identity of Wine: The *Leakey Affair* and the Franco-Algerian Order of Things," *Social History of Alcohol and Drugs* 21, no. 2 (2007): 118–137. On France's postwar contestation over Algerian wine and European competition, see Joseph Bohling, *The Sober Revolution: Appellation Wine and the Transformation of France* (Ithaca, NY: Cornell University Press, 2018), 153–179.

23. Owen White, *The Blood of the Colony: Wine and the Rise and Fall of French Algeria* (Cambridge, MA: Harvard University Press, 2021), 221–227.

24. Hildebert Isnard, "La viticulture nord-africaine," *Annuaire de l'Afrique du Nord: 1965* 4 (1966): 43.

25. Isnard, "La viticulture nord-africaine," 43.

26. White, *Blood of the Colony,* 216–217.

27. Bruno Etienne, "Chronique diplomatique," *Annuaire de l'Afrique du Nord: 1967* 6 (1968): 326.

28. MAEF-N 21PO / 352: Philippe Rebeyrol to Diplomatie, 2820, June 25, 1966.

29. Bruno Etienne, "Chronique diplomatique," *Annuaire de l'Afrique du Nord: 1968* 7 (1969): 205.

30. MAEF-N 21PO / 82: Pierre de Leusse to Brunet, DREE, 17 / SP, January 10, 1968.

31. MAEF-N 21PO / 82: Pierre de Leusse to François de Laboulaye, July 10, 1968.

32. Etienne, "Chronique diplomatique," 235.

33. Bohling, *The Sober Revolution,* 156–159.

34. MAEF-N 21PO / 82: Pierre de Leusse to Bruno de Leusse, Directeur du Cabinet du Ministre, Diplomatie, January 16, 1968. Pierre asked Bruno, his cousin and a French negotiator for the Evian Accords, to read it to the minister. He also sent copies to Tricot, Laboulaye, and Brunet.

35. MAEF-N 21PO / 82: Pierre de Leusse to Bruno de Leusse, Directeur du Cabinet du Ministre, Diplomatie, January 16, 1968.

36. MAEF-N 21PO / DE / 418: Diplomatie to DELFRA Algiers, 98 / 100, "Règlement communautaire sur le vin," January 28, 1970. Giulia Meloni and Johan Swinnen, "The Rise and Fall of the World's Largest Wine Exporter—and Its Institutional Legacy," *Journal of Wine Economics* 9, no. 1 (2014): 24.

37. MAEF-N 21PO / DE / 418: Diplomatie to DELFRA Bruxelles, 169 / 170, "Algérie et CEE," April 13, 1970.

38. MAEF-N 21PO / DE / 418: Basdevant to Diplomatie, 1629 / 1633, "Algérie et Marché commun," June 15, 1970.

39. MAEF-N 21PO / DE / 418: Basdevant to Diplomatie, 4615 / 18, "Régime communautaire provisoire d'importation des vins algériens," October 29, 1971.

40. MAEF-N 21PO / 82: DELFRA Algiers, "Note pour l'Ambassadeur a / s de l'association de l'Algérie à la Communauté économique européenne," December 1, 1971.

41. Hildebert Isnard, "La viticulture algérienne, colonisation et décolonisation," *Méditerranée* 23, no. 4 (1973): 10.

42. White, *Blood of the Colony*, 218–220.
43. Pierre Judet, "Chronique économique Algérie," *Annuaire de l'Afrique du Nord: 1969* 8 (1970): 523.
44. Phillip C. Naylor, *France and Algeria: A History of Decolonization and Transformation* (Gainesville: University Press of Florida, 2000), 96–102, 79.
45. Gérard Destanne de Bernis, "Le plan quadriennal de l'Algérie 1970–1973," *Annuaire de l'Afrique du Nord: 1970* 9 (1971): 209.
46. MAEF-N 21PO / 111: Boumediene address to Secondes assises nationales du secteur socialiste autogéré agricole, April 13, 1971, in Ministère de l'information et de la culture, *Discours du Président Boumediene, 2ème Trimestre 1971, Documents* (Algiers, ca. 1971), 12.
47. MAEF-N 21PO / 111: Boumediene interview with the French daily *Témoignage chrétien,* June 10, 1971, published in *Discours du Président Boumediene,* 41.
48. Bruno Etienne, "Chronique diplomatique," *Annuaire de l'Afrique du Nord: 1971* 10 (1972): 356–357.
49. Bruno Etienne, "Chronique diplomatique," *Annuaire de l'Afrique du Nord: 1976* 15 (1977): 288.
50. Pierre Jacquemot and Michel Nancy, "Chronique économique Algérie," *Annuaire de l'Afrique du Nord: 1973* 12 (1974): 541–542.
51. Giovanni Balcet and Michel Nancy, "Chronique économique Algérie," *Annuaire de l'Afrique du Nord: 1974* 13 (1975): 387.
52. HAEU COM (73) 1987, 1973 / 0353: "Accord entre la Communauté économique européenne et la République Algérienne Démocratique et Populaire relatif à la fourniture de froment tendre à titre d'aide alimentaire," 1973.
53. René Duchac, "Chronique de l'émigration," *Annuaire de l'Afrique du Nord: 1973* 12 (1974): 1064.
54. MAEF-N 21PO / 191: Diplomatie to Bonn, 546 / 51, "Construction d'une usine d'automobiles en Algérie," April 4, 1970.
55. MAEF-N 21PO / 191: Basdevant to Diplomatie, 1098 / 1102, "Visite à Alger de M. Pierre Dreyfus," April 25, 1970.
56. MAEF-N 21PO / 190: Soutou to Diplomatie, 2084 / 2087, "Visite à Alger du président de Citroën," August 1, 1972.

57. Destanne de Bernis, "Le plan quadriennal," 199.

58. Etienne, "Chronique diplomatique," *Annuaire de l'Afrique du Nord: 1971,* 366.

59. Albert Fitte, "La crise pétrolière franco-algérienne de 1970–1971," *Cahiers de la Méditerranée* 4, no. 1 (1972): 42.

60. On the oil shock and integrated Europe, see Giuliano Garavini, *After Empires: European Integration, Decolonization, and the Challenge from the Global South, 1957–1986* (Oxford: Oxford University Press, 2012), 162–200; Aurélie Élisa Gfeller, *Building a European Identity: France, the United States, and the Oil Shock, 1973–1974* (New York: Berghahn, 2014).

61. Algiers Domestic Service, Foreign Broadcast Information Service, Middle East & North Africa Daily Report FBIS-MEA-74-028, February 8, 1974, T1-T2.

62. Gfeller, *Building a European Identity,* 9.

63. Valérie Stiegler, "Envisager le Maghreb à la lumière du renouveau des relations Europe / monde arabe au début des années 1970," *Journal of European Integration History* 23, no. 1 (2017): 124–126.

64. MAEF-N 21PO / 352: Basdevant to Diplomatie, 2882 / 2883, "Recrutement de techniciens britanniques par la Sonatrach," June 23, 1971.

65. MAEF-N 21PO / 352: Rebeyrol, DELFRA Algiers, to Diplomatie, 3433, September 5, 1967; André, DELFRA London, to Diplomatie, 34 / 35, "Relations anglo-algériennes," January 3, 1968; Pelen, DELFRA Bamako, to Diplomatie, 327 / 29, April 11, 1968. The Algerian government kept him detained but refused to allow him to be extradited for execution. See David N. Gibbs, *The Political Economy of Third World Intervention: Mines, Money, and U.S. Policy in the Congo Crisis* (Chicago: University of Chicago Press, 1991), 167–169.

66. MAEF-N 21 PO / DE 417: Soutou to Diplomatie, 268 / 274, "L'Algérie et l'Europe des Dix," January 25, 1972.

67. MAEF-N 21PO / 352: Basdevant to Maurice Schumann, Direction d'Europe, sous-direction d'Europe occidentale, "Commentaires algériens à la veille de la rencontre entre MM. Heath et Pompidou," May 21, 1971.

68. MAEF-N 21PO / 82: DELFRA Algiers, Mission économique et financière, "Note pour l'ambassadeur a / s de l'association de l'Algérie à la Communauté économique européenne," December 1, 1971.
69. MAEF-N 21PO / DE / 418: Burin des Roziers to Diplomatie, 5234 / 48, "Négociation CEE-Algérie," December 17, 1974.
70. MAEF-N 21PO / DE / 418: Burin des Roziers to Diplomatie, 1323 / 1335, "Négociation CEE / Algérie," April 22, 1975.
71. MAEF-N 21PO / DE / 418: Burin des Roziers to Diplomatie, 1323 / 1335.
72. MAEF-N 21PO / DE / 418: Cazimajou to Diplomatie, 1586 / 89, "Négociations avec les pays du bassin méditerranén [sic]," May 9, 1975. Indeed, the Danish delegation continued to attempt to use threats against the Algerian petroleum industry to the EEC's benefit, but later machinations appeared to receive less enthusiasm from their fellow delegates. Cazimajou to Diplomatie, 2143–44, "Négociations CEE / Algérie," June 21, 1975.
73. MAEF-N 21PO / DE / 418: Cazimajou to Diplomatie, 1913–16, "Négociation avec les pays du Maghreb," June 10, 1975.
74. HAEU EN-2405, DGI 1975: E. P. Wellenstein, Dutch, Commission des Communautés européennes Director-General, to Ortoli, Christopher Soames, and Cheysson, "Visite de M. Bencheikh, premier conseiller près la mission d'Algérie," June 2, 1975; MAEF-N 21PO / DE / 418: Cazimajou to Diplomatie, 1811–12, "Dialogue Euro-Arabe," June 3, 1975.
75. MAEF-N 21PO / DE / 418: Cazimajou to Diplomatie, 1816 / 1819, "Négociations CEE-Maghreb," June 4, 1975.
76. Fathallah Oualalou, "La Communauté économique européenne et le Maroc: Le contentieux et l'impact du second élargissement," *African Spectrum* 17, no. 2 (1982): 129–149.
77. AN 19900490 / 182: "Co-operation Agreement between the European Economic Community and the People's Democratic Republic of Algeria," April 26, 1976, CEE / DZ / e, 3.
78. AN 19900490 / 182: "Co-operation Agreement," Articles 38–41, 42–43.
79. AN 19900490 / 182: "Co-operation Agreement," Article 56, 50.

80. "Signature des nouveaux accords d'association entre les Neuf et le Maghreb," *Le Monde,* April 27, 1976; "L'Algérie signe un nouvel accord d'association avec la CEE," *Le Monde,* April 28, 1976.

81. MAEF-N 21PO / 113: Michel Drumetz, for Commines, to Sauvagnargues, DE-CE, "Signature des accords CEE-Algérie," May 4, 1976.

82. MAEF-N 21PO / 113: Jean-François Noiville, DELFRA Algiers, to Diplomatie, sous-direction Levant, "Dialogue euro-arabe," May 13, 1975.

83. Horst was a palynologist, a type of pollen and dust fossil specialist whose expertise was valued by oil companies. I am grateful to Nick Kaplinsky for walking me through Horst's specialty.

84. *Einfuhr- und Vorratsstelle für Getreide und Futtermittel v Firma C. Mackprang* (Case 2 / 75), judgment of the court, May 27, 1975.

85. *Fiege,* opinion of Warner, 1014–1022.

86. *Ulrich Horst v Bundesknappschaft* (Case 6 / 75), judgment of the court, June 26, 1975.

87. *Horst,* judgment of the court.

88. *Directeur régional de la sécurité sociale de Nancy v Auguste Hirardin and Caisse régionale d'assurance maladie du Nord-Est* (Case 112 / 75), opinion of Advocate-General Trabucchi, March 31, 1976, 563.

89. *Hirardin,* opinion of Trabucchi, 566.

90. *Hirardin,* judgment of the court, April 8, 1976.

91. "Opinion of the European Economic and Social Committee on the 'Communication from the Commission to the European Parliament, the Council, the European Economic and Social Committee and the Committee of the Regions—the External Dimension of EU Social Security Coordination,'" COM(2012) 153 final, *Official Journal of the European Union* (January 15, 2013): C 11 / 71.

92. *Tayeb Belbouab v Bundesknappschaft* (Case 10 / 78), Opinion of Advocate-General Capotorti, September 20, 1978, 1928–1929.

93. *Belbouab,* judgment of the court, October 12, 1978, 1925–1926.

94. Wolfgang Seifert, "Admission Policy, Patterns of Migration and Integration: The German and French Case Compared," *Journal of Ethnic and Migration Studies* 23, no. 4 (October 1997): 445–446.

95. Melissa K. Byrnes, "Diplomacy at the End of Empire: Evolving French Perspectives on Portuguese Colonialism in the 1950s and 1960s," *Cold War History* 19, no. 4 (2019): 477–491.

96. MAEF-N 21PO / DE / 418: Soutou to Diplomatie, 1417 / 27, "Déclarations de M. Bouteflika," May 24, 1974.

Conclusion

1. *Daily Mail,* June 16, 2016.

2. *The Sun,* June 23, 2016; *Daily Mail,* June 24, 2016.

3. Nadia Khomami, "Daily Mail Publishes Correction to Story about 'Migrants from Europe,'" *The Guardian*, June 17, 2016.

4. Sara Pursley, "'Lines Drawn on an Empty Map': Iraq's Borders and the Legend of the Artificial State," *Jadaliyya,* pt. 1, June 2, 2015, https://www.jadaliyya.com/Details/32140, pt. 2 June 3, 2015, https://www.jadaliyya.com/Details/32153.

5. Jan Ifversen, "A Guided Tour into the Question of Europe," in *Eurocentrism in European History and Memory,* ed. Marjet Brolsma, Robin de Bruin, and Matthijs Lok (Amsterdam: Amsterdam University Press, 2019), 219; cited in Gabriele Metzler, "Writing the History of European Integration from a (Post-)Colonial Perspective," *Contemporanea* 23, no. 1 (2020): 121.

6. French president Emmanuel Macron's comments following the United States' withdrawal from Afghanistan in August 2021 demonstrate that such rhetoric is not exclusive to the far-right. "Accueil de réfugiés afghans: le discours d'Emmanuel Macron indigne la gauche; la France n'a 'pas du tout à rougir' selon l'Élysée," *Le Monde* with AFP, August 17, 2021.

7. Edward Carver, "Mayotte: The French Migration Frontline You've Never Heard Of," *New Humanitarian,* February 14, 2018.

8. Lydie Arbogast, "Migrant Detention in the European Union: A Thriving Business," Migreurop report, July 2016, 33.

9. Karis Muller has written extensively on these peripheries. See, for example, Karis Muller, "Shadows of Empire in the European

Union," *European Legacy* 6, no. 4 (2001): 439–451; Karis Muller, "'Concentric Circles' at the Periphery of the European Union," *Australian Journal of Politics and History* 46, no. 3 (2000): 322–335; Karis Muller, "Between Europe and Africa: Mayotte," in *European Integration and Post-colonial Sovereignty Games,* ed. R. Adler-Nissen and Ulrik Gad (London: Routledge, 2012), 187–203.

10. Rémi Armand Tchokothe, "'Balladur Visa' or 'Visa of Death'? Questioning 'Migration' to Europe via the Comoros Archipelago," *Journal of Identity and Migration Studies* 12, no. 2 (2018): 68–69.

11. Compare to Aurélie Élisa Gfeller, *Building a European Identity: France, the United States, and the Oil Shock, 1973–1974* (New York: Berghahn, 2014). Gfeller emphasizes the emergence of a particular version of "European identity" with the first enlargement in 1973.

12. MAEF-C 21QO / 1462: DE-CE, "Note a / s le Maghreb et la Communauté économique européenne," October 11, 1962.

13. Todd Shepard, *The Invention of Decolonization: The Algerian War and the Remaking of France* (Ithaca, NY: Cornell University Press, 2006).

14. Observatoire de la laïcité, "Communiqué de l'Observatoire national de la laïcité suite à l'attentat du 7 janvier 2015 à Paris contre le journal *Charlie Hebdo,*" January 9, 2015, https://www.gouvernement .fr/sites/default/files/contenu/piece-jointe/2015/01/communique_9 _01_2015_attentat_0.pdf; Aurélie Collas, "Après les attentats, l'école exalte la laïcité," *Le Monde,* December 8, 2015; Patrick Kessel interviewed by François Darras, "Le communautarisme, voilà l'ennemi," *Marianne,* October 30, 2015; *Les Grandes Questions,* "13 novembre: La faute au communautarisme?" France 5, December 3, 2015; Mattea Battaglia, "À l'école, le nombre d'atteintes à la laïcité plutôt stable," *Le Monde,* October 14, 2020; Francis Chouat, Yves Durand, and Najwa El Haïté, "9 décembre, journée de la laïcité: December 9, 2020.

15. Matthew Carr, *Fortress Europe: Dispatches from a Gated Continent* (New York: New Press, 2012).

Archival and Primary Sources

Archival Series

AD-BdR: Archives Départementales des Bouches-du-Rhône, Marseille
137 W: Affaires traitées par le cabinet de la Préfecture des Bouches-du-Rhône (1952–1969)

AN: Archives Nationales, Pierrefitte-sur-Seine
AG (F): Jacques Foccart papers
C//: Les archives des deux Assemblées nationales constituantes et de la Quatrième République (1945–1958)
2 DE: Fonds Debré (in the midst of recataloging at time of consultation, June 2015)
363AP: René Mayer papers
19771468: SGCI
19820750: Industrie; Direction générale de l'énergie et des matières premières; Direction des hydrocarbures
19880053: SGCI
19900490: SGCI
19950190: Agriculture; Production et marchés (1957–1965)
19980006: DOM-TOM; Direction des affaires politiques, administratives et financières; Sous-direction des affaires politiques (1950–1996)

20000293: SGCI
20040335: DOM-TOM; Direction des affaires économiques, sociales et
culturelles; Sous-direction des affaires économiques (1965–1995)

ANMT: Archives Nationales du Monde du Travail, Roubaix
98 AS N: Conseil national du patronat français

**BDIC: Bibliothèque de Documentation Internationale
Contemporaine,** Nanterre
4° delta 998: Rapatriement des français d'Algérie

CAEF: Centre des Archives Économiques et Financières,
Savigny-le-Temple
Series B: Fonds trésor, relations multilatérales
5A-0000116: Haut-commissariat en Afrique occidentale française

CAOM: Centre des Archives Nationales d'Outre-Mer,
Aix-en-Provence
BIB AOM: Library holdings
23 APC: Octave Meynier papers
100 APOM: Comité central français pour l'outre-mer
1AFFPOL: Ministère des Colonies. Direction des affaires politiques
1AFFECO: Ministère des Colonies. Direction des affaires économiques et
du Plan
81 F: Ministère d'État chargé des affaires algériennes

HAEU: Historical Archives of the European Union, Florence and
digitized
AD: André Darteil papers
AMG: Albert-Marie Gordiani papers
BAC: EEC / Euratom Commissions
CM2: EEC and Euratom Council of Ministers
CM3 / NEGO: ECSC Special Council of Ministers / Negotiations for the
EEC / Euratom treaties
COM: Commission of the European Communities

EN: Émile Noël papers
Online oral history inventory: Jean-Marie Palayret and Anaïs Legendre.
"Histoire interne de la Commission européenne 1958–1973,"
interview with Jacques Ferrandi. Ajaccio, May 28–29, 2004.
archives.eui.eu/en/files/transcript/15190.pdf.

MAEF-C: Centre des Archives Diplomatiques du Ministère des Affaires Étrangères, la Courneuve
0034SUP: Ministère des relations extérieures
20QO: DE-CE
21QO: DE-CE
260QO: Secrétariat d'état aux affaires algériennes / affaires politiques et économiques

MAEF-N: Centre des Archives Diplomatiques du Ministère des Affaires Étrangères, Nantes
21PO and 21PO / DE: Algiers embassy (under restoration at time of consultation, July 2019)
105PO: Bonn embassy
122PO: Brussels embassy
378PO: London embassy

SP: Archives d'Histoire Contemporaine, Sciences Po, Paris
BA: Wilfrid Baumgartner papers
CM: Maurice Couve de Murville papers
MEC: Chérif Mécheri papers
PM: Pierre Moussa papers

Books

Algerian Ministère de l'information et de la culture. *Discours du Président Boumediene, 2ème Trimestre 1971, Documents.* Algiers, ca. 1971.
Drif, Zohra. *Inside the Battle of Algiers: Memoir of a Woman Freedom Fighter.* Translated by Andrew Farrand. Charlottesville, VA: Just World Books, 2017.

Fanon, Frantz. *The Wretched of the Earth*. Translated by Constance Farrington. New York: Grove, 1963.

Gallup, George H., ed. *The Gallup International Public Opinion Polls: France 1939, 1944–1975*, vol. 1. New York: Random House, 1976.

Guernier, Eugène. *Le destin des continents, trois continents—trois civilisations—trois destins*. Paris: Librairie Félix Alcan, 1936.

Kant, Immanuel. "Perpetual Peace: A Philosophical Sketch." https://www.mtholyoke.edu/acad/intrel/kant/kant1.htm#fn8.

Lambert, Jacques. *Manuel de législation algérienne*. Algiers: Librairie des facultés, 1952.

Lemaignen, Robert. "L'Empire, notre espoir." In *La communauté impériale française*, 23–53. Paris: Éditions Alsatia, 1945.

Moussa, Pierre. *Les chances économiques de la communauté franco-africaine*. Paris: Armand Colin, 1957.

Nord, Pierre. *L'Eurafrique: Notre dernière chance*. Paris: Librairie Arthème Fayard, 1955.

Viard, Paul-Emile. *La Communauté française*. Paris: Éditions Renaissances, 1946.

Periodicals

L'Algérie libre

Annuaire français de droit international

Cahiers du communisme

Communautés et continents

Daily Mail

L'Esprit

France Outremer

Frankfurter Allgemeine

Hommes et mondes

L'Indépendant

International Affairs

International Organization

Journal of Modern African Studies

Marchés tropicaux et méditerranéens
Méditerranée
Middle East Journal
Le Monde
Le Monde diplomatique
Revue algérienne des sciences juridiques, économiques et politiques
Revue économique et sociale: Bulletin de la société d'études économiques et sociales
Der Spiegel
The Sun

Official Publications

Algeria

Journal officiel de l'État algérien

Europe

Council of Europe Parliamentary Assembly reports
European Court of Justice reports
Official Journal of the European Communities
Official Journal of the European Union

France

Assemblée Nationale, *Journal officiel*
Assemblée Nationale Constituante, *Journal officiel*
Conseil de la République, *Journal officiel*

Additional Archival Material and Rare Book Repositories

Physical

Bibliothèque nationale de France, François–Mitterrand, Paris
CDHA: Centre de Documentation Historique sur l'Algérie,
    Aix-en-Provence

Online

AEI: Archive of European Integration, University of Pittsburgh, http://aei
    .pitt.edu/

CVCE: Digital Research in European Studies / Centre virtuel de la connaissance sur l'Europe, cvce.eu

Eur-Lex: European Union law database, https://eur-lex.europa.eu /homepage.html

Foreign Broadcast Information Service, online subscription service

INA: Institut national de l'audiovisuel, ina.fr

Légifrance: French law database, https://www.legifrance.gouv.fr/

Acknowledgments

Unless my editor agrees to put out *The Seventh Member State, vol. 2: Gratitude,* I will have to content myself with a few pages to account for the tremendous number of people who have helped me throughout the process of producing this book. My first thanks must go to the two scholars who mentored me and supported this project from the beginning and who continue to do so: David Troyansky and Clifford Rosenberg. David helped me find my own voice in this undertaking and fostered a deep appreciation for spending time—lots of time—in the archives. Cliff guided me to improve this work at every stage, encouraging me to revise that one last draft and to tackle more complex questions. Others provided invaluable feedback and support. Gary Wilder challenged me to think about why this story matters. Fred Cooper offered encouraging words and ideas at critical points and told me to visit Nantes, whose archives changed the direction of the book. Todd Shepard reminded me that this history is not just France's, and I hope the final version reflects this.

I have been fortunate to be surrounded by incredible scholars at all stages of my education. At Northwestern University, I am particularly grateful to Angela Ray, a model for how I want to be in the classroom;

to Abigail Foerstner, who taught me how to write a story; and to Benjamin Frommer, whose class on postwar Europe led me to pursue a doctorate. I learned to love the jumble of European institutional acronyms from Francesco Saraceno at Sciences Po. At the University of London, Institute in Paris, I learned so much from the entire faculty, especially Simon Kitson and Julian Jackson. At the Graduate Center, CUNY, I received support from many faculty members, including Evelyn Ackerman, Dagmar Herzog, Christoph Kimmich, Helena Rosenblatt, Julia Sneeringer, and John Torpey. During my research year, Sylvie Thénault guided me in new directions, and I received a warm welcome and support from Emmanuel Blanchard and Françoise Blum.

At Swarthmore College, I am especially grateful to my colleagues in the history department: Bob Weinberg, Jen Moore, Diego Armus, Farid Azfar, Tim Burke, BuYun Chen, Allison Dorsey, Bruce Dorsey, Marj Murphy, Ahmad Shokr, and Vivian Truong, as well as Celia Caust-Ellenbogen, Maggie Delano, Brian Goldstein, Alexandra Gueydan-Turek, Nabil Kashyap, Micheline Rice-Maximin, Sunka Simon, Carina Yervasi, and many others. I was able to complete this manuscript during a sabbatical year thanks to institutional support, particularly from Provost Sarah Willie-LeBreton's office. Teaching at Swarthmore has introduced me to such impressive, driven students. They, along with the incredible students I met at Brooklyn College, Medgar Evers College, and Sciences Po, Reims, offer a constant reminder of the power of curiosity.

A host of people offered valuable feedback at conferences and workshops: the seminar Pour une histoire sociale de l'Algérie colonisée held at the Centre Malher, at the invitation of Emmanuel Blanchard, Jim House, and Sylvie Thénault; the Re-Imagining Ends of Empire Study Day at the University of Portsmouth, organized by Kelsey Suggitt; a workshop hosted by Didier Guignard of l'Institut de recherches et d'études sur les mondes arabes et musulmans; Columbia University's Beyond France seminar, chaired by Tabetha Ewing and Gregory Mann, with an especially helpful comment by Emmanuelle Saada; the New

York Area French History Group, convened by Jeff Horn and David Troyansky; the Lees Seminar at Rutgers University–Camden, at Emily Marker's invitation; the University of Pittsburgh's European Studies Center, at Jae-Jae Spoon's invitation; and the Philadelphia Area French History Group's inaugural meeting, made possible by Swarthmore's Hungerford Faculty Support Fund.

Generous support for this project came from numerous sources. The Council for European Studies at Columbia University provided grants for my earliest research and, with funds from the Andrew W. Mellon Foundation, a much later writing stage. The Fulbright Scholar Program and the Franco-American Commission afforded me the time I needed to research, and I am especially grateful to Arnaud Roujou de Boubée and Charlotte Goodwin. My time at the Camargo Foundation, already sun-drenched and productive, was made much more rewarding thanks to its director, Julie Chénot, and administrator, Cécile Descloux. The Graduate Center's Advanced Research Collaborative Award for Archival Research in African American and African Diaspora Studies supported a summer in the archives.

The thrill of finding that one *aha!* document after a long day never grows old, and I have had more than a few of those moments thanks to archivists and librarians. I am grateful to the staff of the Archives natio-nales, where Vivien Richard allowed me to consult uncatalogued doc-uments; Anne-Lise Ducoroy at the Archives du monde du travail; the Bibliothèque de documentation internationale contemporaine; the Bib-liothèque nationale de France; the Centre des archives diplomatiques du Ministère des affaires étrangères at la Courneuve and in Nantes, and especially the assistance of Éric Lechevallier at the latter; the Centre des archives économiques et financières; the Centre des archives nationales d'outre-mer; Hervé Noel at the Centre de documentation historique sur l'Algérie; the incredibly friendly archivists at the Historical Archives of the European Union; Olivier Dubois at the library of the Maison méditerranéenne de la science de l'homme; and the Archives d'histoire contemporaine (Sciences Po); as well as the staffs of the departmental and municipal archives I visited while shaping my research topic, and the staff of the Archives de la Préfecture de police de Paris on rue de la Montagne Sainte-Geneviève, where I cut my archival chops. The Graduate Center's Interlibrary Loan department worked tirelessly to locate materials for me. More recently, Swarthmore's librarians, including Sarah Elichko, Amy McColl, and Kerry Kristine McElrone, have made it possible to complete this project.

My friend Daisy Hunter-Haydon once talked about the opposite of schadenfreude and it has stuck with me. In a competitive and often insular field, I have been so lucky to be surrounded by a network of friends who challenge and support me. Scott Johnson's friendship since my first week of graduate school has meant the world, and his incisive comments have improved this project greatly. Jess Pearson's mentorship and friendship have been constants, as has her cheerful willingness to read and reread so many chapters. I wish every scholar had a friend like Miranda Sachs in their corner, both for her kindness and her sharp eye. Chelsea Schields has been a source of humor, grace, and perspective for many years. Her comments on an earlier version of the entire manuscript undoubtedly made the book you have just read much better than it would otherwise have been. I would not have made it through coursework without Andrew Shield and the moments of levity he brings to even the most scholarly of situations. Scott, Chelsea, and Andrew, along with Pete Aigner, Chris Ewing, Kyle Francis, Chris Rominger, Katie Uva, and Katrina Wheeler, made spending inordinate amounts of time near Herald Square enjoyable.

This work has gone through countless revisions thanks to the many people who read and commented on various chapters. They include Kellan Anfinson, Osman Balkan, Tim Burke, Sam Daly, Muriam Haleh Davis, Andrew Denning, Benedikt Erforth, Chris Ewing, Liz Fink, Kyle Francis, Elise Franklin, Thea Goldring, Sarah Griswold, Kit Heintzman, Burleigh Hendrickson, Rachel Kantrowitz, Allison Korinek, Ian Merkel, Terrence Peterson, Chris Rominger, Lauren Saxton, Ahmad Shokr,

Katrina Wheeler, and the members of the Graduate Center's History and the Humanities group. Andi Bartz, while constantly insisting she was "bad at history," offered her incomparable editorial skills to improve the most consequential pages of this project, for which I cannot thank her enough. On countless work-ish dates as the book finally took shape, Emily Marker shared her friendship and ideas.

Over long e-mail exchanges, brief coffee meetings, and conversations at workshops and conferences, I also received invaluable feedback and advice about my project and the process of writing a book from Jeffrey James Byrne, Catherine Clark, Joshua Cole, Herrick Chapman, Sung-Eun Choi, Blandine Descamps-Julien, Lisa Jane Graham, Peo Hansen, Elizabeth Heath, Jean-Robert Henry, Richard Ivan Jobs, Jean Leca, Rostane Mehdi, Marc Michel, Guia Migani, Karis Muller, Eileen Ryan, Emmanuelle Saada, Joshua Schreier, Jennifer Sessions, and Owen White. I am so grateful to the two anonymous reviewers who offered insightful criticism and suggestions, much of which I tried to incorporate. All errors, of course, are my own.

The process of turning this project into a book has been made much more pleasant by my editor at Harvard University Press, Kathleen Mc-Dermott. I am also grateful to Kathi Drummy and Stephanie Vyce, particularly with my myriad questions about images, and to cartographer Isabelle Lewis and indexer Lisa DeBoer. I thank Sherry Gerstein and Joyce Li for their fresh eyes at the final stages of editing and production. Chapters 3, 4, and 5 build on ideas first presented in "Drawing Algeria into Europe: Shifting French Policy and the Treaty of Rome (1951–1964)," *Modern & Contemporary France* 25, no. 2 (2017): 191–208. Helen Drake's and Chris Reynolds's guidance as I wrote that article served me well as I expanded this to book-length.

I would not have been able to complete this project without some necessary distractions. It is thanks to les Bourlier—Diane, Hervé, Isabelle, Marine, Philippine, and their entire (growing) family—that I pursued a career about France in the first place. Also in France, I am so lucky to know Tara Bushe, Hélène Cavarelli, Amelia de Chabert, Ida Falinower,

Florian Félès, Simon Gensowski, Marie Husset, Brigitte Karsenti, Jack McNeill, Philippe d'Orgeville, Unity Payton, Sylvie Rondeau, Nathalie and Michel Toulouse, and a merry band that includes Alex, Mika, Seb, and Sylvain, as well as those who, like me, only pass through on occasion, including Lauren Dolman, Grace Hailstone, and Natalie Kent. Thea Goldring has been a friend to me in many places, starting with when she located Ritz crackers in Paris. In America, I rely on Andi Bartz, Cristina Couloucoundis, Sam Gordon, Daisy Hunter-Haydon, Corrie Leech, Anu Oza, Natasha Palewicz, Meghan Wu, and Jinny VanZanten. Cecily Harwitt, Brent Cebul, Ruth Judge, Semyon Khokhlov, Emily Marker, Sara Mathieson, Aline Normoyle, Abe Taber, and Katherine Treppendahl all help to make Philadelphia feel like home.

My most reliable support system has always been my family. Sam Brown, Sarah McLellan, and Huck McBrown offered real and virtual escapes from the monotony of revising. Rose and John Schonewolf have helped me in many ways, great and small. Kitty's and now Stella's demands for head scratches forced me to look up from the computer. My grandparents did not see the end of this project, but they put up with postcards instead of visits so that I could see it through. From a very young age, my parents, Vicki and Elliot Brown, fostered in me a love of history and a curiosity about France, through family lore, birthday dinners at Chez Napoléon, and deep reads of vacation tour books. Without them, none of this would have been possible, and I dedicate the book to them.

Finally, I am so grateful to Jack Schonewolf, whose own pursuit of learning inspires me every day. Jack infused moments of calm into an often stressful race to the finish, humored me with trips to the Di Bruno's cheese counter and visits to strange museums (who else can say they saw the Musée de la Chasse et de la Nature before they stepped foot in the Louvre?), and showed time and again that he is game for the next adventure, which I have no doubt will be a doozy. I am so glad to have him in my life.

Index

Page numbers in italics refer to figures.